Practical Seamanship Illustrated

Robbert Das
Harald Schwarzlose

This work was originally published in West Germany under the title, *Praktische Seemanschaft in Bildern*.

D1417944

SEVEN
SEAS

©1987 by Highmark Publishing Ltd.

Published by Seven Seas Publishing Company, a division of Highmark Publishing, Ltd.
21 Elm Street, Camden, Maine 04843

Published originally in West Germany by
Delius, Klasing & Co.

10   9   8   7   6   5   4   3   2   1

Library of Congress Cataloging-in-Publication Data

Das, Robbert.
   Practical seamanship illustrated.

   Translation of: Praktische Seemannschaft in
Bildern.
   1. Seamanship—Handbooks, manuals, etc.
2. Yachts and yachting—Handbooks, manuals, etc.
I. Schwarzlose, Harald.   II. Title.
VK543.D3413   1987   623.88'02'02   87-9746
ISBN 0-915160-89-7

Table of Contents

Foreword

I taught myself to sail on a small, man-made lake near Ann Arbor, Michigan. It was named Barton Pond, and a more benign training ground cannot be imagined. Its water was shallow and when the dam gates were opened, the trunks of submerged tree stumps were vexing obstacles for the fleet of daysailers at the sailing club.

My father, a confirmed new England canoeist and white water kayaker, had purchased an old wooden Snipe, which he raced without much distinction. After a series of near disasters that, out of respect for my father, shall not be recounted here, he reaffirmed his devotion to the paddle and challenged me to do what I could with the recalcitrant craft.

On my first solo outing, I was accosted in mid-lake by a neighbor, the elderly Mrs. Stewart, and her collie crew. The dog held the sheets of their Snipe in its jaws as she crawled over the rail, reprimanding me for rigging my boat all wrong. So intimidated was I that for the rest of the summer I avoided sailing whenever I saw their silhouettes drifting about the pond.

Mrs. Stewart had taught me how to hoist the sails and lead the sheets, but I hadn't the foggiest notion how to tack. In fact, I'm not sure I knew whence the wind blew, let alone when to release the jibsheet or how far to trim it. There was something intrinsically wrong-looking about a backwinded jib, but I had no proof.

Fortunately, someone gave me a pocket guide to elementary sailing technique, which I proceeded to study with no little interest. From it I learned the principles of sailing, the points of sail, rough trim for beating, reaching, and running, how to avoid the dread irons! I should like to say that the rest was easy, but of course there is much more to sailing than struggling across a stagnant pond.

The point of course is that much can be learned from reading books. And *Practical Seamanship* is no exception. If we may assume that, given fair warning of potential danger, an intelligent person will prepare himself as best as he possibly can, then Harald Schwarzlose and Robbert Das' book is of considerable value to sailors and powerboaters of many levels.

Nautical titles have a way of crossing the Atlantic as easily as the dreams of an armchair sailor. First published in West Germany in 1985, *Practical Seamanship* was brought to the United States by the publishers of Seven Seas Press, who translated and reset the text, and redesigned the book cover to cover.

There is no other book quite like it. Look at the drawings. These are not great artistic renderings; they are clear, precise illustrations of nearly every situation one might expect to encounter at sea, in harbor, and even before one leaves the dock. What do you do when the engine quits as you cross a roiling New Jersey bar? When a halyard goes aloft as you struggle to change sails in a building gale? When the keel grounds on a lee shore? A crew mate is injured and requires immediate medical aid? These are the sorts of questions that every boat owner must ask himself before undertaking even the briefest outing. He is responsible for the boat, the crew and of course himself, and he'd better know what to do when something goes wrong. His skills derive from experience, but not all experience comes from being aboard. It begins with learning, and for many, learning begins with books.

At the least, a good instructional book gives the reader some notion of what unforseen dilemmas lie in the shoal waters ahead, and gives him a framework to start thinking about how he will attack a problem and solve it. *Practical Seamanship* does just that, by way of lucid illustrations and sage advice organized by 16 topic headings. It is a valuable resource book that should be read at home and kept aboard.

Practical Seamanship was written by Harald Schwarzlose, an experienced yachtsman and editor of the West German magazine *Yacht*. The remarkable illustrations were done by Robbert Das, a veteran Dutch cruiser with an insistence on accuracy. The text was translated by Hyman Rudoff, a retired chemist and engineer who for years sailed a Pearson Vanguard on the Great Lakes and later the Chesapeake Bay. In the 1930s, when he was studying for his PhD, a proficiency with the German language was as essential to chemistry as Latin to pharmacy or Hebrew to a bible scholar. Mr. Rudoff has done an excellent job, painstakingly checking all materials for accuracy, laboring over the nuances of word meaning, and verifying legal requirements with the appropriate U.S. authority.

While most case situations in the book are universally applicable, you will notice that some examples are set in European waters. This is natural enough, given the authors' nationalities and place of first publication. But it is not a liability for the American reader. On the contrary, should you someday plan to cruise the Mediterranean Sea, where else can you get a quick overview of the strategy involved in tying up stern-to a quay? Believe me, I'd like to have studied this book before my first attempt at the quay in Mamaris, Turkey, where a host of international yachtsmen assembled to see how this Yank would guide his stern between the tightly rafted fleet!

It has been said there is nothing new under the sun, and a review of nautical titles seems irrefutable proof! Compare any two texts on seamanship and it is guaranteed there will be overlapping material. It is how the author scours from the existing body of assembled wisdom that organizes his work into something new, and hopefully something of value. *Practical Seamanship* is unique in that it assumes nothing; no minimum level of sea savvy is taken for granted. It is basic stuff, and it is important.

Dan Spurr
Senior Editor
Cruising World magazine

Worry-Free Tying Up

When a boat is made fast securely in a good berth in sheltered water, its skipper and crew can relax. For the moment, at least, no further action is required of them, and no decision need be made. It is a chance to discuss the day's sailing or plan the passage that lies ahead. A secure berth is a haven, so let us begin this manual by introducing the fundamental

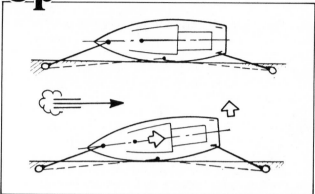

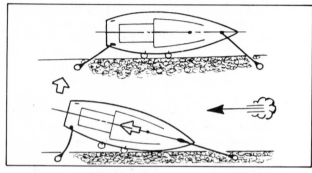

techniques of making fast a boat, after which we'll look at the ways of approaching and leaving a dock or slip under various conditions of wind and current.

The old saw says: An experienced skipper is known by the way he moors his boat. This is undoubtedly true. Therefore, the student of small craft handling should concentrate mainly on the practical side of mooring. The boat must be well secured to the dock or quay so that no damage can be caused.

Proper mooring of a boat is part of the basic knowledge required of a competent skipper. Nevertheless, one continues to observe certain skippers securing their boat to the dock with nothing but bow and stern lines. This will not work, since either current or wind pressure can cause the boat to swing back and forth, displacing the fenders and resulting in a collision with the dock or other boats.

Not much safer is to tie up using so-called false springs, which, belayed to a midships cleat, are then made fast to the same bollards to which the bow and stern lines are fastened. Here, too, the boat has excessive free play, letting the bow and/or stern sway loosely. Particularly when additional boats are docked alongside are false springs considered to be absolutely inadequate for safety.

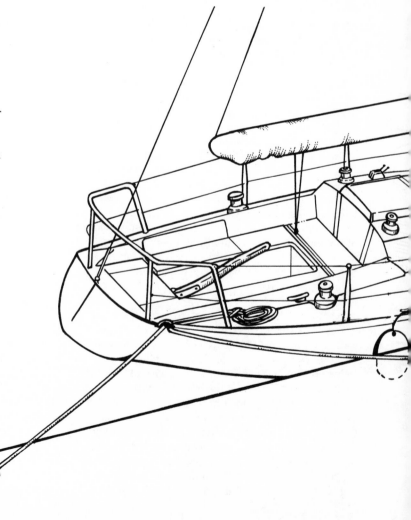

Tying Up Alongside

Shown below is the best way to make a boat fast alongside a dock: Three fenders are in the proper position to protect the boat's topsides. All mooring lines have been passed through the toe rail chocks and belayed to bollards on the dock. The angle of the lines to the boat's sides is large enough to prevent the springs from rubbing against the hull. The bollards for the bow and stern lines are far enough away from the boat. The boat is now well balanced between spring, bow and stern lines.

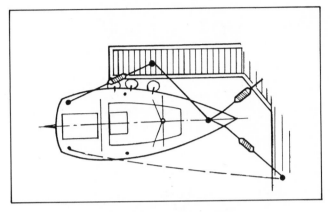

This is the way to moor a yacht to a short spur or extension of a dock. Two bow lines are made fast to the main dock. Rubber shock absorbers ease snubbing in a swell. The appropriate forward and after springs are made fast to a bollard on the spur, with the after spring also receiving a shock absorber. Also, space permitting, a line from the stern to the main dock will moderate the stress on the fenders. Finally, if the wind blew hard on this boat's starboard quarter, she'd need an anchor to windward.

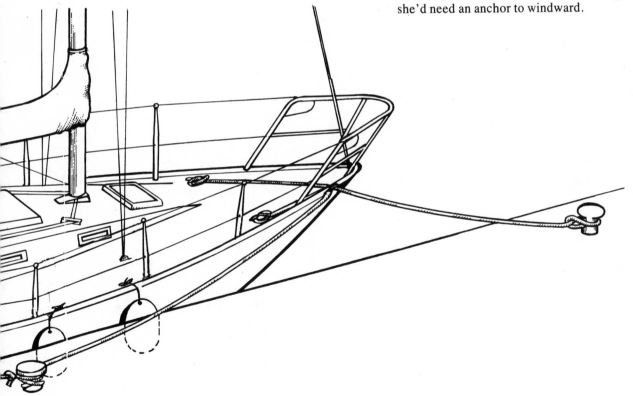

Tying Up in a Pack

Boats that have tied up side by side present a large target to beam winds or currents. Therefore, they must be especially well protected by means of spring lines. Often skippers of the outlying boats forget to use sufficiently long docking lines to connect with the dock or quay. This creates the probability of collisions with earlier arrivals inside.

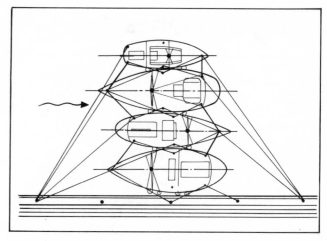

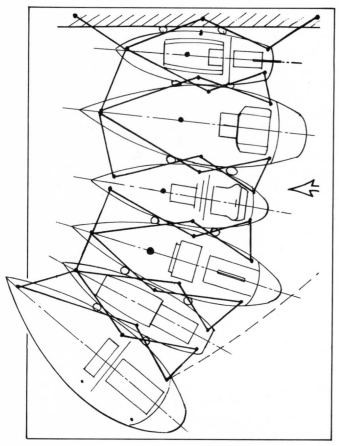

After your boat has been carefully and properly docked, it behooves embarking and disembarking boats to observe yachting etiquette to avoid the wrath of the neighbors. As a matter of principle, one should cross over the foredeck and not through the cockpit, so that the privacy of the crew is respected. When going ashore, wear soft-soled shoes to avoid making a racket.

When two persons simultaneously step onto a boat deck, the owner may be expected to react with some irritation — most likely his morning coffee is spilling in the scuppers or leaking into the bilge. Out of respect, don't step onto a strange deck until another crewmember has already reached the other side of the boat so that the boat heels the least. Never weigh down a boat's side with two or more persons at the same time.

Above, right is the way that several yachts lying side by side are properly secured. If there are swells running in the harbor, each additional boat will dock stem to stern alongside its neighbor. This prevents the masts and spreaders from colliding. Each time another boat comes alongside, it must belay its lines directly to the dock. When larger groups tie together, only the outside boats need to take extra long lines to the pier. In addition, boats on the inside belay lines to the next boat out.

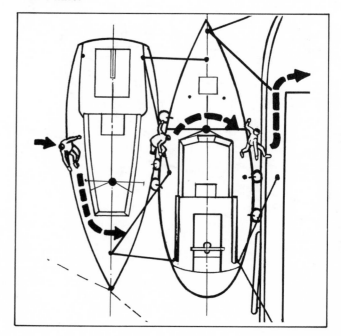

Tying Up in a Slip

If you have a dock space permanently assigned to your boat, the job of docking and setting sail is considerably easier. Lines permanently made fast to the pilings can be run up to two rings on the jetty. They will prevent the boat from drifting against other boats on either side. The crew can use them as handholds to move the boat in and out of the slip in a beam wind by hauling it along the windward line.

In the slip, the boat will lie most quietly when the stern lines are crossed. However, this can cause chafing. This can be prevented by fitting the lines with chafing gear that is free to rotate on the lines.

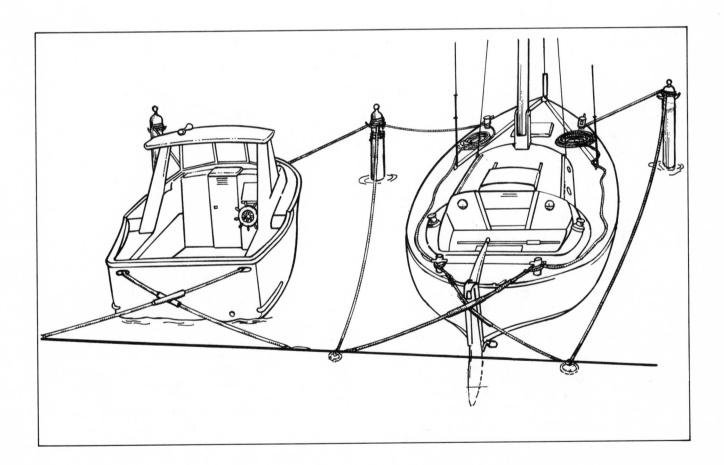

Tying Up in Locks

Sailing into and tying up in strange locks is particularly touchy when the lock is also being used by commercial shipping, which has priority locking in. The hard and fast rule is that pleasure craft may only lock in after receiving signals or verbal instructions from the lock personnel. Responsible pilots and merchant skippers slow their engines when small craft approach. However, this is often not the case; ship's propellers cause strong crosscurrents and undertow which can be dangerous to all small boats (1). Therefore, it is recommended that you maneuver past the merchant ship and tie up in the front end of the lock. This also creates the possibility of leaving the lock as soon as the gates open without any further hindrance or delay.

Under no circumstances should you tie up behind the stern of the ship and wait for it to get under way

first. The propeller wash will force your boat against the lock wall and could cause serious damage. No less dangerous is the wind, which is compressed by the walls of the lock and undergoes a sort of venturi effect when the gates are opened, possibly slamming a small boat against the lock walls or against other craft inside (2). Finally, water pressure flowing either into or out of the lock gates causes a strong flow, which makes mooring and casting off more difficult (3). It is highly recommended that prior to entering strange locks, the small boat owner or skipper takes steps to inform himself of suitable places for tying up. Whoever ties up alongside a merchant vessel will have the fewest problems, since here the water level need not be considered. During the actual tying up, observe the recommendations described on the following pages.

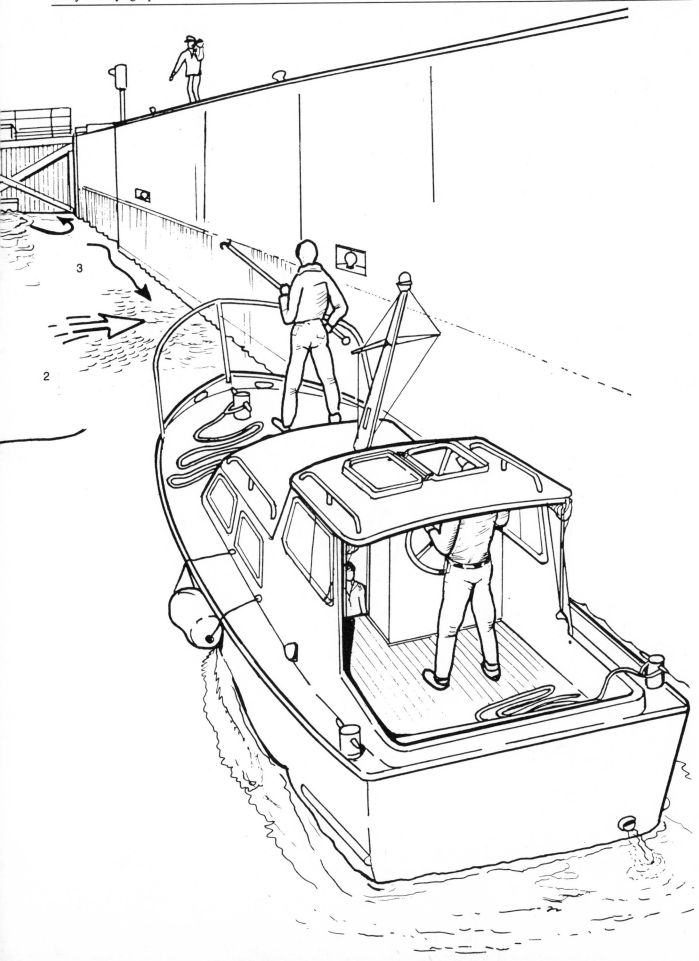

2

3

Locking in with wind, and in some circumstances water pressure astern, is a problem in itself. It is often compounded by the error of making the bow line fast to a floating mooring pontoon before first making the stern line fast, thereby leaving the stern unsecured and permitting it to swing out from the pontoon under the influence of wind, current and any remaining headway. Under these influences, you will find it difficult to get back into your planned position at the pontoon.

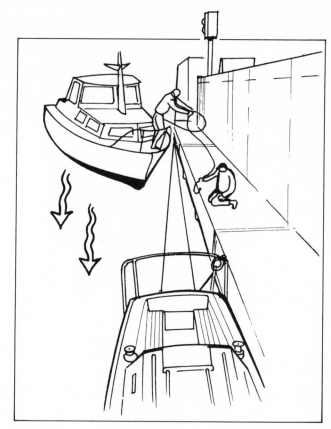

The most favorable situation after locking in finds the stern line passed around a bollard or through a ring in the lock wall (1). The remaining headway is used to reach the bow line bollard while quickly slacking off the stern. Power can be used to assist if necessary. In the meantime, the bow line is made ready on the foredeck and belayed to the forward bollard in such a way that it cannot unintentionally drop into the water (2). The bow line is passed over the bow pulpit if a sharp drop in the water level is foreseen, or under the pulpit if a sharp rise is expected (3).

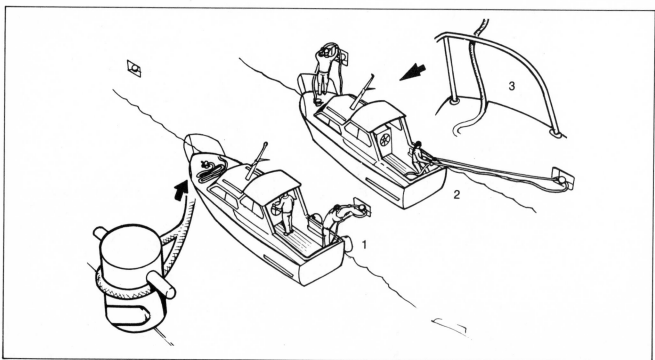

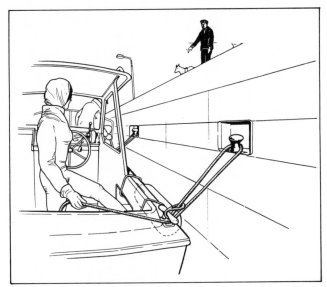

This is the way a functional layout of the mooring lines should look: The ends of the lines (here shown with eye splices) are belayed on board the boat. The lines will be passed around the bollard or through the ring in the lock wall and then brought back on deck to the cleats, ready to slip. There they should be secured and hand held by a crewmember, ready to ease off or haul in depending on the water level.

In locks with little water turbulence and/or slight water level differences, it is possible to forego the mooring lines and to hold the boat against the lock wall by means of boathooks (above). With little drop in the water level, it is practical to hang the fenders horizontally so as to keep them from being soiled by algae on the lock wall below the high waterline.

How a boat can be held in position by a single person in a lock chamber which has no floating tie-up pontoon is shown in the drawing below: The bow and stern lines are passed through the same ring on the lock wall to the deck amidships, where they can then be handled by a single deckhand, who depending on the water level eases or hauls in as the case may be. A special hook can be used for this purpose.

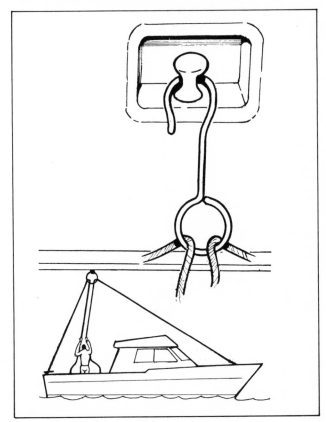

Below is the proper way to make fast to a floating pontoon in tidal waters or in a lock: As a matter of principle, only the bollards or rings on the pontoon are utilized to belay the mooring lines. Under no circumstances should the chains or the pilings to which the pontoons are secured be used for tying up.

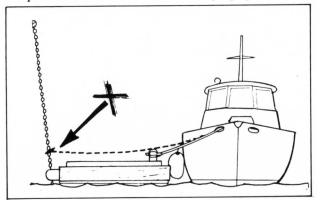

Tying Up in Tidal Waters

If you tie up at a dock or quay in tidal waters, you must constantly take care that the boat does not dry out on its seaward side at low tide. This can be avoided by attaching a snatch block to a halyard and securing it by a short line to a bollard or ring on the quay. During the ebb, the block will slide up the halyard and hold the vessel erect at low tide.

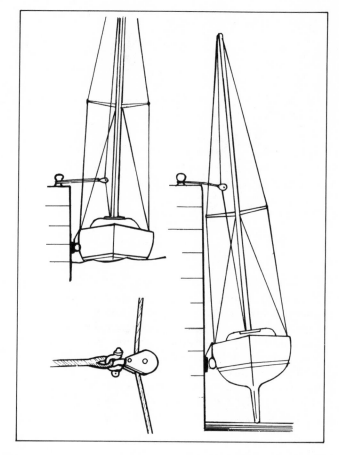

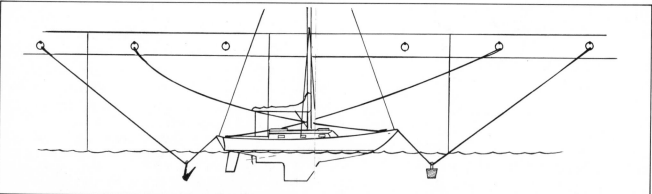

If you must tie up to a quay in a tidal area, it is essential that all mooring lines be paid out to their greatest length, so that they can compensate for the range of the tide. A rule of thumb is that a three-foot (one meter) difference in the water level requires lengthening the mooring lines by a distance equivalent to one-half the boat's length. In order to permit the bow and stern lines to retain their holding ability when the water is rising, the lines should be weighted down.

Mooring Lines

There are several ways to belay a line to a bollard ring on a dock or quay.

1. A double round turn with two half hitches prevents the line from chafing. This is the way professional skippers make fast their heavy ropes.

2. If the line has an eye splice, it is easy to form a noose and bend the line to the bollard.

3. A bowline also can be used to make a large loop. This has the advantage of being belayed or cast off either under or over the lines of other boats.

4. The mooring line also can be belayed to a ring bolt. The drawback is that, if the ring is rusty, the line will chafe itself to bits in a hurry. It is therefore better to take a round turn around the ring prior to making the bowline.

5. The best and quickest way is to belay the line to the ring bolt with a double turn and two half hitches. The double turn immediately reduces slippage while even an untrained sailing guest can tie the half hitches.

Various types of chafing gear, particularly plastic hoses, have proven their worth wherever mooring lines must be passed through chocks or openings in the bulwarks or toe rail. Ship's chandlers sell them in the proper sizes to fit the usual sizes of lines. When buying chocks be sure that the opening is large enough to accommodate your lines and chafing gear.

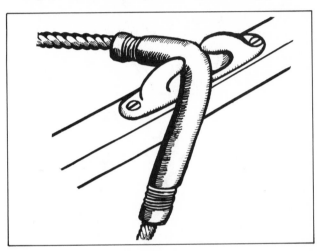

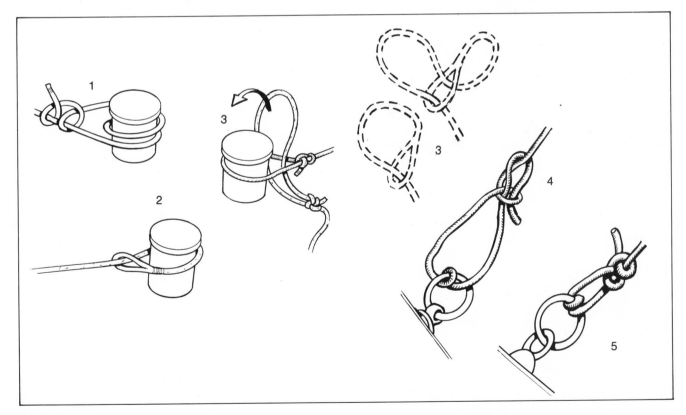

Chafing gear must be securely fastened to the lines since it can shift under pressure.

1. It is difficult to sew PVC hose to the line since the hose is very tough and difficult for a sail needle to penetrate.

2. A simple method is to wind duct tape around the ends.

3. Knots in the lines prevent slippage; however, the knots tend to reduce the tensile strength of the lines.

Below is one way the mooring lines for a larger yacht can be rigged: A shock absorber composed of a steel spring is shackled directly to the ring bolt. The mooring line, with an eye splice and thimble, is shackled to the shock absorber. The chafing area of the line is protected by PVC hose. To safeguard against a possible malfunction of the shock absorber, a short length of chain is attached to each shackle. A rubber shock absorber may also be used in place of the steel spring.

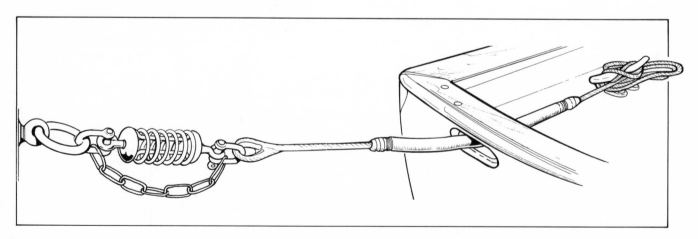

Fenders

Fenders should be hung over the side before docking. A rule of thumb maintains that at least three fenders are needed to protect the boat's side, one midships and one each fore and aft. The easiest, though not the best, way to hang the fenders is to knot them to the lifelines with a clove hitch, with an additional half hitch to prevent loosening of the knot. If there are several boats moored side by side or if wind and swell are pressing the boat against the dock, the fenders have to withstand heavy pressure. So that they remain fixed in their positions, it is best to knot them to the foot of the lifeline stanchions with two round turns and a clove hitch. When heavy swell is expected, the fenders must be made fast to sturdy deck gear such as cleats.

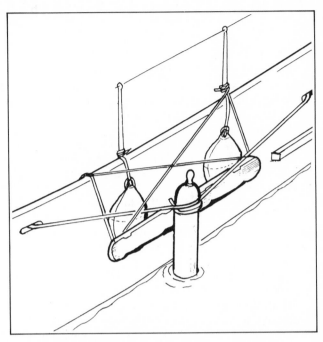

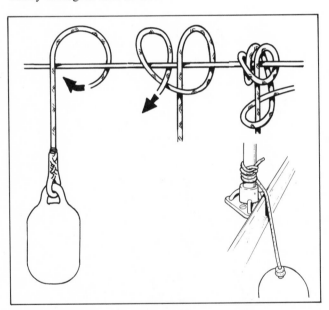

A simple and practical solution for fending off from pilings is the use of fender boards, which present a lengthy area of contact and cannot be squeezed to the side by the pilings. Fender boards also are recommended for yachts that must often tie up to dirty quay walls.

When there is swell in the harbor, it is often better to hang fenders lengthwise along the boat's side. This way they can roll up and down, adapting to the movement of the boat without chafing on the side of the hull. This also fixes their positions along the side. It is better to hang the fenders below the rubbing strake if possible.

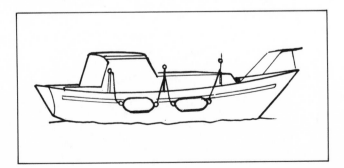

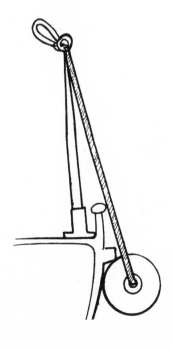

Docking Techniques

On leaving a berth at the helm of a new or unfamiliar boat, anyone will experience some slight trepidation. However, with proper attention to certain basic rules, casting off and leaving a berth is one of the simplest routines, provided:

Before letting go any lines you check that there are no loose rope ends hanging in the water. It is all too easy to foul the propeller. Take care in placing the lines on the dock **(1)**.

It is best for a crewmember to take one of the stern lines aboard. For safety's sake, the line made fast to the dock cleat or bollard should be made ready to slip **(2)**, while the other stern line is lifted over the lifeline and hand carried amidships **(3)**.

The bow lines remain coiled on deck, belayed to their cleats until the maneuver is ended **(4)**.

While fending off the next boat, do not press against the lifelines or their supports, as their mountings are often too weak to prevent damage to the deck. Instead, one should use a boathook with a soft, round plastic tip which can push against the toe rail **(5)**.

Loose sheets or lines lying on the deck are dangerous. It is easy to slip or stumble on them. Therefore, execute all movements on deck slowly and carefully **(6)**.

Boundary ropes between slips can be used to haul the boat out of the berth by hand **(7)**.

And now the most important rule: Ease the boat slowly backward and don't panic **(8)**. That is the key to success.

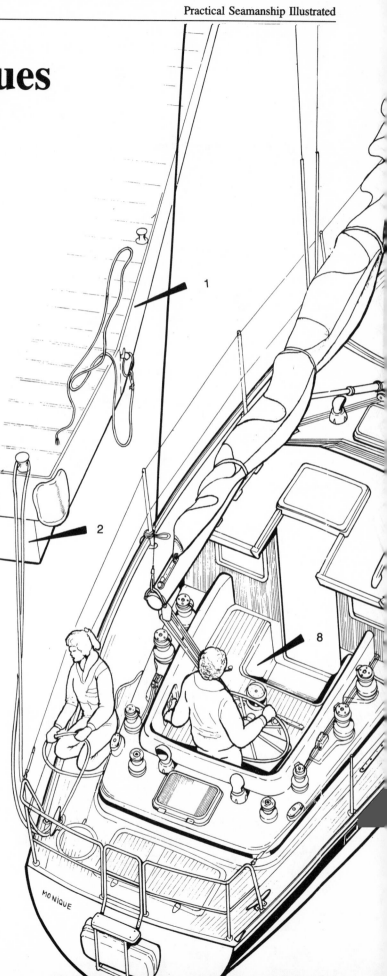

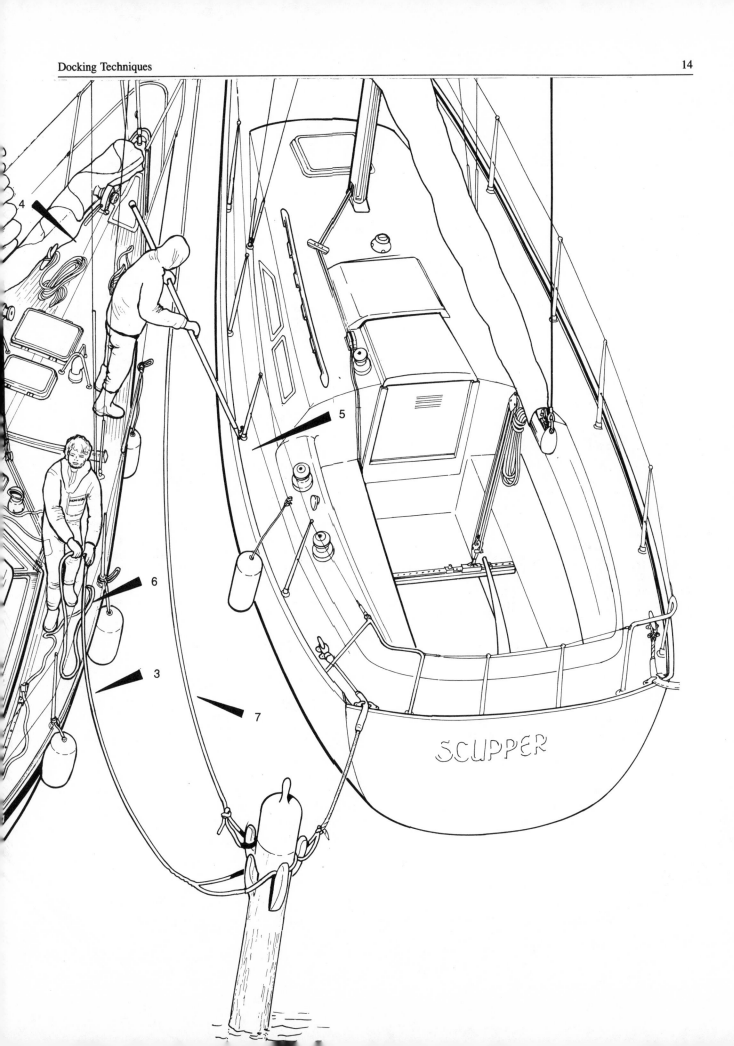

SCUPPER

Clear the Lines

It's the same old story: A yacht approaches its mooring amid hectic scrambling. The mooring line is clawed out of the rope locker and passed to the dock. Naturally the line is all twisted and fouled up and in the scramble the end of the line goes overboard into the water because the skipper completely forgot to belay his end...

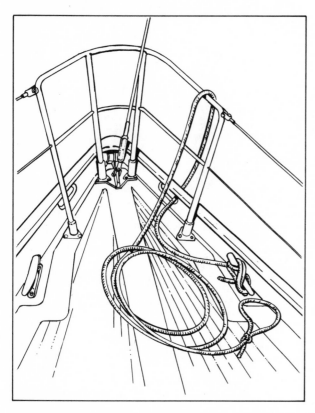

Insufficient preparations are the cause of most abortive docking maneuvers. The skipper fails to instruct the crew as to where and how he wants to dock the boat. What often happens is this: The crewmember on the bow tries desperately to clear the messed-up bow line, while the skipper, unable to get to the stern line, hangs onto the piling, half in and half out of the boat. In the meantime, the boat is adrift at the mercy of wind and current, colliding with pilings and other boats.

...That's why the first commandment, prior to docking, is: Clear the mooring lines! The lines are carefully belayed and then passed through the chock or hawsehole and over the lifeline and neatly coiled on the deck. As a matter of course, the mooring lines are made fast on the dock with the boat alongside, using the least amount of line. Haul the major portion back aboard and make it fast on deck.

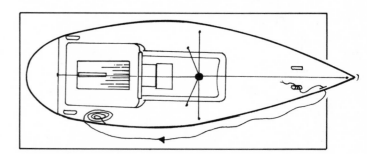

Prior to docking, the bow and stern spring lines must also be cleared. Each spring must be passed from its cleat through the hawsehole or chock and outboard, all the way to the bow or stern as appropriate, then back on deck and neatly coiled.

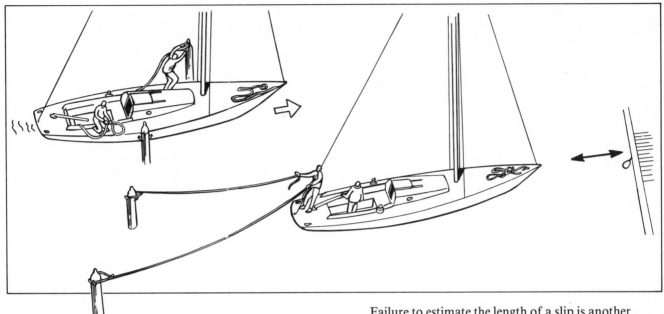

Failure to estimate the length of a slip is another prevalent cause of abortive docking attempts. Stern lines are coiled on deck while entering the slip and are too short. The bow lines cannot reach the dock. Result: The boat drifts crosswise and damage to the boats on either side is probable.

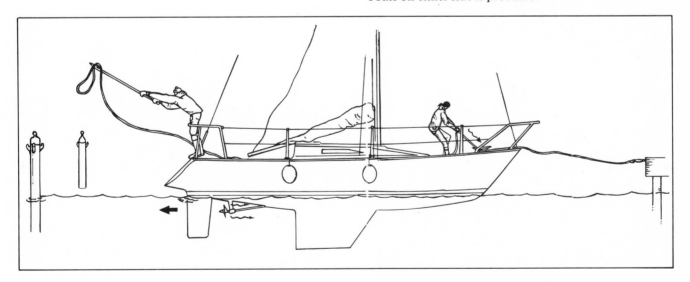

Should it be impossible to secure the stern lines to the pilings while entering the berth, the best procedure is to first secure a bow line to the dock and use the engine to move backward, while the foredeck crew promptly slacks off the bow line. It is helpful if the skipper takes large bights in the stern lines and uses the boathook to loop them over the pilings. Never tie on to wooden piling cleats, the true function of which is to prevent docking lines from sliding down the pilings. As a rule, they cannot withstand heavy lateral loads.

Berthing in a Crosswind

Approaching a slip in a strong beam wind is difficult. One must move with sufficient momentum as closely as possible to the windward piling and in passing take a turn around the windward piling with the windward stern line. This line will be slacked off until a crew-member with a long line can jump over to the dock. This line is immediately made fast far to windward, and is then used to haul the bow around. Standing in the bow, the foredeck crew hauls the bow into the proper position so that bow lines can be passed ashore. Not until the bow lines are belayed to the dock should they be slackened and the windward stern line tautened so that the leeward stern line can be made fast to the leeward piling.

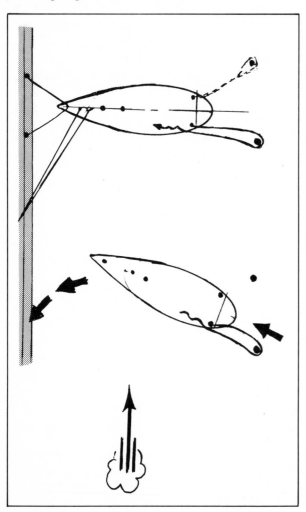

Berthing with Wind and Current Abeam

It is difficult to berth in a beam wind and current. Trying to move with the wind and current may force the bow against the lee piling; the stern then swings about quickly and the boat is drawn right back out of the berth. Under these conditions, it is almost impossible to tie onto the pilings with the stern lines. However, this maneuver succeeds if the boat moving upstream and upwind under power is turned into the berth using a lead spring line belayed to the leeward, rear piling. As soon as the stern has swung close enough to the windward piling, it is secured there. Not until the boat has swung completely into the slip can the lead spring be slacked off and taken astern to be the second stern line. There the stern is secured while the boat is moved to the dock quickly and bow lines are secured.

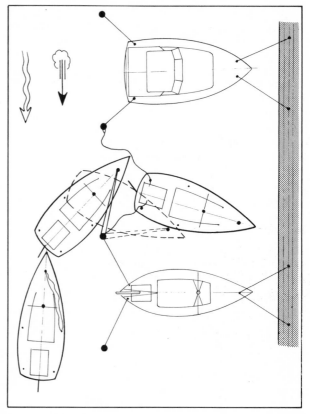

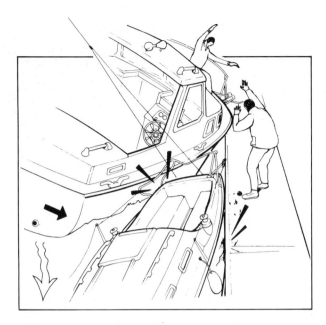

Docking in a Current

The serious damage that can result from an improper mooring attempt is shown here.

The skipper of a motorboat saw an empty berth just behind a sailboat tied to the dock. Disregarding the fact that he was moving both downstream and downwind, he headed directly into the berth. The bow line was passed to the jetty and secured.

Meanwhile, the stern swung far out into the stream. The boat drifted rapidly in a 180-degree turn and collided with the stern of the sailboat, which was slammed against the dock, fracturing the hull. This accident demonstrates that, as a matter of principle, you should always approach a dock or mooring heading upstream and/or upwind. The speed of the current is the primary consideration, assuming that its speed is at least one-half to one knot.

(1) When moving downstream toward the berth, the skipper must come about while allowing for a proper distance between the boat and dock prior to entering the berth.

(2) When the berth is abeam, the boat is allowed to drift in at the slowest possible speed, with its rudder toward the dock.

(3) If possible, the hull should be fendered all along the dock side. The bow line is secured first.

(4) Immediately thereafter the stern spring must be secured, because it determines the position of the boat at the dock. This line has the most important job.

(5) Follow with the forward spring and finally the stern line **(6)**, which has very little load to carry.

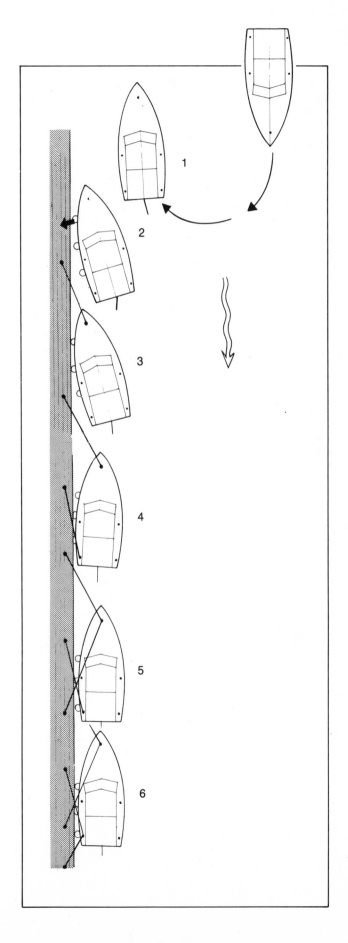

Docking with a Bow Anchor

The predominant method of docking in southern European ports is stern to the shore, utilizing a bow anchor. To successfully use this procedure it is vital to know whether the boat has a right-handed or left-handed propeller because when going astern the boat will turn to starboard or port according to the direction in which the propeller rotates. Not knowing the proper rotation might cause one to miss the gap between boats.

Yacht **A**'s propeller, when in reverse, turns in a clockwise direction. Therefore, the skipper must start backing down while the boat is still about 45 degrees to the anchor and quay.

After the anchor is let go and the rode paid out, the boat is powered astern to the quay. The stern swings to starboard and the berth is hit on the nose.

Yacht **B**'s propeller turns counterclockwise in reverse. She is moved past the opening to the berth far enough to approach the anchor position from an angle of 45 degrees, but this time with the anchor to port. After the anchor is let go and the engine run in reverse, the stern will swing to port.

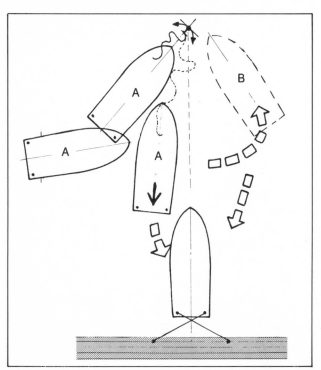

Docking in an Onshore Wind

Providing the strength of the wind is used with caution, docking in an onshore wind is simple. When tying up alongside a dock, the boat should be well fendered and eased into the dock bow first, since in both motorboats and sailing vessels the bow pays off before the wind **(1)**. At this stage, the forward spring must be made fast without delay. The wind then pushes the stern against the dock and the docking is finished without any trouble. In a very strong onshore wind, the boat is stopped parallel to its berth permitting the wind to force the bow against the dock **(2)**. If there is a heavy swell breaking on the pier or jetty and there are no stern pilings available, then it is preferable to

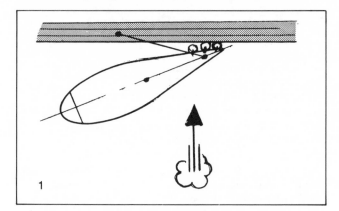

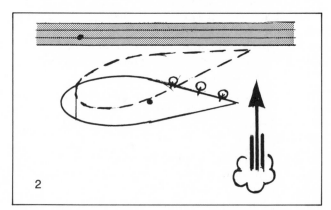

anchor an appropriate distance from the pier and pay out the anchor rode, letting the boat drift astern until the stern lines can be made fast **(3)**. However, there is a risk that the anchor may drag and cause the rudder or the stern to collide with the dock.

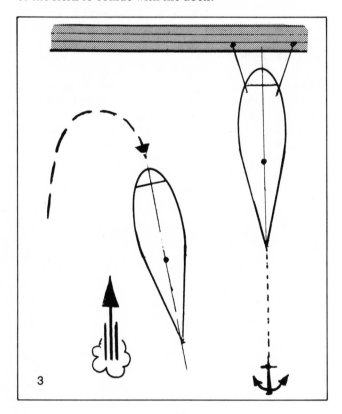

Docking in a Tight Space

Tying up to a dock or float is always a problem when the open berth is at best no longer than your boat. The answer is to call on the forward spring. The well-fendered bow must be eased into the dock so that the foredeck crew can step across and make the line fast — as far astern as possible. The skipper turns the rudder away from the dock and powers ahead slowly. The stern then slowly swings into the dock.

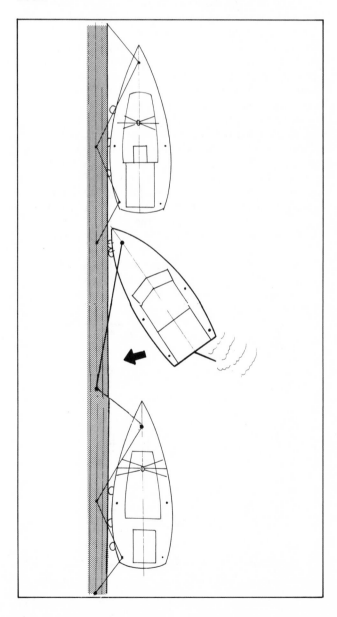

Leaving the Slip in Beam Winds or Currents

Take advantage of the lines connecting your boat to the pilings and dock to facilitate departure from the slip. First cast off the leeward bow line and prepare to slip the windward bow line. This line must be long enough to steady the bow until the row of pilings is reached. Thereafter slip the leeward stern line (1). If this is impossible, it must be postponed.

The boat is hand-hauled out of the slip by two crew-members while the bow line is slacked off and the stern line is hauled in. When the stern is next to the piling, remove the remaining stern line from its cleat and prepare to take it midships (2). If the current is too strong, it may be necessary to reeve an emergency line to a midships cleat. If you haven't been able to cast off the lee stern line before this, it must now be accomplished by slacking off the windward line and letting the stern drift toward the lee piling. Then, while slacking away the bow line, haul the boat backward until the stern line is amidships (3).

Now the bow line should be cast off, the rudder turned into the current or wind and the boat backed under power in that direction out of the slip. In the meantime, the erstwhile stern line is carried forward by hand until the bow clears the neighboring boat or the lee piling (4).

Whether the propeller is right- or left-handed is immaterial in the procedure since the current and/or wind exercises greater leeward pressure on the bow than on the stern.

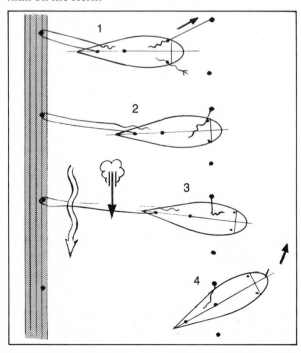

Leaving a Dock in an Onshore Wind

It is difficult to cast off in an onshore wind, especially when other boats limit the area of your berth. We must again rely on the forward spring. With the rudder toward the dock and the boat making slow speed ahead, move the stern as far from the jetty as possible (1). In this situation, the bow must be particularly well fendered. If you are sure the boat can move astern without striking another boat, turn the helm to starboard and move slowly astern under power. Not until you are absolutely certain the boat is moving clear astern out of the slip should the forward spring be cast off (2). As soon as there is sufficient clearance to safely avoid the slip, the boat moves ahead with the helm kept to starboard (3).

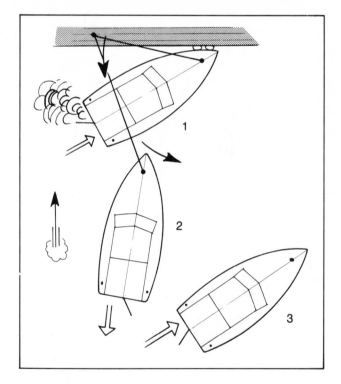

Casting Off into the Current

As a matter of principle, casting off against the current succeeds whether moving ahead or astern. First (when going ahead) cast off the stern line (1), then the forward spring (2). The bow line also can be cast off while the crew on the dock keeps the bow from swinging, since the after spring is holding the boat safely in the current (3). This spring should be ready to slip, so that it can be released and hauled in.

The foredeck crew pushes the bow away from the dock and boards amidship. The skipper heads into the current and powers slowly ahead (4).

Not until the boat has swung far enough to make way should the after spring be slipped (5). Be careful to avoid hitting the dock with the transom.

Casting Off Downstream

This is considerably more difficult than standing off against the current. Here again the proper operation of the spring line is essential.

First cast off the bow line (1). The forward spring is made ready to slip. Next the after spring is cast off (2), and then the stern line (3). To swing the stern away from the dock smoothly, the helmsman gives power slow ahead with the rudder pointing dockward (4). The bow must be well fendered. Now the current will quickly swing the stern farther around. Then the forward spring must be slipped quickly and the boat moved astern under power with the rudder pointing toward the channel (5).

Not until the boat has completely cleared the dock should forward motion be initiated (6).

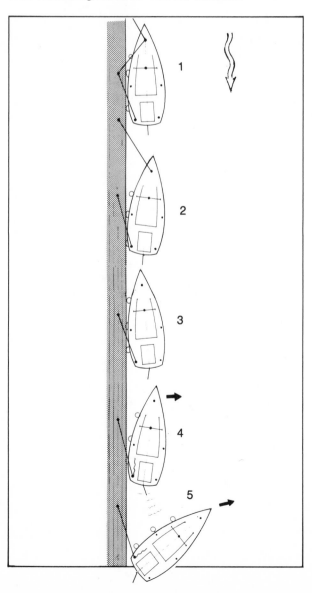

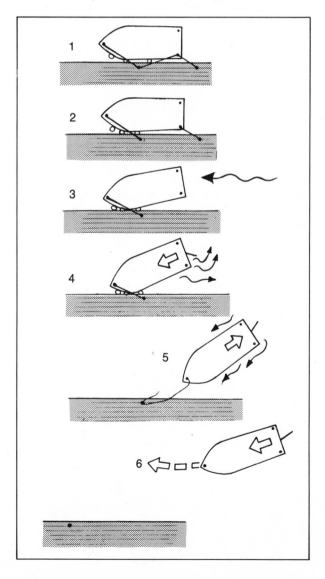

Ready to Anchor

One universal anchor suitable for all bottoms does not exist. Therefore, it is recommended that a boat carry at least two anchors on board; each should have the highest possible degree of effectiveness for its particular type of bottom. One should be a conventional heavy anchor that will hold in rocky bottom or in a bottom overgrown with weeds. The other one should be a modern, lightweight-type anchor with large flukes that can hold in sandy bottoms.

Most Commonly Used Types of Anchors

This drawing elucidates the utilization ranges of the most common types of anchors.

1. The traditional fisherman or kedge anchor is close to being the most universally usable anchor. It holds on rocky, stony or coral bottoms and also in bottoms overgrown with seaweed.

2. The plow anchor is principally used on sandy or muddy bottoms.

3. The Danforth® anchor is one of the lightweight-type anchors used for holding in sandy, muddy and shingle bottoms.

4. The relatively heavy Navy anchor also has good holding ability in sandy, muddy and shingle bottoms, but is suitable only for larger yachts.

5. Unusual, but nevertheless trustworthy in the right conditions, is the Scandinavian Sea-Grip anchor, whose flukes may be turned around each other for stowage. It will hold in sand, mud, shingle and rocks as well as a bottom with seaweed growth. However, the fact that only one fluke digs in at a time tends to restrict its holding ability.

6. The well-established folding-type anchor holds well when hooked into boulders, shingle and coral growths as well as mud, but seaweed growth, hard clay and packed sand bottom cause problems.

7. The grapnel anchor has similar characteristics, with the exception that this anchor's flukes have little holding power in a soft mud or sandy bottom. On the other hand, these same flukes can penetrate seaweed growth and work themselves to a hold between plant roots.

8. Relatively new is the Bruce anchor from England, which was developed originally for mooring around tidal bore islands and anchoring in the North Sea. The characteristics are similar to those of the plow anchor as it holds well in sandy and muddy bottom. In seaweed it does a very bad job of digging in. It is reputed to have good holding power; however, it requires a long chain rode or a long chain leader when using rope, because this type of anchor will only dig itself in properly if the stock is parallel to the bottom. It mounts simply and accommodates itself well to the shape of the bow.

Sand   Shingles   Coral

Stones   Mud   Weeds

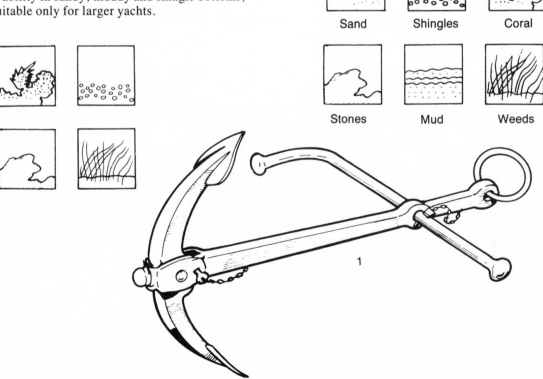

1

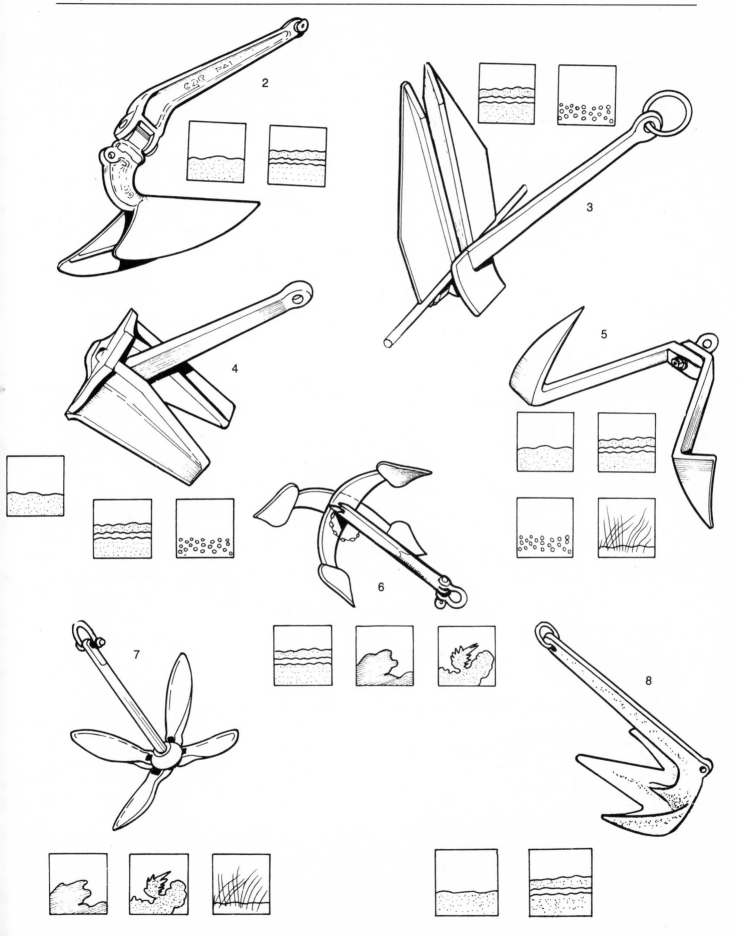

Why Doesn't the Anchor Hold?

Anchoring can be deceiving. Many skippers are astonished to find their boat dragging its anchor, when this has never happened before. Why isn't the anchor holding? There can be a host of reasons:

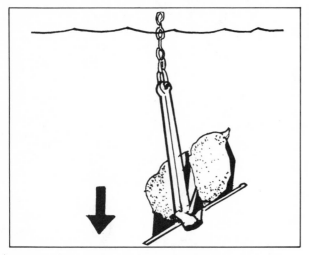

1. Sometimes you must weigh anchor because you have encroached on the anchorage area of another boat. If while sailing to another nearby anchorage the foredeck hand does not haul the anchor all the way into the boat, he fails to see large mud balls caught in the flukes. On arrival at the new or substitute anchorage the anchor is let go but does not dig itself into the holding ground in a proper fashion due to the mud balls.

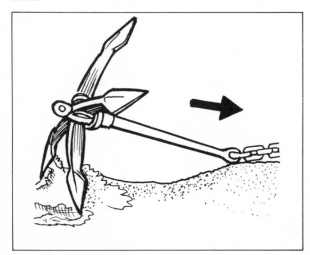

2. Folding and grapnel anchors have four flukes which can be spread out like a fan. Frequently they fail to dig themselves in properly because the angle of the fluke to the stock is too obtuse to grip the bottom.

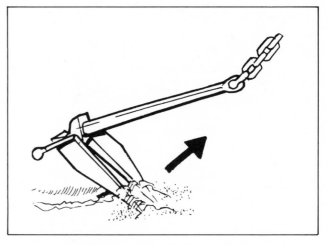

3. The chain rode or chain leader should be paid out to a sufficient length so that the anchor stock lies parallel to the bottom and the pull is horizontal. If the chain is too short, so that the stock is positioned at an angle to the ground, the flukes are unable to dig themselves into the bottom.

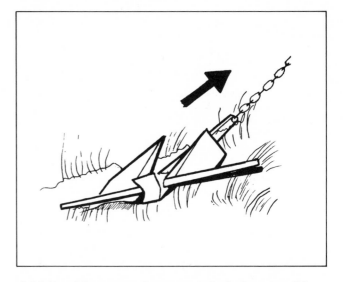

4. Lightweight-type anchors are particularly susceptible to short rodes. The nature of the holding ground is also of major importance, because weedy growth or stones, coral branches and shingle prevent the broad flukes from digging in. In fact, when they are lying in seaweed, they often slide right over it.

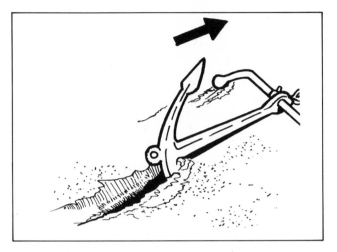

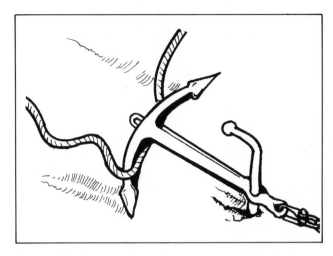

5. In a soft bottom, a fisherman's anchor may simply dig a groove unless it catches something firm on which to hold.

6. And finally not a few skippers have unknowingly let their anchors go right over some obstruction on the bottom that prevents the anchor from digging in.

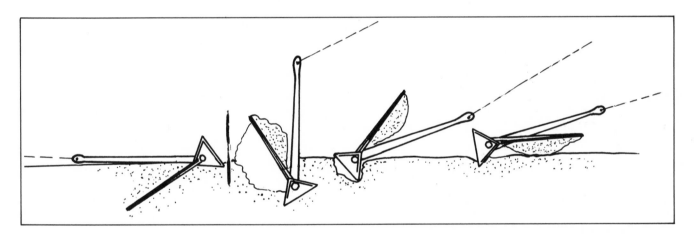

The unexplained drifting away of a boat in tidal waters also can have another reason: Clay or thick mud will often adhere to the broad flukes of light-weight anchors when being tipped over. For instance, when the direction of current changes, so does the direction of pull on the boat; the broad flukes tip over and fail to bite.

Chains and Rodes

The proper scope of a rode or chain depends substantially on two factors: on the depth of water and on the material weight. By its nature, chain weighs more than rope and, therefore, is more likely to keep the stock of the anchor parallel to the ground, thus preventing its breaking out. When anchoring with an all-chain rode, scope should be at least four times the water depth. With a chain leader (no shorter than the length of the vessel) on a rope rode, scope should be at least six times the water depth, and when anchoring with all rope, a scope of 10 times the water depth is required.

An overriding rule about anchoring is that you need more scope proportionally in shallow water than in deeper.

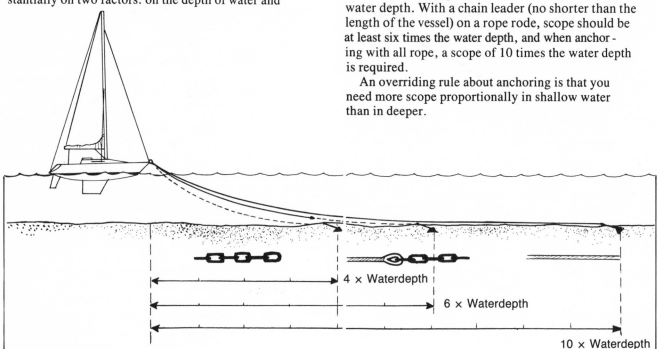

4 × Waterdepth

6 × Waterdepth

10 × Waterdepth

Adding a Back-Up Anchor

Supplementing your main anchor with another — usually lighter — second anchor is a possible means of increasing holding power in high winds and seas. In the illustration, a lightweight anchor is connected to a fisherman's anchor with at least a 15-foot (five meter) length of rope or, preferably, chain.

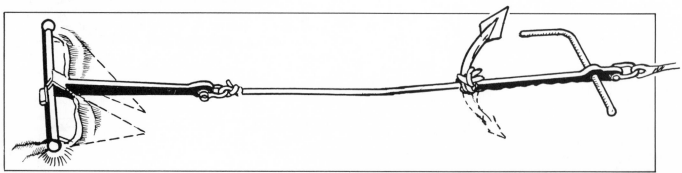

Catenary Weights

A catenary anchor weight made fast to the rode and lowered to the bottom can materially enhance the holding power of the anchor or shorten the length of necessary rode. There are special sliding shackles for this purpose. A thin line can be fastened to the catenary weight to facilitate raising it prior to weighing anchor.

It is possible to make do with a sail bag or sack loaded with a piece of chain or a heavy tool, fastened to the rode with a standard shackle.

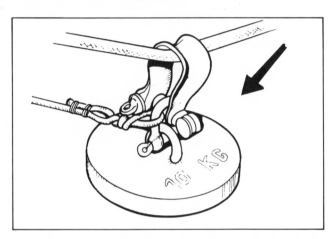

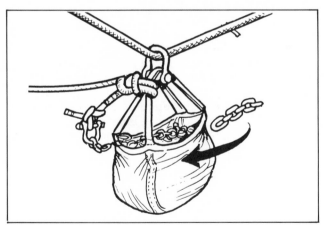

Anchor Mounts

For a boat with six tons displacement and a length overall of about 35 feet (10 meters), the following has proven to be the appropriate amount of anchoring equipment:

1. In the stem is the anchor bed with a plow or similar anchor fastened in such a manner that the fluke points cannot damage the bow. This means that the anchor rollers must extend over the stem. To hold the anchor in place, a security pin in the roller bracket is required.

2. For manual operation, there should be a windlass available in a boat of this size. The windlass must be located directly abaft the bow rollers so that the chain can be fed directly into the wildcat and then free-fall into the chain locker.

3. It is recommended that the windlass also have a gypsy for handling rope.

4. The anchor locker must be situated behind the windlass so that the reserve anchor and line can be utilized handily.

5. A strong cleat or samson post securely bolted to the deck is necessary to take over the chain or rope from the windlass when necessary.

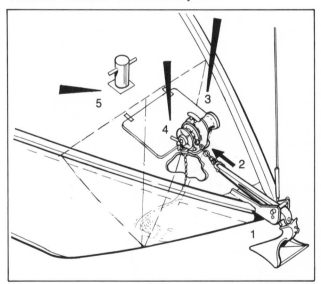

The Anchor Locker

More than a few yachts have gone adrift helplessly after anchoring, because the rode wasn't made fast on deck or in the anchor locker. It is important that the rode be connected to an eyebolt in the anchor storage area by means of a short, strong safety line. Under no circumstances should chain be shackled directly to the eyebolt since, in an emergency, the chain cannot be let go in a hurry. The last link in the chain is made fast by means of a line and knot that is easily untied under tension. The eye must be securely bolted and able to withstand the load placed on it by sharp, jerky motions of the rode. While anchoring, of course, the rode should be secured on deck — don't count on the safety line and bolt. Many anchoring procedures have been frustrated by fouled chains. If there is sufficient free space between the hawsepipe and the pile of chain, it will not become fouled under normal circumstances. However, in some boats, the chain is led through a long pipe into the chain locker. When the top of the chain locker is too low so that the chain stops running in freely, it can get snarled and jam when running out. If it can run freely in, it will run freely out.

Ideally, the anchor locker should be divided lengthwise into two compartments so that the chain can be stowed in one and the chain leader with rope in the other. It is beneficial if the hatch is large enough so that the reserve lightweight anchor can be passed through it. The anchor locker must be separated from the rest of the forepeak by a sturdy, water-tight bulkhead and have a drain. The stemhead fittings should have two bow rollers and a locking bolt so that two anchors can be used simultaneously.

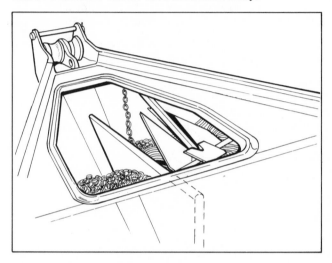

Anchoring Aids

Above, right shows one proven method used by singlehanded sailors to let go the anchor without leaving the cockpit. The anchor, cleared to let go, is hung over the bow roller, while a shackle on a short line belayed to a bow cleat prevents the chain from letting go. However, the shackle is not closed by a threaded bolt but by an unthreaded pin that can be

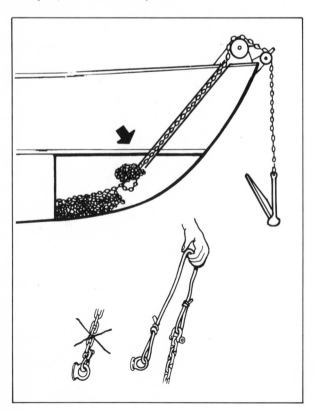

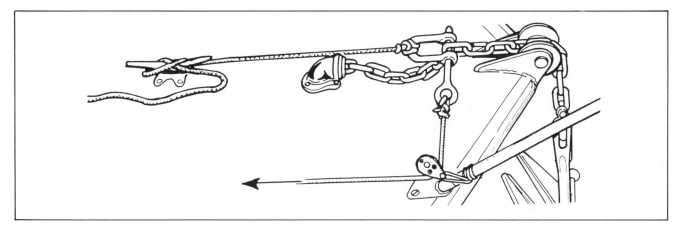

easily withdrawn and that is connected to the cockpit by a line and block. This same device can be used as a spring to prevent jerking or jolting of the chain when anchored in a seaway, though the line would have to be securely shackled and sufficiently slackened off to reach at least three feet (one meter) over the bow roller.

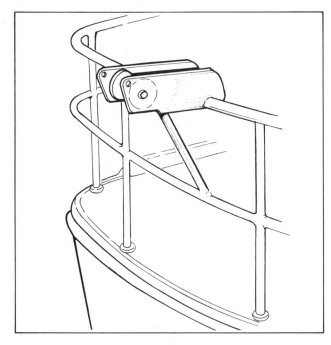

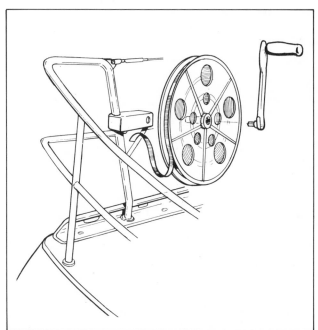

A new type of webbing strap has proven itself as an anchor rode for the stern anchor. It is wound on a plastic reel, which is mounted on the stern pulpit and which can be turned by a winch handle. When the anchor is let go, the strap unrolls off the reel without difficulty. The breaking load of the strap is very high, so that it offers the same safety factor as a traditional rode.

At times, such as in a constricted anchorage, an anchor led from the stern is desirable to keep the boat from swinging. To facilitate letting go and weighing the stern anchor, one can use an anchor roller on the stern pulpit. An appropriate fitting can be welded directly to the steel pipe of the pulpit. If the anchor cannot be weighed by hand, the rode can be passed over the roller to a sheet or halyard winch. The rode is belayed by taking it out of the roller and making it fast to a stern cleat.

Anchoring by "Shooting Up"

When anchoring a sloop under sail, only the mainsail is used. As soon as the proper anchorage has been selected, the jib is taken in and the anchor rode is flaked on deck with the end cleated. Be sure it is made fast to the anchor (1).

The helmsman sails into the wind or current, estimating the distance the boat will coast to the spot where he wants to drop the anchor (2).

When the boat has stopped, he commands, "Let go the anchor!" The rode is paid out smoothly hand over hand as soon as the boat starts drifting astern (3).

Not until the amount of rode considered to be adequate has been almost paid out is the boat snubbed to come to a stop (4).

Then the remainder is paid out and the boat is observed to see whether it turns into the wind. The crew signals the helmsman that the anchor has bitten. For safety's sake, it is recommended that the bite be reinforced by moving the boat astern under power for a short distance. Bearings are taken on two land-marks, one behind the other, to determine whether the anchor position is maintained (5).

If the wind is against the current, you also shoot up before letting go the anchor so as to lower and furl the sail while you are facing into the wind. Then feed the anchor out slowly, hand over hand until it touches the bottom. Then smoothly pay out several yards more rode or chain and belay on the bow cleat. The anchor will take hold as the boat falls astern. The boat will then swing until it lies to the current. Only now do you pay out the rest of the line. When the anchor is firmly set, you finally make fast.

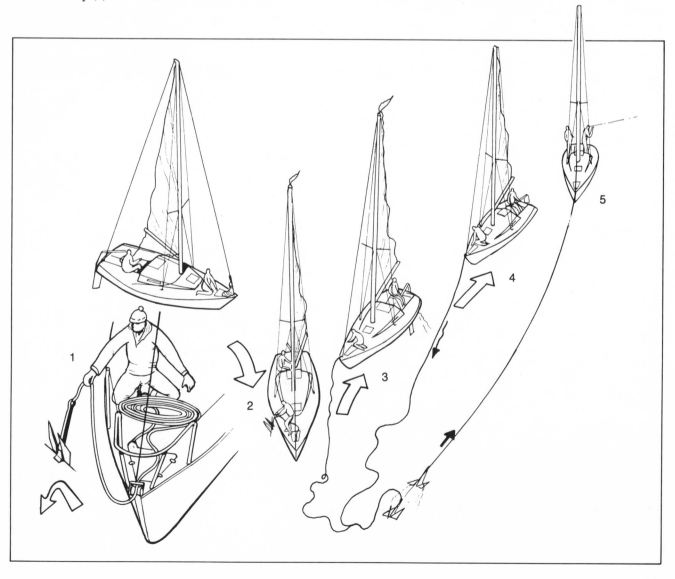

Anchoring the Motorboat

Anchoring a motor boat as well as a sailboat under power is accomplished while heading into the wind or, as the case may be, into the current (**1**).

As soon as the boat heads into the wind, the helmsman puts the motor in reverse (**2**), and then commands, "Let go the anchor!" when the boat starts drifting astern.

In smaller motorboats, the anchor is normally slacked sidewise off the deck, because it is dangerous to be leaning over the bow if the helmsman mistakenly accelerates backward in a hurry. It is therefore important to carefully clear the anchor rode outside of the pulpit and belay it to the foredeck cleat (**3**).

Shortly before the rode is fully paid out, the foredeck hand stops it and slackens the remainder out hand over hand, while the helmsman observes the course astern (**4**).

As soon as the rode is safely belayed, the helmsman gives more power astern to dig the anchor in (**5**).

Immediately thereafter, a visual bearing is taken over a nearby object, if available, to a point or points on shore, to gain information on whether or not the boat is holding its position (**6**).

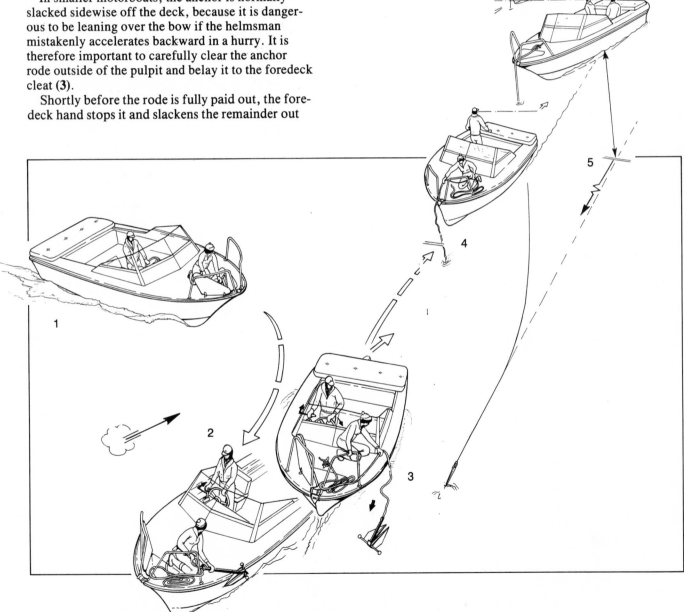

Watch Out for Coils

The following anchoring incident can become particularly dangerous: The foredeck hand has coiled a part of the rode on the deck and has unwittingly stepped into a bight. When the anchor is let go the person could be snatched overboard, unable to free himself from the heavy anchor which pulls him underwater — for a singlehanded sailor a deadly peril.

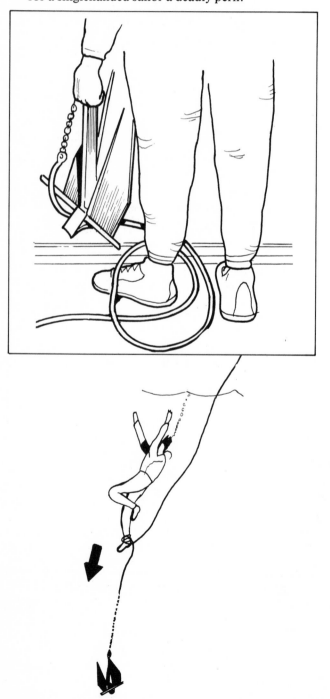

Special Anchoring Methods

The swinging of an anchored yacht can be reduced by having her lie to two anchors. The heavier anchor is in this case also the main anchor. This anchor is let go first and its position is marked with an anchor buoy (1).

As soon as the main anchor holds, the boat is headed under power at an angle of about 35 degrees to the anchor buoy until it reaches a position abeam of the buoy (2).

At this point the second anchor cannot be let go, because it would then lie at the same distance from the boat as the main anchor and could foul it should both anchors be dragged together in a high wind. So the boat is powered ahead for several boat lengths and then the second anchor is let go (3).

Now the boat is permitted to drift astern for about one-half the distance to its proposed anchorage; there the rode is belayed and under reverse power the second anchor is made to hold (4).

Then the boat is allowed to drift back on the wind until both anchors are holding (5).

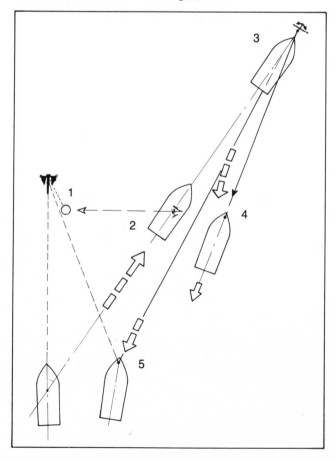

The tiresome swinging back and forth can be alleviated for small boats lying at anchor by another means. The anchor rode is made fast to the bight of a rope, approximately two boat lengths long, whose ends are belayed to the bow cleat and the windward midships cleat (below, left).

The length of the rope end leading to the bow cleat should be somewhat shorter than that leading amidships, so that the boat rides with the wind off the port bow. In this manner the boat is given a constant leeward drift and is stabilized in its position.

Mooring ship is a technique often resorted to in natural harbors on the North Sea coast where tidal flows require a boat to use less swinging room (1).

The main anchor is let go against the tidal current (2). Then the boat is allowed to drift astern downstream (broken line) until twice the normal amount of rode is normally necessary has been paid out (3).

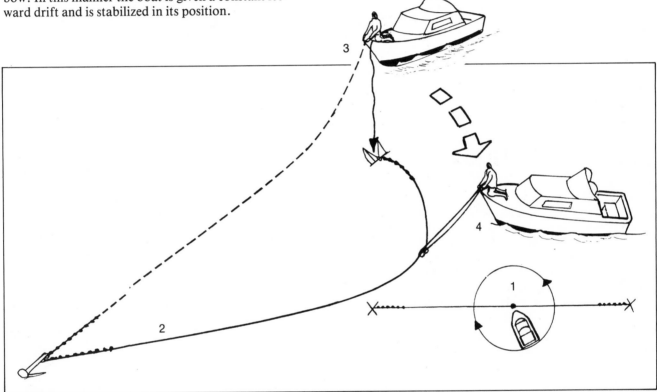

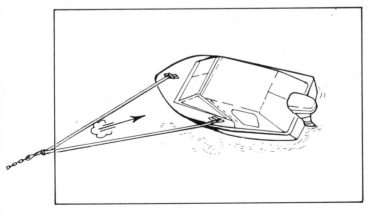

Now the second anchor is let go with ample rode paid out. Then the boat is hauled against the current along the rode of the first or main anchor until it reaches a point approximately halfway between the two anchors. At this point, both rodes are either shackled or lashed together at such a depth that the boat's keel will not foul the rodes as it swings (4). Alternatively, each rode can be belayed to separate bow cleats in a Bahamian moor.

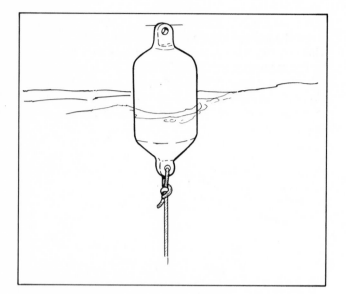

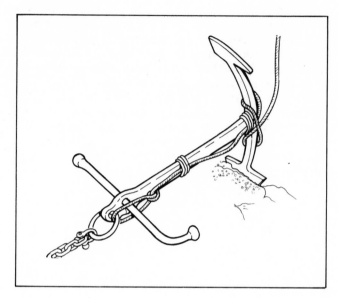

The Anchor Buoy

In a crowded anchorage you should always use an anchor buoy. This will indicate the position of your anchor to the other skippers, and will make it easier to retrieve your own anchor if it gets fouled by some- one else's chain. A buoy will work only if it is made fast directly to the crown and is not fouled around a fluke or under the chain. A fender or detergent bottle will serve as a buoy, provided it has enough buoyancy.

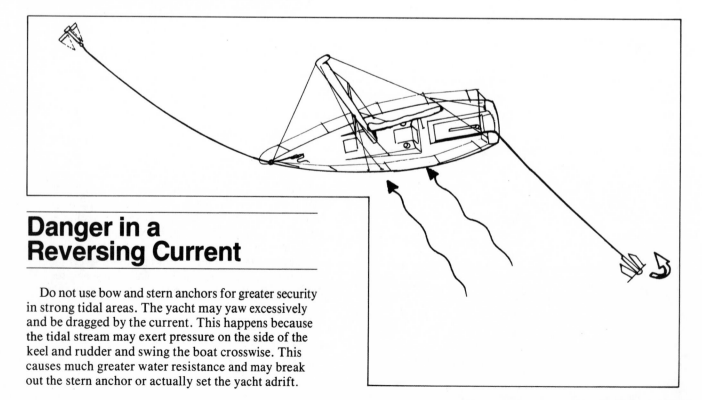

Danger in a Reversing Current

Do not use bow and stern anchors for greater security in strong tidal areas. The yacht may yaw excessively and be dragged by the current. This happens because the tidal stream may exert pressure on the side of the keel and rudder and swing the boat crosswise. This causes much greater water resistance and may break out the stern anchor or actually set the yacht adrift.

Keeping the Tender Off the Topsides

If you are lying to bow and stern anchors near shore in a cove when the wind is offshore, there is a simple trick to keeping the tender away from the yacht if the wind suddenly rises and veers, which often happens in coves with steep shores. Set the spinnaker pole in one of the holes in the toe rail or at a chain plate, lash it outboard and run the painter through a block at the end of the pole, as in the detail drawing.

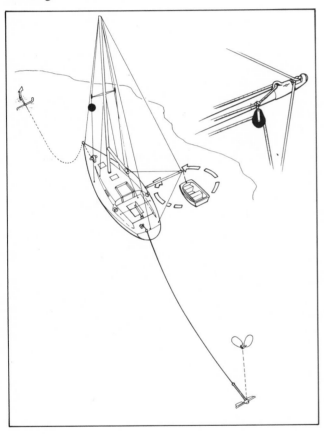

Ensuring Swinging Room

To prevent grounding you must choose your anchorage and the length of your chain and rope with great care. Whenever possible, anchor where there is room for a 360-degree swing without any obstructions. The distance from shore must be great enough to allow some drift before the boat grounds. Your anchor must be dropped in such a position that even a 360-degree swing will not cause you to touch another anchored boat (1).

There's usually an illusion that the anchorage is, of course, too crowded for several yachts. For that very reason one must be certain that they will not collide when they all swing the same way with a change of wind direction (assuming that there is no current acting against the wind) (2).

It is important when the stern is toward the shore that there be no danger of collision with boats astern that might be lying to two anchors, or might actually be made fast to shore (3).

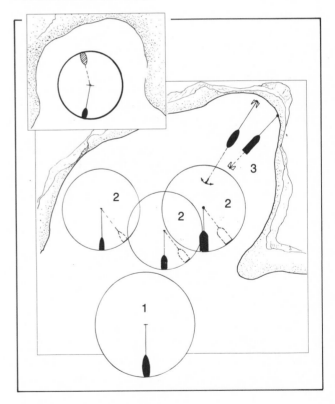

Upon anchoring in an unknown bay whose depths are not charted, the swinging radius has to be sounded using the tender and a hand lead. At the same time, search out underwater obstructions. If you find shallows or if the shore is too near, you must either anchor farther off or set a stern anchor to prevent excessive swinging.

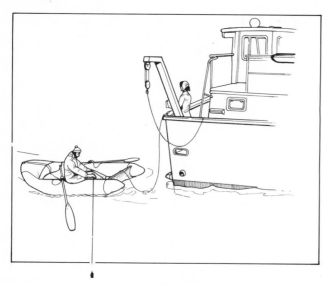

In tidal waters a boat is frequently anchored too close to shore. With a change of current, the boat swings as much as 180 degrees. Sometimes, if the wind remains constant, it works with the current to swing the boat in a half circle at the full extent of the rode. The boat may ground and, as the water ebbs away, dry out and fall over against the face of the shore with ensuing damage.

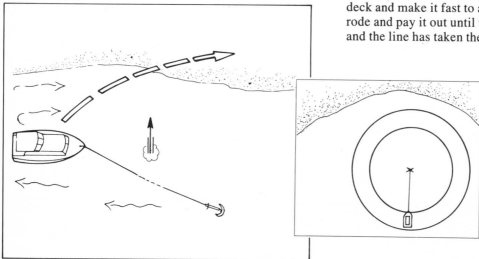

Clawing Off a Lee Shore: Under Power...

In a narrow bight the boat will naturally use a stern anchor to prevent swinging onto a lee shore with a change of wind. Because this second anchor is usually a lighter one, and because the depth to seaward often increases rapidly, this anchor must be equipped with a chain and rope twice as long as usual. This can be done only when there are no yachts anchored directly astern. Mark the position of the anchor with a buoy —even better, with a line of buoys consisting of three or four fenders—so that arriving yachts will know just where your anchor is.

Important: You must load the whole line of buoys into your tender before you set out, because if you drag the whole thing astern of the tender you will not be able to steer properly away from the yacht (1).

When the wind comes around onshore, the lighter stern anchor has to hold the boat in place. Under these conditions you must immediately move up toward your main anchor (2).

In order to do this, you must pay out more stern rode until you can haul up the bow anchor (3).

Now the boat is turned around while lying to its stern anchor and moved up under power, until you can haul in the rode gently and with care (4).

When you have reached the anchor buoy, come up over the stern anchor, break it out and leave the anchorage under engine and mainsail (5).

Here's how to turn the boat around in this example: First make a line fast to the stern rode with a rolling hitch. Lead this line outboard to the foredeck and make it fast to a bow cleat. Now cast off the rode and pay it out until the boat has swung around and the line has taken the strain.

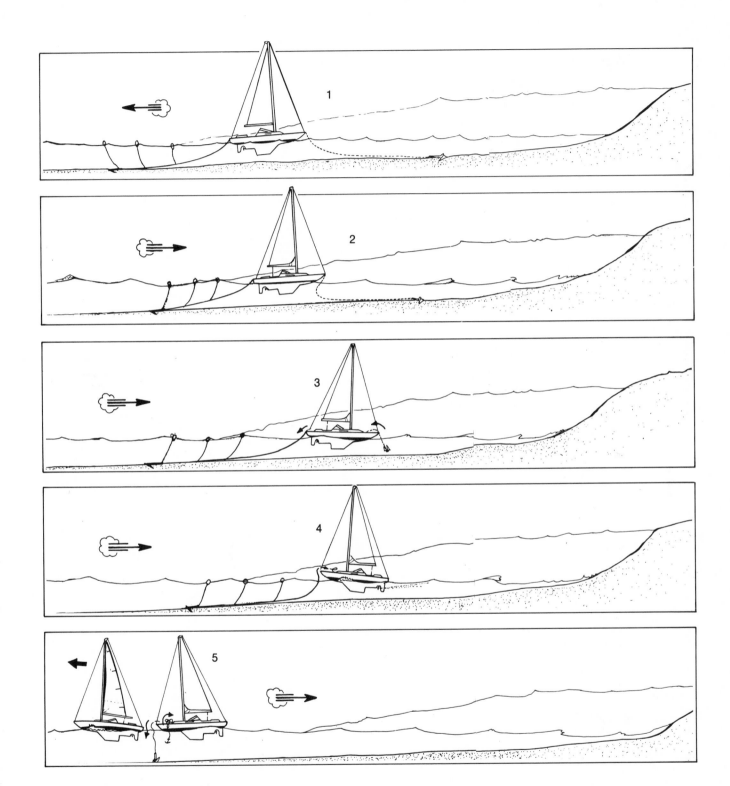

. . . . And Under Sail

If for any reason the engine will not start, you must leave the anchorage under sail. Here's how to do it.

1. First, set the main while the small working jib lies on the foredeck ready for use. (You use this jib even when the wind is light.)

2. Sheet the main in tight and slowly and smoothly sail up to the chain or hawser, until the foredeck hand calls ''Up and down!''

3. Next, the anchor is broken out. Immediately ease the main to a beam reach trim and steer a beam-reaching course to the extent that the coastline permits. This gets you going.

4. If the situation permits, sail slowly upwind with the main sheeted in very tight. With sufficient way on, come about.

5. Set the jib on the new tack as quickly as you can.

This maneuver, to claw out of an anchorage on a lee shore under sail, is much more difficult with larger yachts and their heavier anchors, because the anchor windlass may be overloaded. Hence the anchor would have to be broken out under way— "sailing the anchor out" (see below).

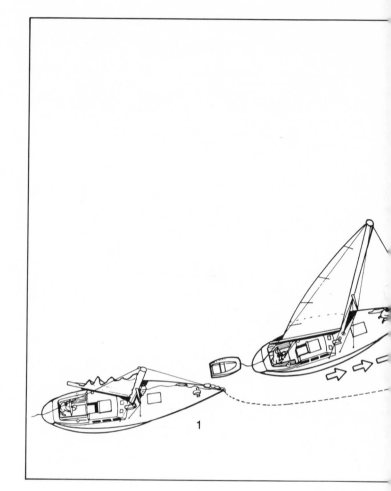

1. In heavy wind take a reef in the main.

2. Just before you come up to the anchor line, the second crew sets the main.

3. Now he immediately goes back to the helm, hardens in the main and falls off a bit. As soon as the ship is making some headway, the foredeck hand stops hauling in the anchor chain or rode and sets the jib.

4. The jibsheet is at once trimmed in hard by the crew in the cockpit. Now take in as much rope or chain as possible.

5. As soon as it is tight, come about and back the jib. Now the yacht will drift over its anchor.

6. As soon as there is no more slack to take in, make the rode fast. Then trim the jib on the new tack and the yacht will break the anchor out due to the pressure of the sails and its own momentum. This done, the anchor can be hauled up without difficulty, while the yacht is steered on a safe course under sail.

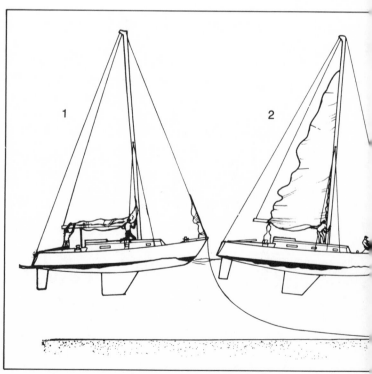

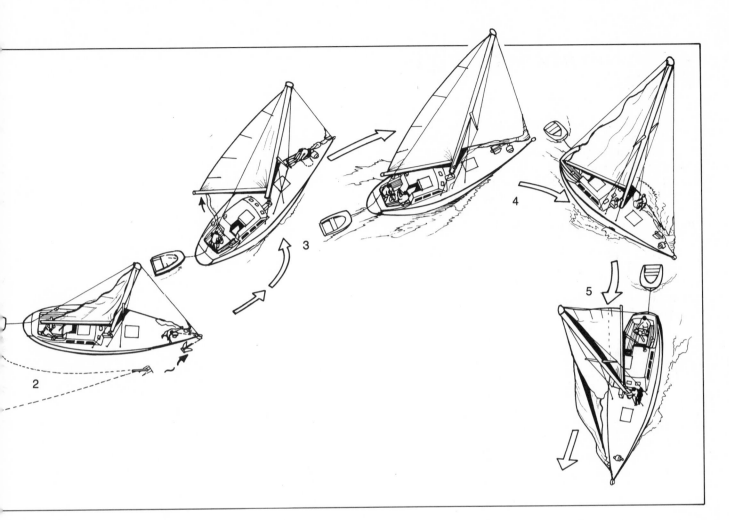

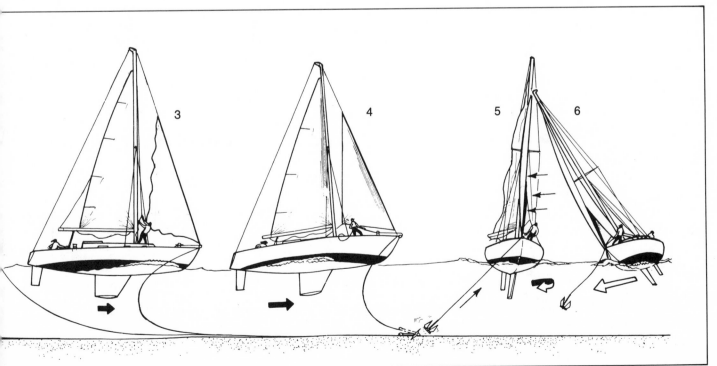

When the Anchor Won't Break Out

It is usually quite possible to break out a well dug-in anchor by redistributing weight, even in the case of light-displacement and trim-sensitive boats.

Start with the entire crew on the foredeck, who haul the rode as tight as possible and make it fast. Now have the whole crew run to the stern and try to start the boat pitching. This will at least loosen the anchor so that you will probably be able to break it out and haul it up without difficulty.

If there is a swell in the anchorage, you can make use of the waves. Haul the chain as short as possible with the windlass. The pitching of the boat will break the anchor out and the helmsman can motor out at a low forward speed.

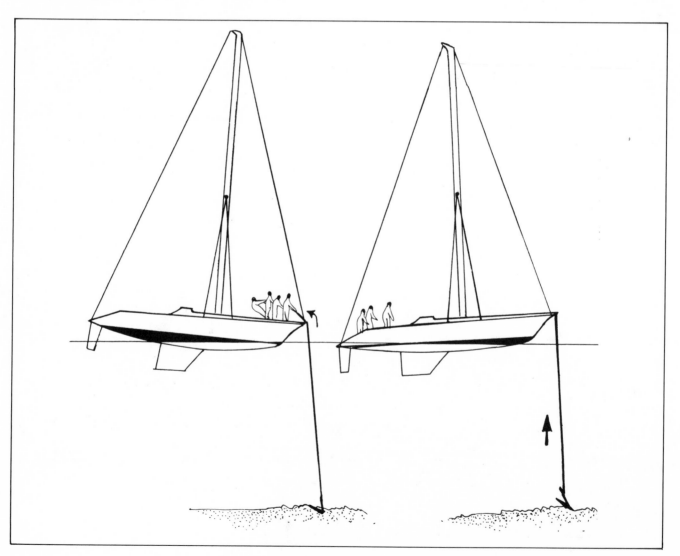

If there is no wave action in the anchorage, you will have to use engine power to break the anchor out. In this case, too, you haul the rode in as tight as possible on the windlass and cleat it down. Now power over the anchor with the wind or current. Be very careful with your engine speed, so as not to overload fastenings and cleats.

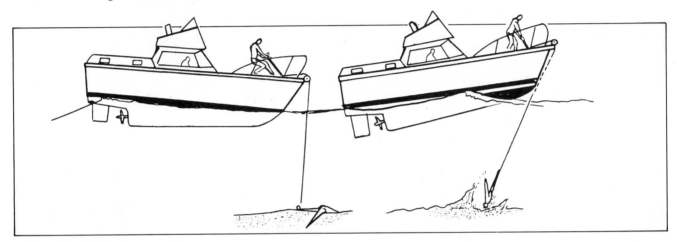

Fouled Anchor

Because the wind may change direction suddenly, the boat may not lie straight downwind but may swing back and forth. Thus a turn may form around the anchor system somewhere. If the rode or the chain gets under the anchor of another yacht, the other anchor may be broken out (1).

Often, a light sideways pull on the anchor will cause a considerable loss in holding power and the breaking out of the anchor (2).

If your anchor is lying under someone else's chain, you might try to catch his chain with a grapnel. Lead this as close as possible to your fouled anchor. As soon as you have grabbed the chain, haul the grapnel up by hand or with the windlass until the anchor is cleared.

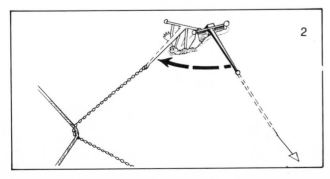

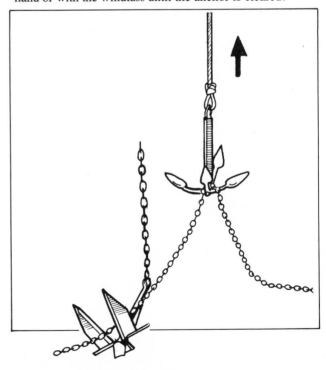

Towing with Understanding

Towing is an operation that doesn't call for much description, so long as the weather is calm and the speed is right for the job, but things surely look different when the sea builds up. Then, a sudden jerk of the towed boat sternward may part the towline. Fasteners may be ripped out. Worst of all, a towline snapping back presents a deadly danger to the crew of the towing and the towed boats.

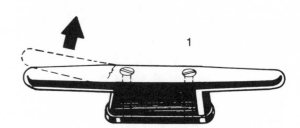

Towing Cleats

Marine suppliers offer a great many models of cleats for the most varied installations. Quite often types of cleats unsuitable for towing or even making fast are mounted on the deck. Or they may be inadequately fastened. Under towing stresses, a horn may break off (1), or the whole fitting may be torn out, particularly if it is held merely with wood screws (2).

Sharp-edged types can cut right through a towline (3).

If a cleat is to hold fast under heavy load, it must be held to the deck with thru-bolts. But even this is inadequate if the deck cannot withstand the pressure when the nuts are made up tight, so that its surfaces are squeezed together. This is often the case with cored decks (4).

On motorboats especially, you may find bow cleats that are thoughtlessly modeled after old automobile designs. They are more ornamental than useful. These ''dressy'' cleats are utterly useless for emergency towing because one cannot securely make a bitter end fast. Small motorboats must be fitted with a thru-bolted towing eye (5).

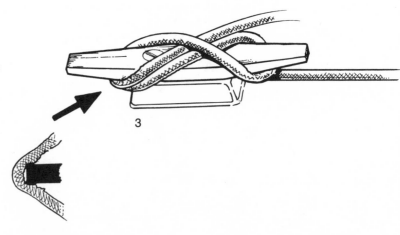

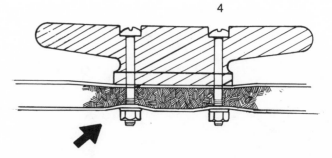

It is possible to make a foredeck cleat more suitable for towing. If the space between the horns and the deck is too small, it can be enlarged by inserting a plywood spacer between the upper and lower parts of the cleat. In the case of one-piece cleats, the spacer simply goes underneath. In either case, a plywood backing plate goes under the deck. Obviously, strong bolts go through the whole assembly and the deck and the nuts are made up tight down below. Holes may have to be enlarged (6).

Figure 7 shows how you can install a really effective reinforcement for a towing bitt. Such a precaution is clearly needed for wooden yachts if they don't have thru-deck bitts or samson posts. In fact, a towing bitt tie-rod and turnbuckle can be retrofitted in modern reinforced fiberglass boats, too.

Badly designed chocks are often responsible for the parting of towlines. These chocks have sharp edges and are set into the toe rail so that the towline is acutely bent and soon chafes through. You should always take a close look at the chocks on a strange boat before leading the towline (8).

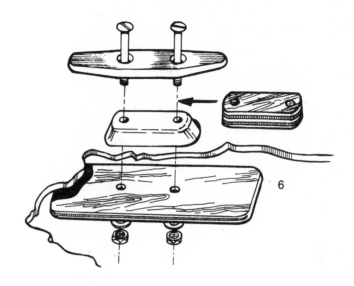

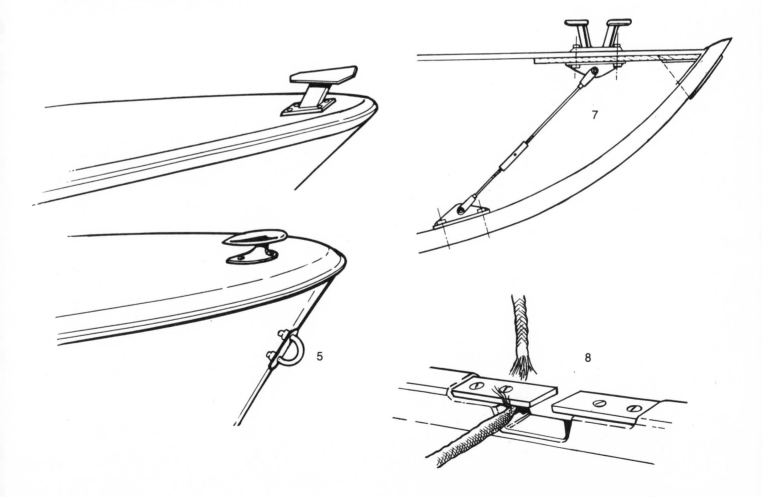

Passing a Line to a Commercial Vessel

If you need a tow by a commercial ship, you cannot expect that she will maneuver close to you to take the towline. Instead it is the yacht that must carefully approach the larger vessel. And whose towline? There is a general rule: For a courtesy tow, the party who wants the tow supplies the line. In emergency situations, as for example when hauling off, the towing vessel will often pass a very heavy line to the vessel in trouble. Normally the yacht comes up to one side of the ship from astern, taking care to maintain sufficient clearance. Meanwhile, the ship is going ahead very slowly (1). When you are amidships, approach a little closer and heave the first few yards of the carefully coiled towline (2). Don't heave the whole line! The man on board the towing ship will make it fast.

Now under way again, let yourself drop astern and pay out as much line (and no more) as necessary. Don't let the bitter end of the towline lie slack on deck as it could go under the boat (3). And only when the whole line has been paid out do you give the go-ahead signal (4).

Unfortunately, some skippers take off as soon as the line has been made fast. Therefore you must try to take up your position astern as quickly as possible or haul in the last few yards of the towline hand over hand and belay it. Since it is almost impossible to do this under tow, the line must be carefully made fast on the boat beforehand.

This example assumes, of course, that your boat is maneuverable. If it is not, then you will have to talk the skipper of the towing vessel into maneuvering close enough to you, so he can heave or float the towline to you.

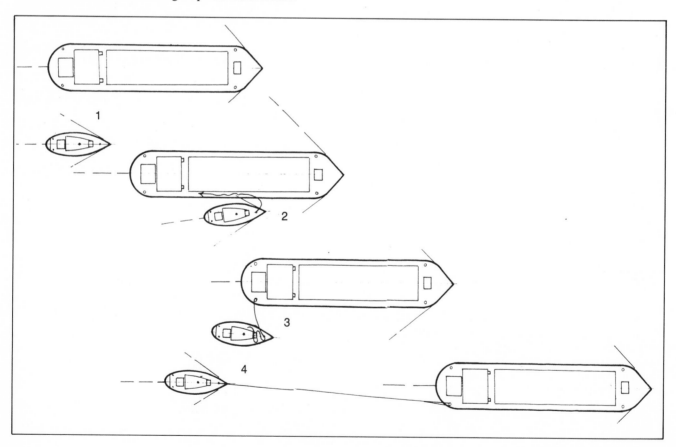

Getting Along with the Towline

The coiling and heaving of a line is an art, but one that you can learn. Whether you are right-handed or left-handed, you start by coiling the line in large uniform turns which you hold in your non-throwing hand. Then, in the throwing hand, you hold as many turns as will span the distance you want and a little more. You heave these with a side-arm or underhand toss to the man on the other boat. The turns uncoil while in flight. You should heave over a minimum of line; pay out the rest only after the end has been made fast.

Handling of the Towline

A fully controlled belay of a towline is possible only with a samson post, because one or two round turns will enable you to exert your full holding strength with confidence. After the full length of towline is out and you are under way, you can then make it fast.

The drawings below show the proper way to belay the towline on the towing bitt. You can use either a

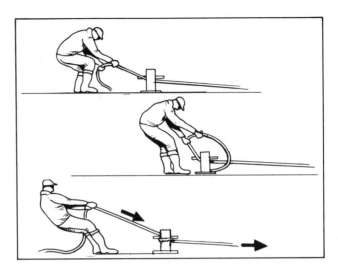

clove hitch (1) or, if a samson post is available, a round turn and several half hitches (2).

Since a clove hitch draws up very tight, you could take several round turns about the post and make the line fast with a half hitch. In this case you bring the end around under the towing part before belaying it (3). This last method is really far preferable to the first two.

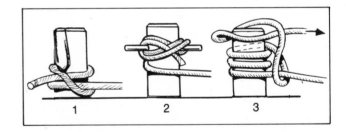

On the double bollards of a large ship, the crew usually takes several figure-eight turns of the towline so that individual turns tighten under load. The turns readily absorb the towing stress.

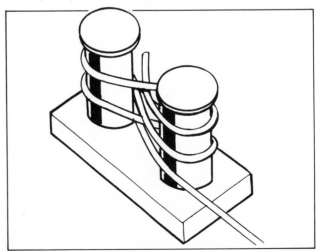

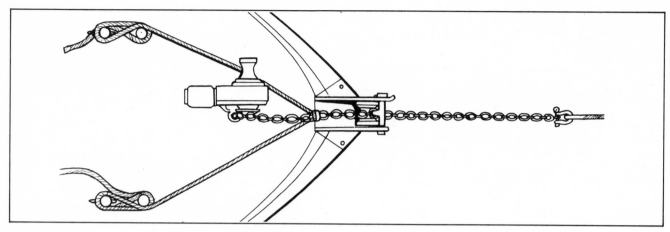

On heavier motor yachts, the load is best taken through the anchor chain. Auxiliary lines reduce the load on the anchor windlass and also act as springs. Pay out just a few yards of chain, otherwise the shock loads may become excessive. The towline — not the chain — must bridge most of the distance between the vessels. It is vital, too, that the chain be prevented from jumping the roller by means of a bolt or pin.

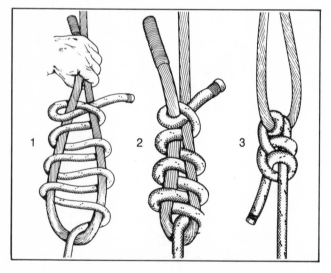

Because rescue vessels nearly always tow boats in distress with wire hawsers, you should give some thought ahead of time to the kind of knots suitable for attaching your own towline to the steel hawser. Sketch (1), shows a method whereby a solid, hard material — in this case a steel wire rope — can be attached to a soft elastic one. Under the pull of the tow, the bight which you have made and held together by hand, is drawn tight (2). If the wire has an eye, you can take two turns around the wire followed by half hitches (3). A bowline is possible, too, but that gives you only one turn of line through the eye.

Hand Signals

There are no prescribed rules for towing maneuver signals but, in practice, there are certain common gestures.

1. The one who wants the tow stands on the boat with the coiled towline in one hand and swings it up and down.

2. When the line has been made fast, he holds his arms crossed in front of his belly.

3. The signal to start towing is a circular movement of the raised hand.

4. Control of towing speed is indicated by upward or downward movements of the outstretched arms with the hands held palm down.

5. To signal that the tow is finished, or that the line may be cast off, cross the arms across the chest and separate them sharply once.

6. The extended fist with thumb up is universally known to mean OK.

Towing Mistakes

Many mistakes are often made in towing larger yachts and can lead to serious accidents. It is absolutely essential that the master of the towing vessel be able to observe the maneuvers and to regulate the towing speed accordingly. But this is often impossible owing to the restricted vision from the pilothouse or bridge (1). If the towline has been led over the sharp edge of a deck, it is in danger of chafing or parting (2). Very often the towing speed is too high (3) and/or the towline too short (4).

A towline run unsecured through the bow pulpit can break it right off if there is a sideways pull (5). It also endangers the forestay and the two members of the crew who are forward of the point where the line is made fast (6). Before towing, all halyards should be made fast (7), the jib removed and the main lowered and covered (8). The towline should not be fastened to the mast if the latter is stepped on deck (9). The mast step is often not thru-bolted and can scarcely withstand a sideways pull. Moreover, the pin that secures the heel of the mast is often inadequate to resist a large overload (10). It is especially important to keep the towing speed down in short choppy seas as, for example, under wind-against-current conditions.

In the case of large motor yachts having inadequate cleats on the foredeck, it is advisable to fashion a bridle outside the vessel to which the towline is fastened. This can certainly be provided if the yacht has a broad vertical transom and it is possible to secure the bridle above the waterline at the stern. Anti-chafe protection must be placed at the sharp corners of the transom to protect the rope. In addition, the bridle must be secured to the stanchion bases at the desired height on the vessel's sides.

In certain cases, the swim ladder has to be protected from damage by having a baulk of timber inserted between it and the transom (1). For safety's sake, the helmsman steers from the pilothouse (2). A bowline is best for fastening the lines together in front of the bow; it is made with both parts of the bridle together. The longer free end is led back on board and made fast, just taut enough to hold the bridle up.

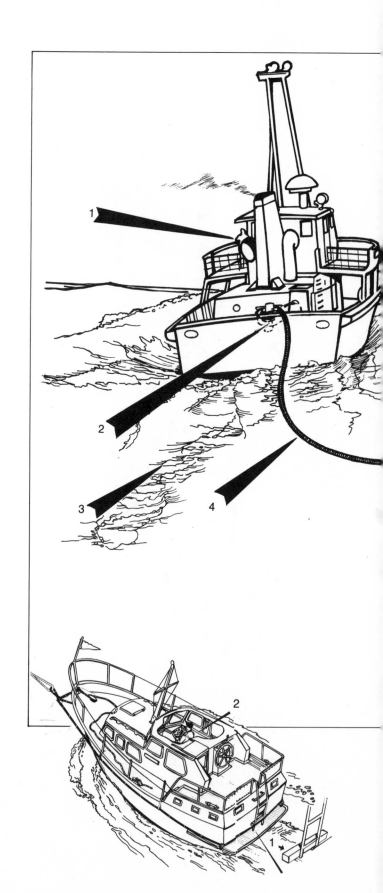

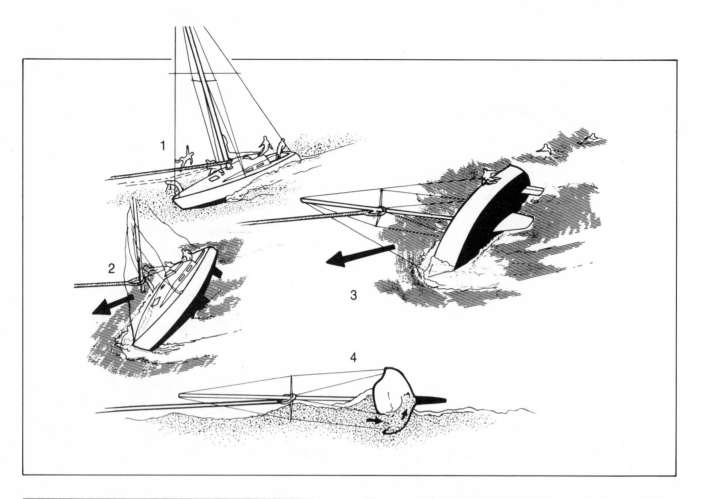

An Unsecured Towline at the Mast Step

This scenario shows what may happen when the towline to a seagoing yacht is improperly fastened at the foot of the mast: As the boat slides down the face of a large sea, the towline, unsecured at the bow, rips the pulpit from its fastenings and flings overboard the crewmember who sat on it watching the towline **(1)**. The bight of the line around the mast slides up the mast and breaks it out of its step **(2)**. The whole rig then comes down. There can be fatal results even if the mast holds. The bight in the end of the towline can go up the mast to the spreaders, heeling the boat over and dragging it into a position beam to the line of travel **(3)**. This can lead to a capsize with a resulting inrush of water via the cockpit and the companionway **(4)**. If this happens, the rest of the crew would be very lucky not to go overboard — and all because of difficulties with a simple towing job.

The towline, especially from a large vessel, must be securely fastened *down*.

Keep Out of the Danger Zone

The following accident happened in the English Lake District. A motor sailer was to be hauled off a lee shore. Since the towing vessel had to pull from the side, the bow cleat sustained a very powerful sideways force. When the cleat was broken out of the deck, the

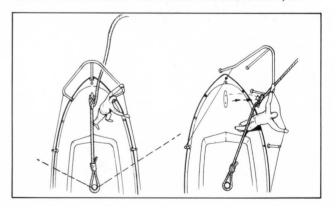

towline ripped the bow pulpit out of the deck and broke both legs of the crewmember who was standing watch over the operation. The dashed line shows the limiting angle forward of which no crew should stand. Anywhere beyond this angle is the danger zone.

Group Towing

Light racing yachts are often towed to the starting line by an escort boat. In order to prevent collisions, the lengths of the towlines are adjusted so that no two boats overlap. Since these boats generally have no anchor rollers, you run the towline between the forestay and the stanchion base(s) to the bow cleat. To prevent chafing the line at the forestay, the helmsman steers off a bit on the side opposite the one where the line comes aboard. Only yachts with towing eyes or rollers take a course right along their keel lines.

Right the Day Sailer Before Towing

Through ignorance, capsized day sailers are often towed back into harbor without first being righted. When this is done, the mast often strikes the bottom, which inevitably results in damage to the rig. In

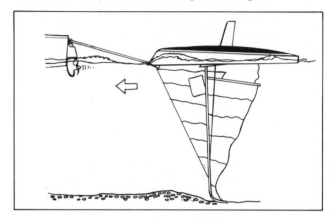

addition, water forced into the hull causes pressure that can break it up bit by bit. A capsized day sailer towed at too high a speed has been known to tear the whole transom out of the towing boat.

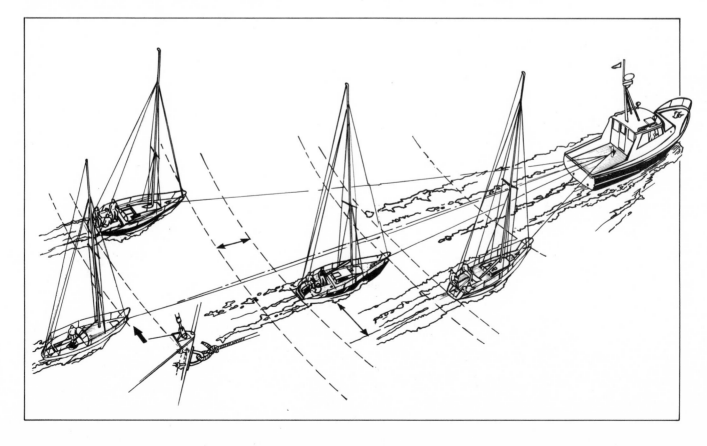

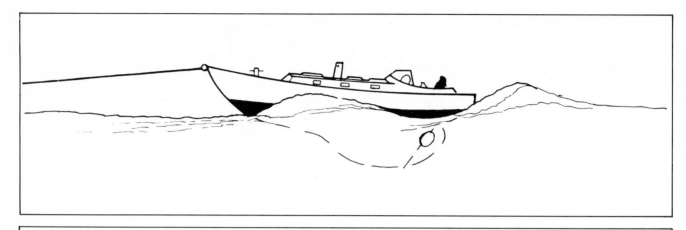

Towing Speed

Sailing yachts that cannot plane because of their hull shape are particularly endangered by excessive speed, such as that reached by a commercial vessel. If the theoretical hull speed is exceeded, an extra large bow wave is formed and a stern wave as well. As speed increases, the stern of the towed boat sinks deeper into the trough, and the stern wave becomes steeper, breaks and engulfs the after part of the boat. In a matter of seconds, the undertow can increase the size of the wave to the point that it forces the stern underwater and the crew is washed overboard.

On the other hand, a motor yacht towed too fast can cut into the large sea that is formed when its extra large bow wave meets a natural crest. Such an accident happened in the western Mediterranean when a Grand Banks trawler in distress was towed too fast by a fishing vessel and its forward part was drawn under. The motor yacht was lost.

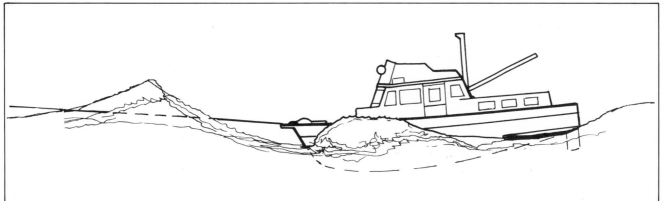

Precautions to Note

There are vital points to observe when a 30-foot yacht finds itself in difficulties, say due to a grounding or a heavy sea, and wants to be taken in tow by a powerful tug.

1. If your engine is OK, it's obviously ready to start but don't engage the propeller.

2. Have the helmsman stand for best vision all around.

3. Close the companionway hatch and insert one hatchway board. Have the crew go below and pay attention to the helmsman.

4. Lash the boom and mainsheet to one side to give the helmsman maximum vision forward.

5. Close all hatches and ventilators.

6. Lead a strong line the length of the boat on each side through the jib lead blocks to the winches and cockpit cleats and lash them to one side of the cleats on the foredeck. The lashings at the cleats take part of the towing load so they must be protected against chafe by parceling.

7. Tie the ends of the two lines together in such a way that they form an eye some six to 10 feet forward of the bow. Fasten the towline to the eye with a bowline. It's a good idea to prepare such an arrangement, appropriate for your own boat, beforehand, and to keep it on board. Emergency vessels will usually pass a steel hawser to the distressed boat. Such a hawser cannot be made fast anywhere on board even if it is accompanied by a rope haul-in line. You must tie or shackle the hawser to your own towline.

You can devise this bridle system if you have large sheet winches and solid backing plates. The commonly published solution — to run the ends aft around a sailboat's cabin structure — is seldom practical and may even be dangerous because the cabin's after bulkhead is usually at a slant, so that the bight of the towline can slide up. Besides, in modern sailboat designs the distance between the cockpit coaming and the cabin top is so small that there is nowhere for the towline to be held. Moreover, under heavy loads, the ends of the cabin trunk could be crushed.

There are similar objections to running the bridle around the stern for, in many sailboats, the transom slants too. You can hardly secure a towline in such a case.

8. Another preparation you must take is to get your life ring in its bracket with the heaving line clear.

9. Put on your work gloves.

10. Make sure that your towline is at least five times as long as the yacht.

11. It's dangerous to remain in the cross-hatched sector of the inset drawing. Modern synthetic ropes are very elastic and for that very reason, liberate enormous energy when they part and snap back. Serious accidents have occurred as a result, some with fatal consequences.

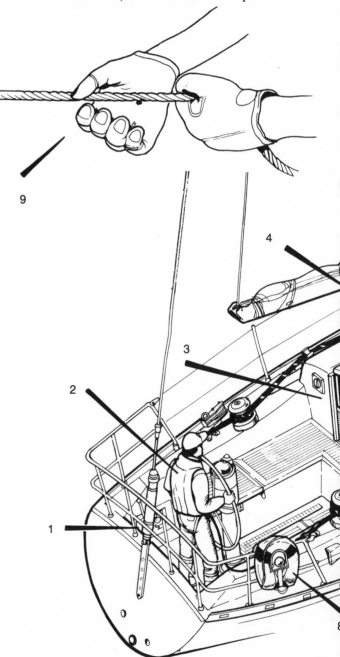

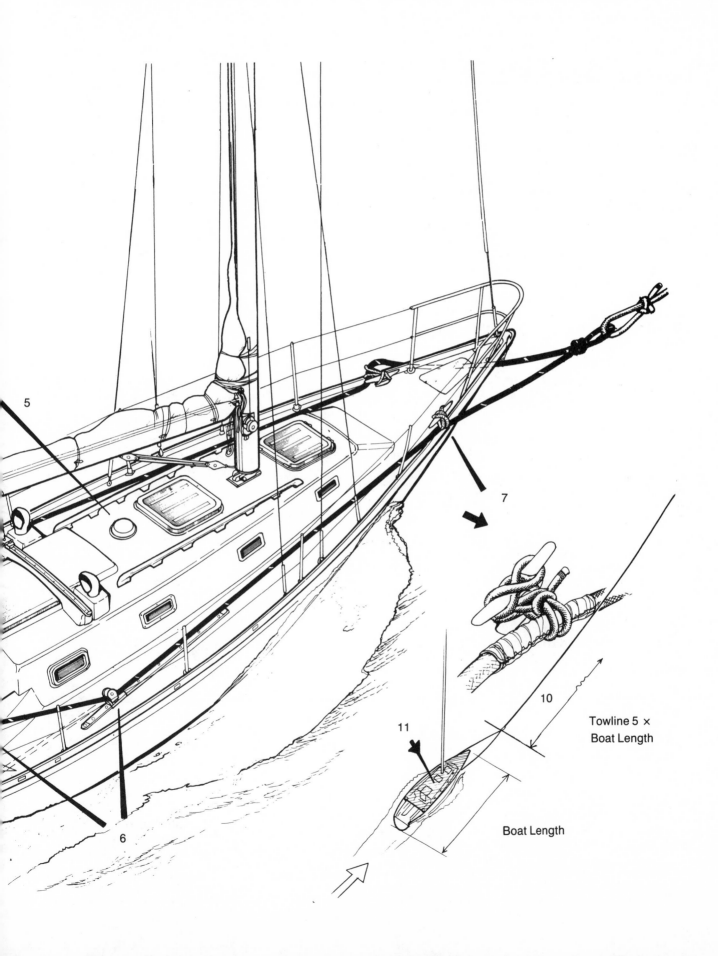

5

6

7

10

11

Towline 5 ×
Boat Length

Boat Length

Towing Day Sailers

1. Modern day sailers often have no towing cleats on deck. As a result of ignorance, the towline is often knotted around the forestay instead of the mast where it should be. The forestay fittings were never designed for these loads. The result? You could break the stem fitting or tear it out of the deck, quite possibly leading to the loss of the mast or other damage.

2. Secure the end of the towline with two round turns around the mast and a couple of half hitches. If you use this method, be sure to fasten the line at deck height (no higher) to prevent subjecting the mast to a bending moment. If the mast is freestanding, take the turns around the mast but run the bitter end of the towline back to the mainsheet deck fitting or to the track and make it taut and fast. Secure the towline to the forestay fitting with a short line.

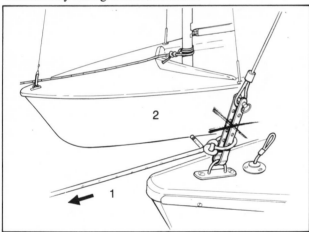

4. It's best to provide the motorboat with a long towline having a number of eyes in it, separated by more than the length of one boat. The racing crews have only to hold on to these eyes, or to tie a short strop between the eye and the foot of the mast.

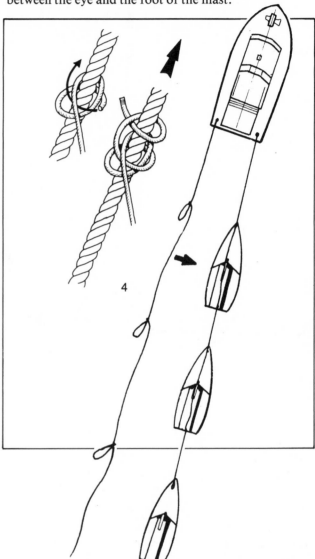

3. If you have to tow two day sailers and are not using individual towlines, you will usually find it difficult to make the towline fast on the last one if the first boat doesn't have a stern cleat. In this case, take two turns and two half hitches around the mainsheet traveler as close to one side as possible to keep from bending it.

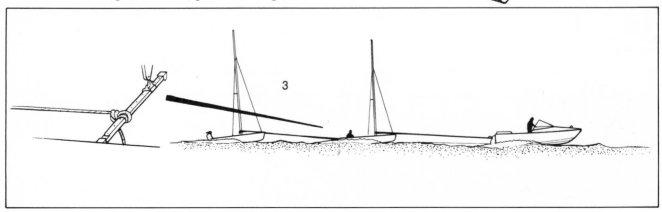

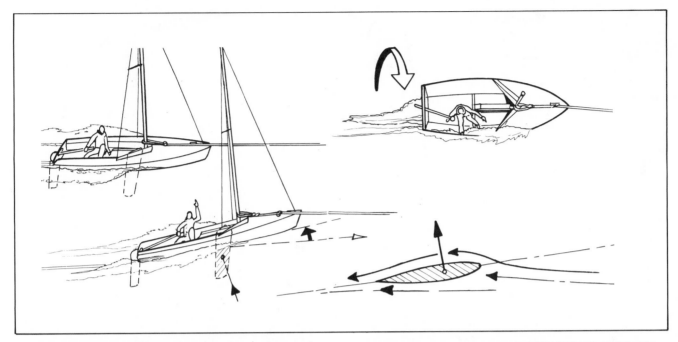

Planing dinghies and larger boats are less endangered by towing because at higher speeds their hulls ride up on the surface, greatly reducing resistance to movement through the water. But the slightest lack of attention by the helmsman may lead to a capsize, especially if the board is down. Even a small divergence from the towing course causes the board to exert a strong lift, which can cause the boat to heel with lightning speed. Therefore, at higher towing speeds, raise the centerboard altogether or at most lower it just a couple of inches.

Towing Alongside

If neither boat has a long towline or if the channel is very narrow, as in a lock for example, so that you have some difficult maneuvers to make, towing alongside is worth a try. To do this, first fender both boats very carefully. The towing load is taken mainly by the towing boat's forward spring. You adjust the bow line to keep the two boats from coming too heavily together. While under way, adjust the lines so that both boats just touch the fenders.

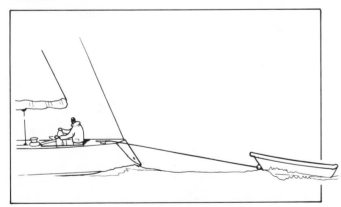

Towing Your Tender

Rigid tenders are usually easy to tow. Inflatables, however, develop a considerable undertow at the stern and can fill from aft or be flung around by the wind. In any case, pay out enough line so that the tender rides up on the boat's stern wave. Otherwise its bow may dig into the wave and fill the tender.

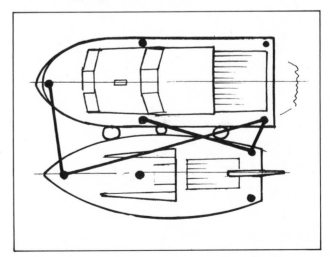

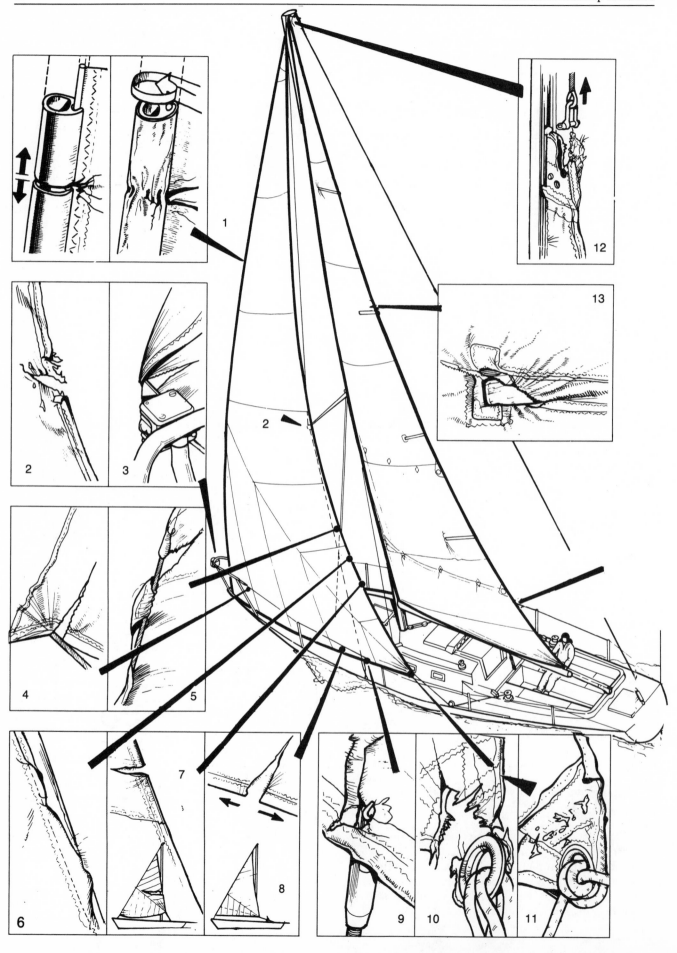

Sails Damaged? Help Yourself

Sails must be expected to suffer minor damage with use as time goes on. You may overlook the damage or merely be inattentive. But what will happen later on when the sail must work hard in a rising storm? Under wind pressure, unnoticeable chafe or a slightly opened seam can suddenly lead to a gaping tear.

Sails usually suffer most damage by chafing against part of the rig or fittings. The drawings show the most dangerous spots.

1. Roller-furling installations are often made up from sections of special aluminum extrusions. At the joints between sections, inappropriate design or sharp edges caused by corrosion may pinch the wire or rope luff or cut the sail itself. In modern construction, fairing pieces or plastic inserts between the sections tend to minimize both problems.

2. Don't sheet your jib in so tightly that the leech comes up against the tips of the spreaders. Have mercy!

3. On courses off the wind, the jib can easily be caught behind bow fittings such as running lights or the pulpit itself. You can tear the sail if you don't notice this before you sheet it in with the winch.

4. Don't chafe the foot of the jib by letting it rub on the lifelines.

5. You endanger the leech by hauling it past the baby stay each time you tack.

6. Further, frequent and severe flogging or chafing on the shrouds is very dangerous as it can very soon tear the sail's leech line.

7. If you have set a bad lead for your headsail sheet so that its pull comes down too vertically to the lead block, you can cause a tear across the sail.

8. On the other hand, if you bring the lead aft too horizontally, you may overload the foot and it may tear.

9. Other danger spots for a low-cut genoa are the cotter pins used to secure shroud turnbuckles.

10. Excessive flogging of the headsail under storm conditions can quite possibly tear out the clew cringle.

11. It is even more likely that the seams of the reinforcing patch will start to let go first.

12. Too much tension on the mainsail halyard endangers the headboard. If you set the halyard up too tightly, it may tear the headboard cringle out.

13. The most common sail damage generally occurs at the batten pockets. They are considerably endangered by the constant movement and pressure of the battens. Watch them carefully or you may have a rip right to the luff.

14. A common error is to take in too much on the leech line to reduce fluttering. When setting the mainsail, one often forgets to ease the topping lift. Then, while beating close-hauled, the skipper suddenly remembers it. If the topping lift is abruptly let go, the sudden load can part the leech line, resulting in a tear at the leech.

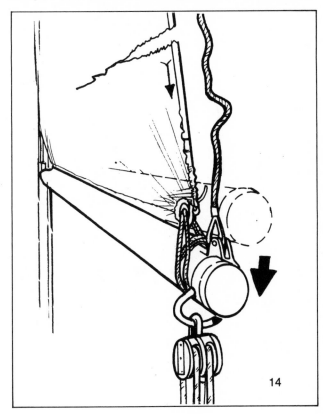

14

Mainsail Chafe

On downwind courses, the eased out mainsail usually touches the end of a spreader **(1)** or shroud **(2)**. Considerable chafe occurs in these areas, leading to holes or tears in the cloth. You would be well advised to haul in on the mainsail until its lower parts do not touch the shrouds or spreaders.

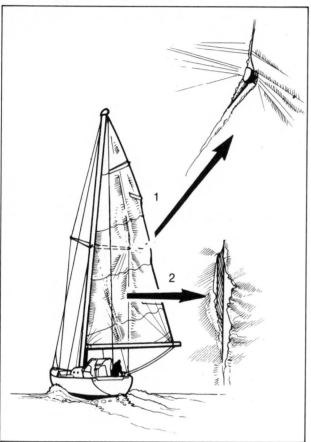

Reefing Problems

Many yachts are fitted with roller reefing. If you do not ease the main halyard enough while rolling the reef in, a good deal of tension will develop in the luff rope as it rolls up into a thick bundle. You can end up with a tear in the luff. In the case of a tied-in reef, if you forget a reef point that is still tied, you may tear out a reef point cringle when you reset the full sail.

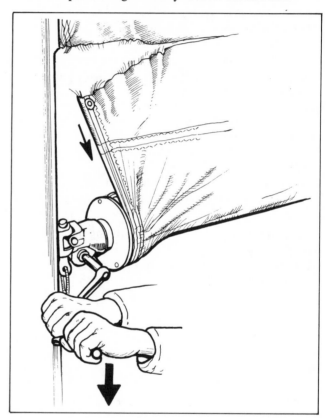

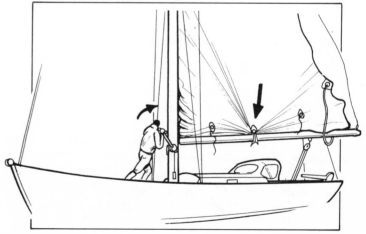

Water in the Genoa

Seas coming aboard can overload a low-cut genoa to such an extent that it tears right out of its boltropes. This has happened repeatedly in ocean races. In heavy air and high seas, change down in time to a smaller sail with a high-cut clew.

With adjustable sheet leads, you can reduce the load on the foot or the leech of a damaged or torn headsail. If you move the lead aft, you reduce the pull on the leech; a position farther forward eases the tension on the foot.

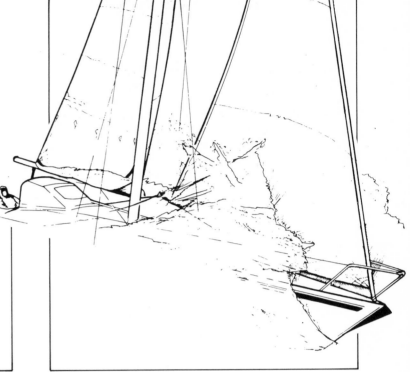

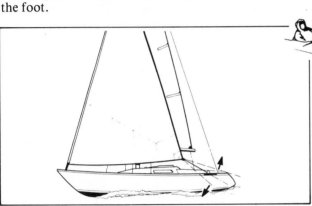

Jibing Instead of Tacking

Under storm conditions, when the headsail sheet is cast off in preparation for tacking, the sail can flog so violently that it may rip immediately. The drawing shows how you prevent this disaster. Bring the boat around on the new tack by jibing. In this method, both windward and leeward sheets are held in tight when the boat reaches the downwind position. You ease the old leeward sheet only after the boat is again on the wind.

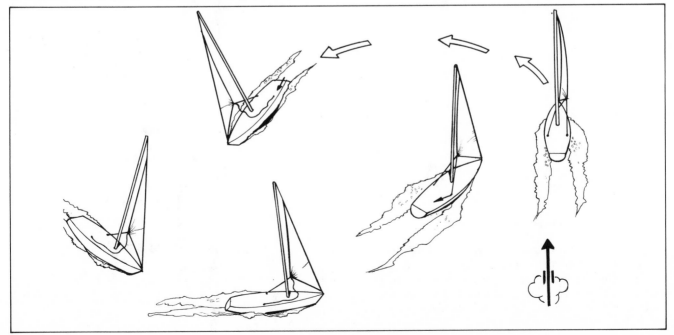

Roller-Furling Problems

A roller-furling genoa is rarely taken down, even in harbor. Take great care that as the sail is rolled up, the line turns are wound tightly around the drum. If there is noticeable looseness, the wind could unfurl the sail and very soon tear it. Then individual pieces of the sail's panels unroll still more and are plucked away by the wind. After several days of heavy weather, many an owner has been confronted with a totally demolished roller-furling jib.

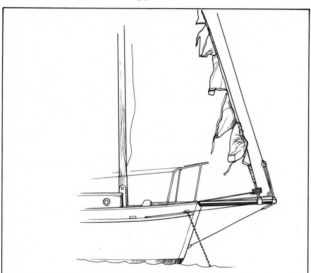

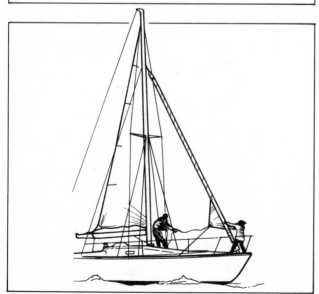

Quality is the prime requirement of a roller-furling system. If there are mechanical deficiencies, you may — depending on conditions — find that you can neither pay out a rolled-up sail nor roll it in. In emergencies, you should be able to easily change the sail.

Jammed Genoa Halyard

Similarly, you have to foresee when the genoa can no longer be lowered, for in heavy air the boat may actually be endangered. When a storm has begun it is next to impossible to wrap a genoa around the forestay by hand, roller fashion. The wind yanks the sail out of your hand time after time and bellies out the first few turns into flogging bights.

The usual cause of a jammed halyard is a damaged or badly worn turning block at the masthead (below). The halyard fitting or the shackle itself is usually so tightly jammed between the structure of the masthead and the block that it can be freed only by hand; this

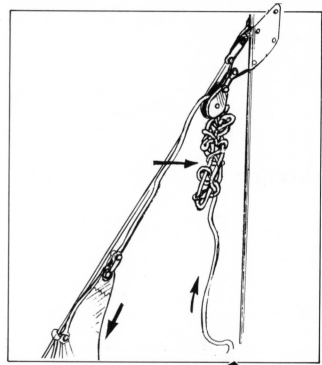

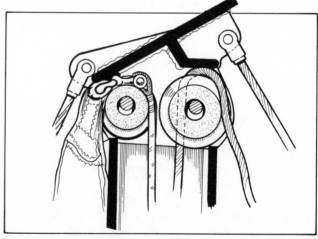

means winching a man to the masthead. You must
make a regular inspection of the sheaves during winter
layup.

Before letting the halyard run, be sure there are no
tangles in the rope — ease the halyard hand over
hand. Don't let the whole thing go suddenly! This
could cause turns and knots to form, stopping the
halyard at the block or turning sheave.

Up the Mast

When a halyard gets jammed at the masthead,
someone may have to go up the mast even in high
winds and seas. This dangerous operation is possible
only on larger boats and calls for an adventurous
crew. You really should not try to make repairs on
the mast on a small boat at sea, unless a serious
emergency demands you do so. Before starting, set
the mast up firmly with the backstay and baby stay
(1). The person going aloft must use a boatswain's
chair and safety harness. Steer the boat on the course
that will produce the least motion. The person hoisting must be very careful with the winch. If a second
halyard is available, use it on the boatswain's chair
as a backup.

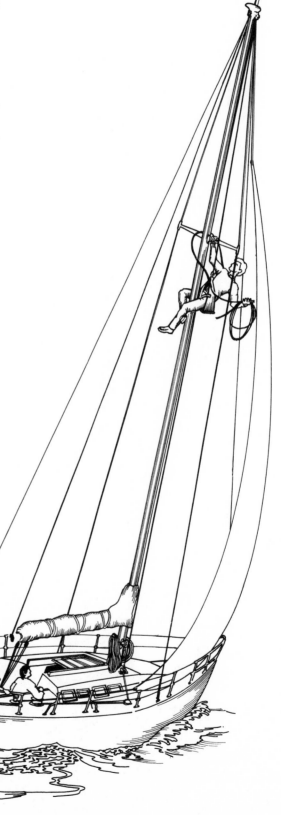

Halyard Tips

The following methods of retrieving a halyard from the masthead have been established by experience: As part of normal fitting out, a light steel ring is seized to the wire halyard just above the shackle. Then, in an emergency, you bend a clothes hanger into a hook and tape it to a spare halyard. You can snare the ring at the masthead with this hook and haul the halyard down.

An additional boat snap (or carabiner) hooked around the forestay makes sail changes easier as the halyard cannot get away (1).

Here's a good way to attach the main halyard to the head of the sail. The extra slide in the mast track stabilizes the headboard and leads the halyard fair to the turning sheave at the masthead, where the slide and the light shackle prevent jamming. You have to

use two shackles on the halyard — the light, stabilizing one for the slide and the main shackle between the halyard and headboard. This presents no problem with today's elegantly designed shackles.

Seize a ring to the main halyard, too, so that you can get it down if it runs up the mast (2).

To blunt the sharp ends of the spreaders, there are several things you can do (bottom). For almost any size of metal spreader you can buy a commercial boot that stretches over the end (1). Another standard item is a variety of ring-shaped standoffs that are good on wooden spreaders as well (2). The do-it-yourselfer can saw out a couple of wooden discs (3), put them in place and screw them together (commercial plastic discs are widely available). The simplest method, no less effective, is to tape the whole end (4). You must always tape the cotter pins or rings at the turnbuckles (5). Note that there are available plastic boots suitable for every size of turnbuckle. Just be sure to draw the boot down over the lower part of the assembly all the way over the stanchion base (6).

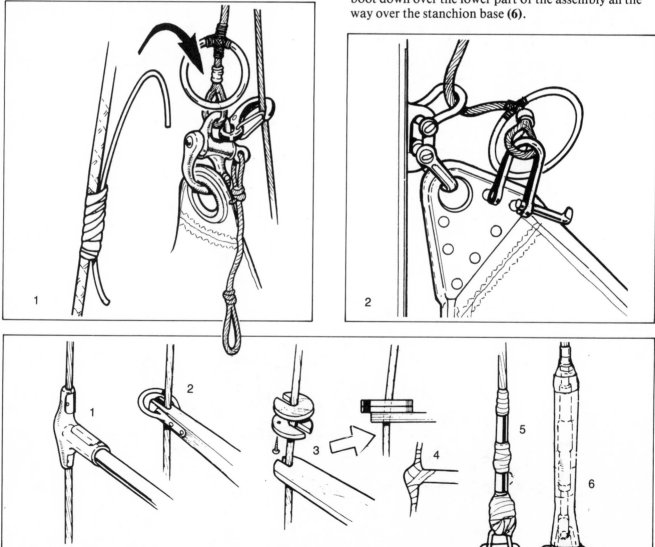

Anti-Chafe Protection

Use tape and rope—which are not expensive—to cover up ill-placed fittings and parts of the rig on which a jib could hang up.

You can cover your running lights with a board. And for safety's sake always tape your cotter pins. A simple means of preventing the halyard from flying up when the sail is lowered is to fasten a shock cord at the bow pulpit; it can be clipped to the halyard shackle or to the halyard ring mentioned previously.

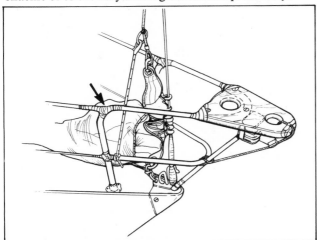

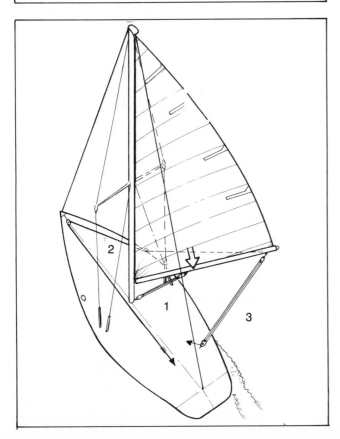

Damage to the mainsail by abrasion on the shrouds and spreader ends, on courses off the wind, can be prevented by keeping the boom absolutely immobile. This can be done by combining these three steps: First tighten down on the boom vang (1). Second, haul in on the preventer, which you can do from the cockpit if you have provided a turning block on the foredeck so that the line is led aft (2); and third, trim in the mainsheet (3) a bit so that the whole combination is under tension and the boom is kept off the shrouds.

Spinnaker Problems

The ends of the spreaders are dangerous for the leeches of the spinnaker, too. If a spinnaker collapses to leeward behind the spreader, the leech sometimes gets hooked and there are times when you cannot free it. The next time it fills it literally tears itself away.

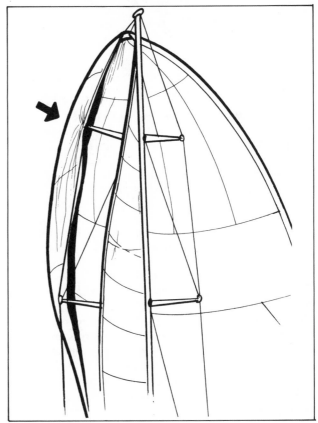

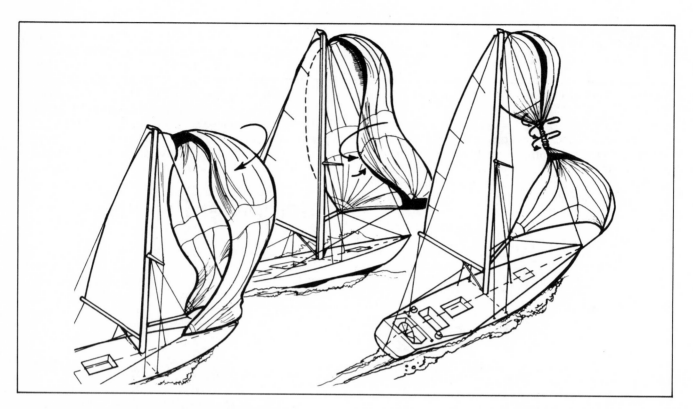

Spinnakers can be damaged in many different ways. The commonest cause of a torn panel or even the total loss of the spinnaker is the infamous "hourglass wrap." With a sudden gust from ahead, the spinnaker wraps itself several times around the forestay in such a way that it forms two big bulges, one above the other, that flog madly about. In stronger winds at sea, it is often impossible to unwind this hourglass. The only chance is to detach the sheets and wrap the sail even more tightly around the forestay. Unfortunately, you won't be able to use a headsail. When conditions allow, it becomes possible to unwrap the sail, but you will have to send someone up the mast. Cases have been reported in which the "repair" required the use of a sharp rigger's knife!

You can prevent the dreaded hourglass by setting a jib in addition to the spinnaker. On courses broad off the wind, the jib will work with the spinnaker so long as it is drawing. Of course, this jib should be cut narrow and high clewed so as not to blanket the spinnaker too much. Sailmakers offer special headsails for this purpose (right).

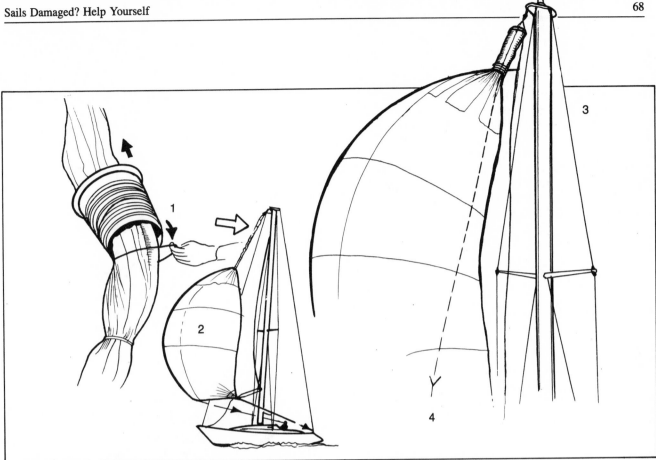

Two methods are recognized as being effective in preventing wraps while the spinnaker is being set: Cut the bottom out of a bucket. Stretch a number of rubber bands around it. Hoist the whole length of the spinnaker through the bucket and as it goes up slip one band after another off the bucket and around the sail (1), thus "stopping" it. In this way you can set the stopped spinnaker. Now, when you haul on the sheets, the rubber bands break, starting near the foot and then all the way up. The spinnaker fills smoothly (2).

Several kinds of commercial spinnaker "socks" or rings work in a similar way: After the spinnaker "sausage" has been set, the sock is hauled to the masthead on a special halyard where it remains in a semi-collapsed state (3). Conversely, the sock can be hauled down with an additional halyard while the spinnaker is still full, thus drawing it together before it is taken down (4).

Sail Repairs

The most durable repair to a sail with a tear (1) or an extensively abraded area is made with a sailcloth patch. The patch must be substantially larger than the damaged area (2). Fold the edges of the patch inward and pin the patch in place on the sail (3). Then mark

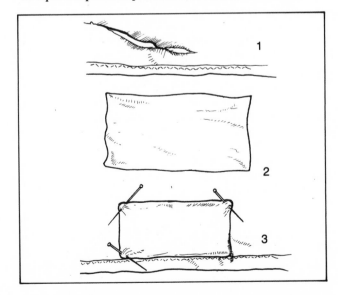

around the tear, outlining the patch (4). Cut the torn part as nearly as possible to a rectangular shape (5). Then replace the patch over the area, folded edge under (i.e., against the sail). Hold it between your thumb and forefinger and sew around the edges with a simple round stitch (6). Now turn the sail over and fold the edges of the rectangular opening inward under the patch (7). Then sew this together, too (8).

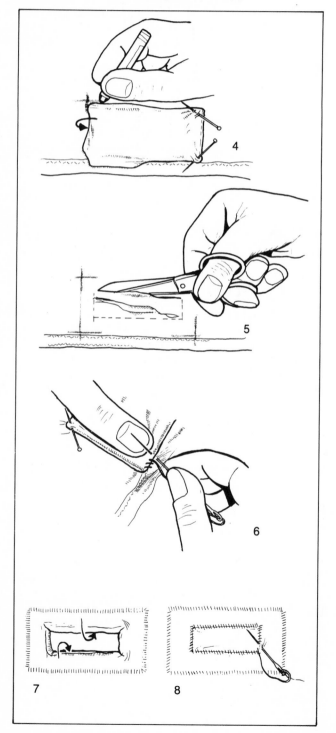

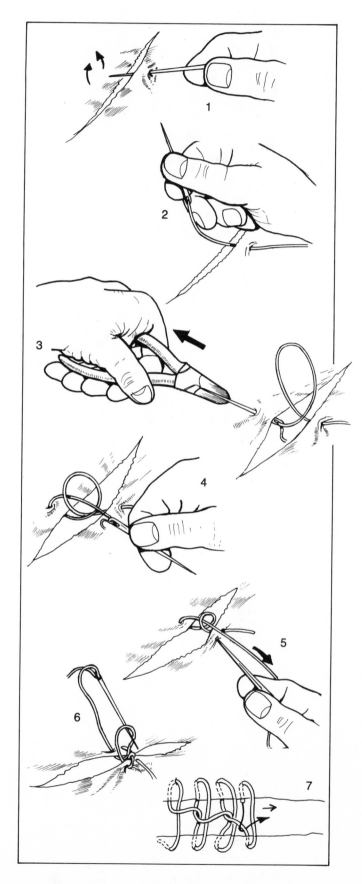

Rips in the sail are most easily repaired with a "bosun's seam." For this you will need a medium-size sail needle, suitable synthetic twine and flat-nosed pliers or a sailor's palm. Push the needle *down* through the edge of the cloth near the tear **(1)** and lead it *upward* through the tear **(2)**. Form a loop right over the tear and run the needle back through the other side of the tear from *underneath*. This is easy to do with the pliers **(3)**. Now lead the needle back through the loop **(4)** and take the next stitch in the same way, a fraction of an inch farther along **(5)**, forming the loop as before **(6)**. Obviously you must tighten all the stitches just enough so that they draw the edges of the tear together without overlapping **(7)**.

You can make temporary sail repairs with sail repair tape. This is a material with extraordinary adhesion and strength. It's available at chandleries and should be carried on board at all times. Opened seams and loose threads can be repaired with tape on one side only, but use tape on both sides of a tear and reinforce with several vertical strips.

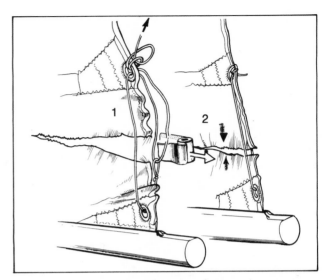

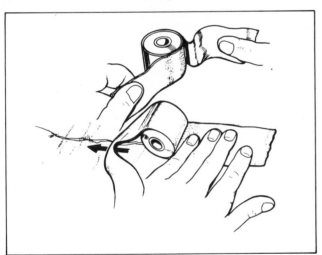

A torn leech is especially hard to repair because it has to withstand considerable tension. To take the load, rig a hauling line consisting of several parts from the nearest reef cringle to the boom end or the headboard **(1)**. Draw the edges of the tear together with this line, being careful not to cause another tear by trimming the mainsheet too tight. It's a good idea, too, to stick several strips of sail repair tape on both sides of the torn area **(2)**.

Keep the following items on board at all times so you can repair your sails: **(1)** plastic mallet, **(2)** flat-nose pliers, scissors, sail twine, **(3)** sailor's palm and a selection of sail needles, **(4)** wax to lubricate the twine, **(5)** rigger's knife and marlinspike, **(6)** sail repair tape, **(7)** sailcloth for patches, **(8)** spare shackles, awl, **(9)** strong sail twine, **(10)** spare sail slides and jib hanks.

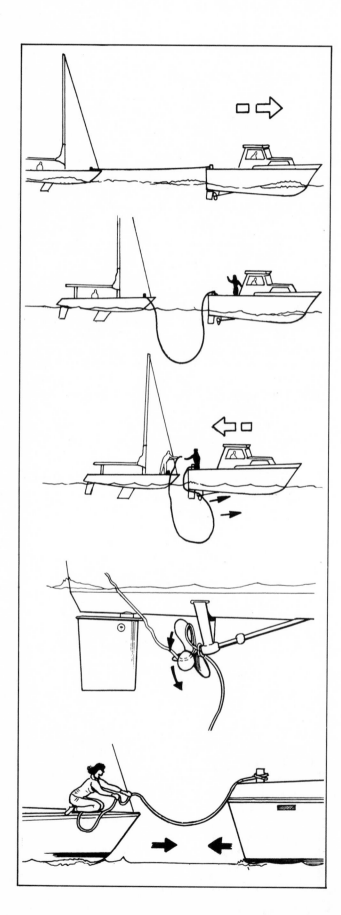

Complications Under the Keel

The crew if often responsible for a jammed propeller, for a line that has slipped overboard from your own vessel is enough to stop the engine. Even flotsam can be pretty annoying. Particular nuisances are floating plastics, which, despite appeals by world-famous people on behalf of animals, are often encountered. Dangerous, too, is fishing tackle set out near shore; be extra careful when traveling canals, which are common places for fishing tackle. Novice sailors, in particular, tend to underestimate the distance that a line can reach into a channel. So, when you see an angler, keep as far off from the slope of the shore as you can.

Crews of boats that carry diving equipment on board can make good use of it when they have let a rope bring their engine to a stop. Sometimes, even when all the necessary tools are on board, it may be difficult to remedy the situation in the shortest possible time. And sometimes it may be that the diver simply cannot effect a repair. Then there is only one way to go — tow and haul out.

Rope in the Propeller

A common cause of a line wound up in the prop is the poorly executed ending of a tow. While the towing boat is going astern, the towed boat keeps coming up on it from aft. As a result, the line is sucked into the prop wash and winds around the propeller.

Here's how to prevent this trouble: A crewmember on the foredeck of the towed boat hauls in the towline hand over hand until it has been cast off and the boats are no longer tied together.

You have to watch carefully also when docking and undocking in harbor, especially if you are single-handing. If you are leaving a slip by going astern, it may well happen that one of the after mooring lines is drawn under the hull and wound around the screw. This misfortune happens particularly when the pilings are a good distance from the catwalk and the boat is relatively small with respect to the length of the slip. The mooring lines then have to be rather long.

Under these conditions it is best to haul in the stern lines by hand to take them aboard or to hang them on the pilings. This you can do easily and correctly without using the engine. Only after the bow lines have been cast off do you haul the stern over to one of the pilings by hand and coil up the mooring line. Then you haul the stern over to the other piling and secure the other mooring line. Only now do you slowly maneuver the boat out of the slip.

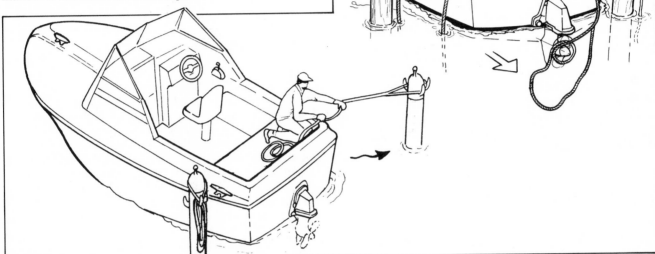

Lines Dragging Over the Side

Every racing skipper knows this situation: While motoring to the start you hank on the sails and lay the sheets out on deck. The spinnaker sheets especially are very long and have to be laid out just before sail handling begins. Therefore, they are allowed to lie loose on deck, and they can easily slide overboard and thus into the propeller. In some very bad cases, the sheet is wound up so tightly that it develops considerable tension; in some instances, this can also lead to the damaging of the knotmeter sending unit. Indeed, it may become questionable whether one reaches the start at all. . . .

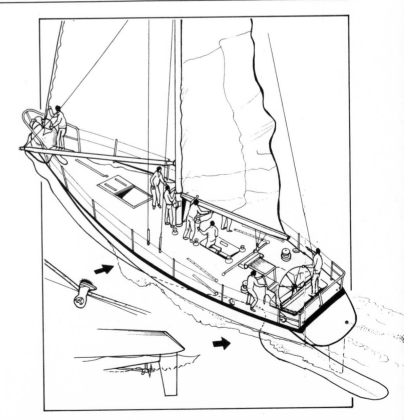

Through inattentiveness, many a skipper has found himself in acute trouble while entering harbor. Usually one lays out mooring lines on deck before motoring in. It is very possible that under wind pressure and the motion of the sea a mooring line goes over the side. As soon as it hits the water, the vessel's speed snatches it aft into the propeller wash, which drags it under the boat. The result? A stalled engine during the dangerous phase of entering harbor.

Propeller Killers

Be careful approaching piers stern first. In berths along the pier or quay there is often all kinds of rubbish, plastics and old floating synthetic lines, particularly abundant during an onshore wind. Besides, in many harbors, dirty old mooring lines hang down from their rings into the water. These can easily be wound around the propeller and shaft to the extent that you cannot fish them up with a boathook.

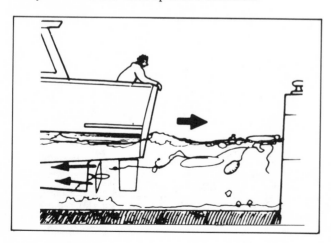

Fish Nets

Near shore, fish traps are marked with buoys, which usually have lines to the shore so that the traps can be hauled in from the land. Because these lines are mostly underwater, they can endanger boats that hug the shore too closely. Outboard runabouts have often snagged these traps and dragged them away.

Along many coasts, fixed nets are commonly set out near the shore. They are held by stakes that form a line extending out from land at right angles. The net

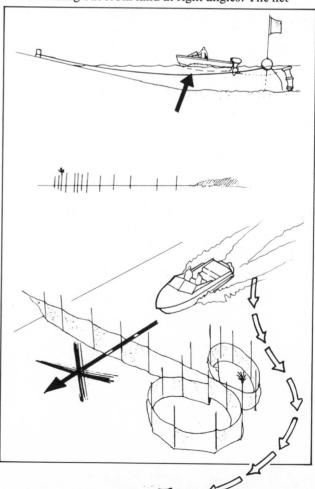

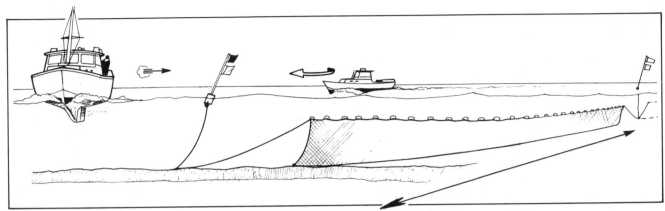

ends in a pair of enclosures that form a sort of rough cross. The upper edges of these nets are at the surface and are usually pretty hard to see. Many a skipper who has tried to go between the stakes has regretted the resulting damage. The end of the fixed installation is generally marked with some item such as a broom on the outermost seaward stake. You may be sure that hardly any of these layouts are lighted at night, though some may have radar reflectors.

Fishing buoys with small colored pennants mark fixed nets or traps on the bottom. Usually the nets or traps lie so deep that one may safely pass between the buoys (the drawing above shows the layout). But this depends on the depth at the moment and the draft of the boat. Note the buoys and go around them to windward (or upstream if a tidal current is running). The lines between the nets and the buoys may be very long, so the buoys can drift fairly far with the wind.

Dredge Hawsers

When, through the inattentivesness of the skipper, a yacht drifts down with the current on the anchor cable of a dredge, serious damage is likely. The cable may get caught between the keel and rudder. If so, the current or wind drives the yacht ever closer to the dredge so that it cannot be freed. The crew of the

dredge can neither ease the cable nor cut it; the help of a tug is then required, for the yacht's engine cannot be used.

Dredges show the side on which you should pass by displaying two diamond shapes, one above the other (at night two 360-degree green lights). Pleasure boats must note these signals carefully in canals or river channels, because dredges often have cables led to shore that are difficult or impossible to make out. (The forbidden side is indicated by two balls one above the other, or at night by two 360-degree red lights in the same position.) Damage to the hull, keel, rudder or propeller by collision with a cable under tension can become very great, even leading to loss of the boat.

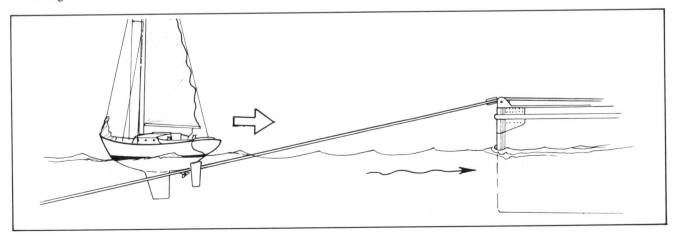

Propeller Damage

1. The frictional heat developed by a line wound around the propeller shaft is so great that synthetic rope can be very quickly melted — despite the surrounding cooling water.

2. A fishing line wound around the shaft can lead to particularly critical damage: The friction melts the line into a compact mass. If the engine is kept running in spite of the entanglement, the hot line can be drawn into the shaft bearing (depending on the design of the bearing). Running a little longer leads to the complete failure of the bearing. Repair is possible only upon haul out.

3. It is much the same with plastic bags and films caught in the propeller; these also melt where the shaft exits from the bearing and weld the shaft strut, shaft and propeller blades together. Plastic bags are often drawn into the propeller because they have the unpleasant habit of drifting 18 to 20 inches below the surface. In murky water, you just can't see them in time.

   When going astern be particularly watchful for driftwood. The propeller's suction forces the drifting material under the bottom of the ship where it can jam or cause a bent propeller blade. A bent blade leads to severe imbalance with associated bad vibration, making further motoring impossible. If in spite of this warning you try to keep going, you will badly damage the bearing and sometimes water will pour in around the base of the strut, which has been literally torn away from the hull.

   A similar collision can be serious in the case of a sail drive (bottom sketch at right). The shock of the impact with the flotsam may break the retaining pin and result in the loss of the propeller. It all depends, of course, on the particular design. Some drives have—like outboards—built-in shear pins to prevent further damage. When the pin has been sheared, the drive remains intact and the propeller can eventually be used, but the boat has to be hauled to replace the pin. However, most manufacturers now use a slip clutch instead of a pin to protect the propeller. Thus the drive will withstand even a heavy blow without damage.

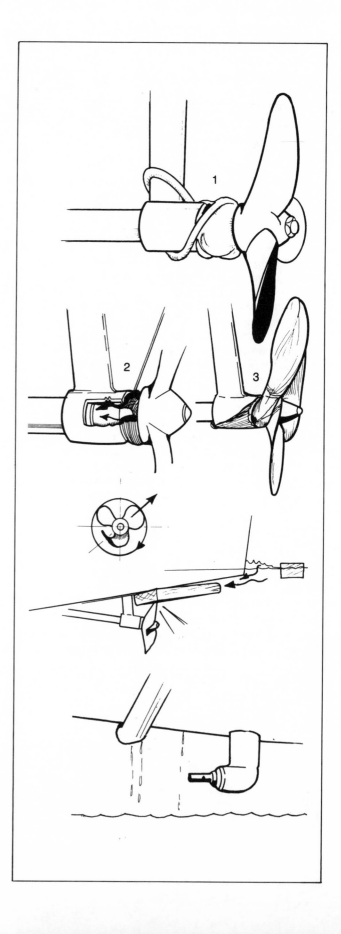

1. The propeller is most effectively protected when it is placed in an aperture in a skeg; this structure keeps lines and flotsam away. Obviously, of course, it is difficult to retrofit a skeg. Consequently, voyaging sailors should give thought to the design of the rudder when considering the purchase of a new boat.

2. and 3. On the other hand, one can retrofit the boat with anti-rope protectors. A strip of stainless steel or wire can be fastened as a connecting piece between keel and rudder. In addition to the use of bolts or screws, it can be laminated to the structure as well. The advantages of such an arrangement far outweigh the small loss of speed.

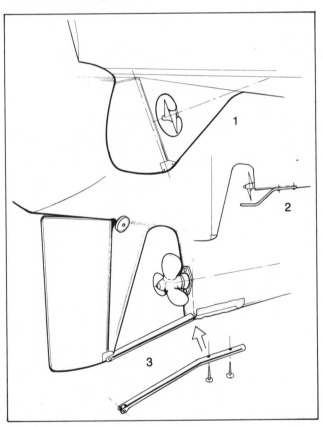

A Rope in the Rudder

1. Freestanding spade rudders are particularly effective rope catchers. Matters become critical when a line is caught between the upper edge of the rudder and the bottom of the boat. Balanced rudders nearly always catch lines with their leading edges. If the line becomes wedged near the rudder bearing it may make the vessel unmaneuverable.

2. A small protector, made of stainless steel and screwed to the hull forward of the rudder's leading edge, can prevent such damage. It may also be laminated to the hull.

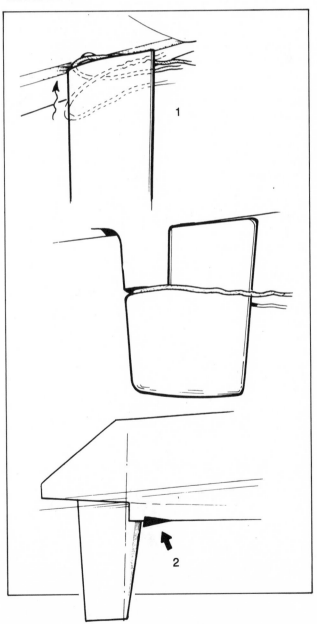

Clear It with the Boathook

If a line under load or net is caught under the hull between the keel and rudder but is not wound in the propeller, try using the boathook to lead the line under the rudder and free it aft. But most boathooks are far too short! The boathook must be long to reach from hand height above the deck to the lower edge of the rudder.

You can also use a spinnaker pole for the same purpose. Since pole-end fittings are all rounded, you will not be able to catch the line with the pole. However, you can lash a boathook to the spinnaker pole as shown. If you don't have a boathook on board, you may still be able to do the job by lashing an anchor to the end of the pole.

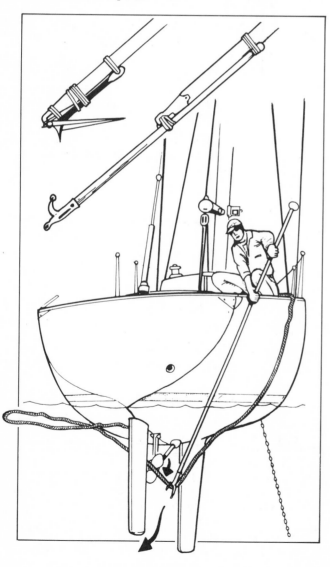

Working Underwater

When diving is the only way to free the propeller from a line, the diver must be well prepared and equipped before undertaking the task.

1. The most useful devices are divers' goggles and snorkel.

2. If there is no wet suit with weighted belt on board, the diver must protect himself from the cold water with warm underwear and an oilskin overall. Such clothing provides warmth even when wet.

3. A line should be snapped to the diver's belt and held by a crewmember on deck **(4)**.

5. All the tools must be strung together on a safety line. You can work with only one hand, since you have to hold yourself in place with the other; all tools must be usable with one hand.

6. Protect your feet from the cold water with warm socks.

7. Wear flippers to stabilize your body underwater and to reach the trouble spot quickly.

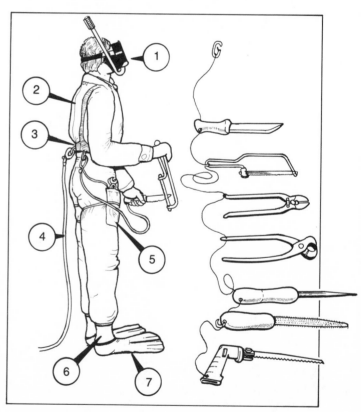

These tools are essential: knife, hacksaw, flat-nose pliers, wire cutters, steel awl, large round file, rat tail file, keyhole saw.

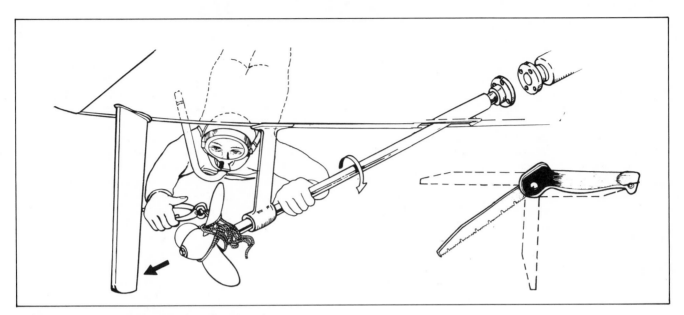

If you ascertain during the first dive that there are many turns of line around the propeller, but no welding, you may be able to use this trick: Uncouple the shaft from the engine or transmission and withdraw it slightly. Now you can easily rotate the shaft in the correct direction to unwind the rope. If the engine or transmission can be manually rotated without uncoupling the shaft, you may not have to unbolt it.

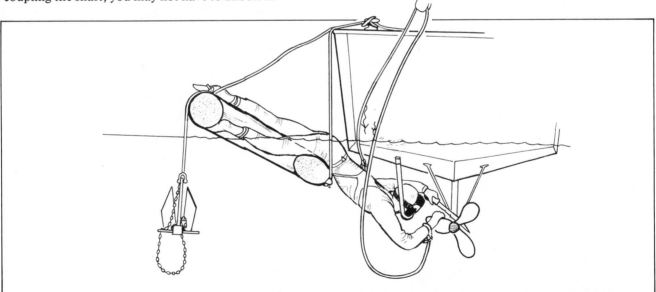

An item very useful for cutting free a melted synthetic rope is a folding pocket saw. If you do not want to dive to free the screw, or can't, you still have two options. Either hoist the after end of the boat with a crane, or move all the people and the heavy weights to the bow. With modern boats that have their propellers far aft, you should be able to reach the screw from the tender.

You may also be able to get at the screw from some larger float, such as an air mattress or a partially pumped up inflatable. When using an inflatable, hang an anchor from the side you are not using as a counterweight.

In this case, too, you must use a safety line and belt. However, this method makes it more difficult for the diver (in the position sketched) to get himself out from under the bottom of the boat and back to the surface.

Beware of Thunderstorms

At sea, few things really scare an experienced skipper. However, a thunderstorm must be reckoned as a force worthy of respect, for it can be very violent, especially in the tropics. Despite expensive protective installations, a boat cannot be lightning proofed.

It has been stated again and again that lightning cannot strike you on the water and that pleasure boats are therefore not endangered. This is totally false. The number of boats struck each year is considerable. Especially great is the probability of a strike during rainfall or when sails and spars are wet. Crew sitting on deck near the shrouds (shown in white in the diagram) of a racing yacht are scarcely aware of the deadly danger they are in.

Lightning strikes on a yacht can have devastating effects, ranging from relatively minor damage to the rig to the total loss of the yacht.
ing from relatively minor damage to the rig to the total loss of the yacht.

The drawing below shows how lightning usually goes to ground (the water) on a sailboat: Most commonly, it travels from the aluminum mast via the wiring system to the propeller shaft and/or electronic components (depth-sounder transducer, knotmeter impeller) or grounding plates set in the hull. Less often it is grounded through the shrouds, stays and chain plates. Often both paths are followed.

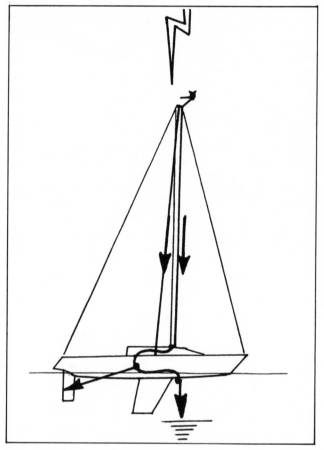

Lightning Damage

Destruction and damage to boat and crew depend on the construction material. The best protection of the crew is afforded by a steel ship, because its continuous metal skin acts as a Faraday cage, which conducts the electricity away along its outer surface. It's another matter with a wooden boat. The lightning seeks a path from the metal rigging to ground at the water's surface, releasing enormous energy. In doing so it strikes right through wooden planks, sometimes tearing out whole chunks, which can quickly sink a yacht.

A strike is even more dangerous to a fiberglass yacht. A smoldering cable can set the laminate afire with very rapid development of extremely poisonous fumes (1).

Less often the lightning is conducted from the upper shrouds and chain plates through the hull into the water (2). On boats with aluminum masts, it tends to follow the mast extrusion itself, because this has very low resistance due to its large cross-sectional size. It then branches off belowdeck through the boat's electrical system. In such cases, the equalization of poten-

tial occurs through the engine and the shaft, possibly destroying the alternator and the starting motor. The strike can also reach the water by way of the transducer and the knotmeter impeller. Even opening the main switch offers no sure protection, because lightning may easily jump it.

Electronic instruments are usually destroyed (3). In the worst case, the thru-hulls of the depth-sounder and knotmeter may be melted right out of the hull, threatening to sink the boat (4). Leading the strike through the propeller shaft is always a problem, because it can destroy the bearings (5).

Leading the lightning via the shrouds and chain plates can pose nasty problems on a fiberglass yacht: The laminate may smolder or melt through at the chain plate fastenings. If these are below the waterline, the water will pour in at once.

The drawing at right shows the protective measures that can be taken. The objective is to make the lightning's path to the water as easy as possible. Carefully ground all turn-buckles and fittings that can handle the electrical energy.

1. The backstay can function as a conductor, in addition to the grounded aluminum mast. However, grounding is difficult if the backstay serves also as an antenna.

If so, it will be equipped with two insulators, one near the masthead and the other just above the turn-buckle. These interrupt the flow of electricity, but you can buy special insulators that lightning can jump but the antenna potential cannot.

2. You cannot ground a steel topping lift going from the masthead to the end of the boom. Use rope instead.

3. It's much better if the lightning can be led from the upper shrouds directly into the water via the keelbolts or grounding plates.

4. The best thing to do before a storm is to get all sail down. Wet sails are particularly good conductors of electricity (some think they even attract it).

5. Because the mast is the main lightning conductor, it must be grounded as directly as possible to the keel or grounding plate.

6. Both the bow pulpit and forestay castings should also be grounded. If the boat has a continuous metal toe rail, these, along with the stern pulpit, can be grounded to the keel, too **(7).**

8. Thorough grounding of the engine and the fuel tank(s) is essential.

9. If the chain plates for both upper and lower shrouds were not electrically connected to the keel during construction, then a grounding cable must be retrofitted, also tied to the keelbolts or grounding plate. Nothing smaller than AWG #8 (American Wire Gauge) wire should be used.

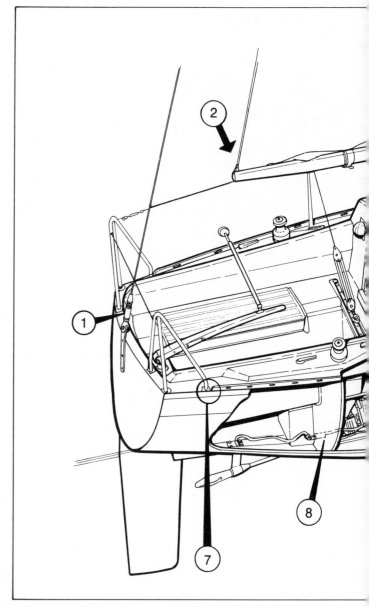

10. A glassed-in ballast keel cannot serve as a ground. Fully effective grounding becomes difficult with this construction. Required is a grounding plate of at least several square feet in area, attached to the hull or the side of the keel. This plate may also be laminated into the hull structure in the mold, under the first layer of mat. This plate requires a thru-hull connection for the grounding cable or strap. When using the plate, all grounding cables must be led to a main ground strap whose cross-sectional area is not less than 0.04 square inch.

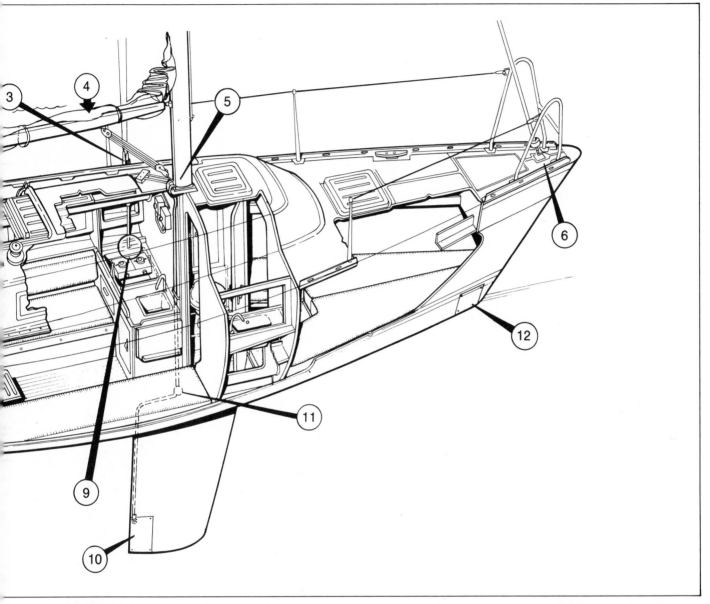

11. If a lead or iron keel is bolted to the hull, it suffices to connect the main grounding strap from the mast and shrouds to a keelbolt.

12. Preferably the forestay should be grounded to a similar plate in the bow area. This is not absolutely essential if the forestay has been grounded to the keel as described but it should serve to bleed off some of the voltage that otherwise would exist on a wet jib.

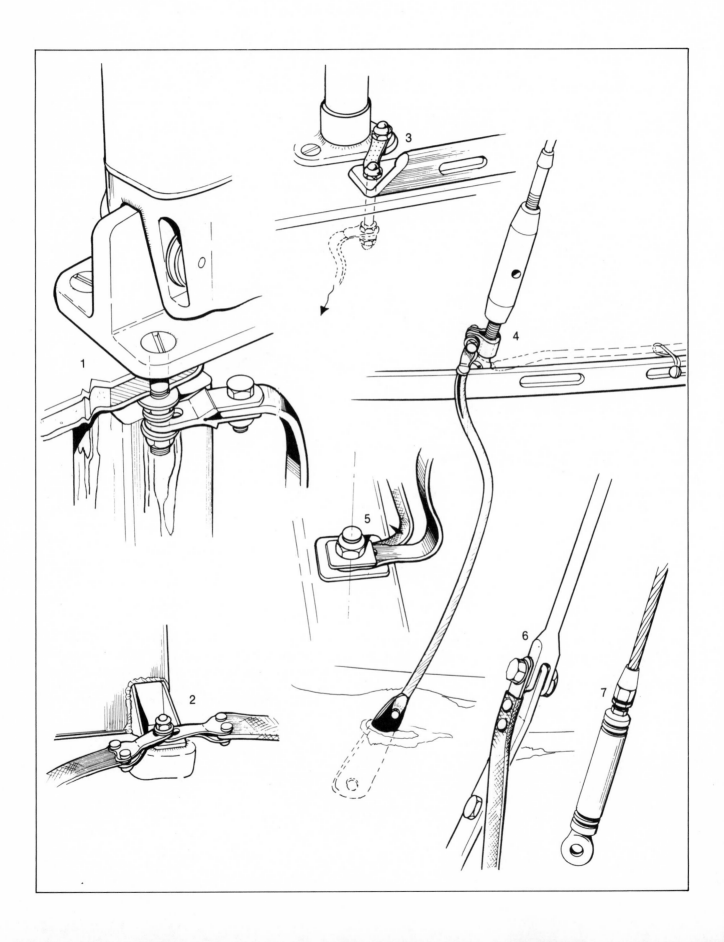

1. The drawing shows how to connect a cable to the mast step under the deck. It is important to use as large a bolt as possible. Further, the cable terminal (or strap terminal, as shown) must have a large contact surface in order to present the least electrical resistance.

2. Metal tanks with electrical gauges have to be grounded to the keelbolts just like stanchions and toe rails **(3)**. It is adequate to run short conductors from the stanchion bases to the port and starboard toe rails respectively and to ground the rails to the keelbolts.

4. A copper cable, attached to a shroud and hung overboard, would appear to keep you out of trouble, but it doesn't guarantee that the stroke will be entirely led off to ground via this cable alone. Still, it's better than nothing at all. It is essential that the cable be at least AWG #4 in diameter; #2 would be better. And it should lead to a large conductive area underwater, for instance, to a thru-bolted copper plate. Never connect the cable to the shroud with a mere cable clip. You must use a bolt-on system with a large surface.

5. All grounding conductors leading to the keelbolts must be AWG #4 or equivalent. Large contact areas between conductors and bolts are important. Use good-size steel plates under the connections to distribute the compressive load.

6. The same rules apply in dealing with the chain plates belowdeck. Contact must be as large and solid as possible so that no "intermittents" can occur. When connections are made as shown, the usual clevis pins and cotter pins are not used.

7. This illustration shows an antenna insulator for the back-stay, which serves as a lightning arrester. The lightning jumps a gap in the device and goes to ground. The lower voltage of the radio signal cannot jump the gap; it is not connected to the hull in any way. Various models of this accessory are available on the market. These lightning arrestors are useful with single sideband radios.

Safety Spacing for the Crew

The position of the crew on board during a thunderstorm is not a matter of indifference. Experiments have shown that the minimum distance from the lightning conductors — in this case mast, shrouds and stays — should be about five feet. The most suitable spot is in the cabin near the after bulkhead, so that the cabin top serves as additional protection, provided that there are no electronic instruments nearby. Stay as far forward in the cockpit as possible, i.e., near the companionway. Avoid the foredeck altogether, because only on large yachts can you maintain a safe distance from the conductors. In order not to endanger the people in the cockpit, unshackle your wire topping lift and make it fast at the mast. Use a rope halyard instead. Best of all is to use a low-stretch rope topping lift from the start.

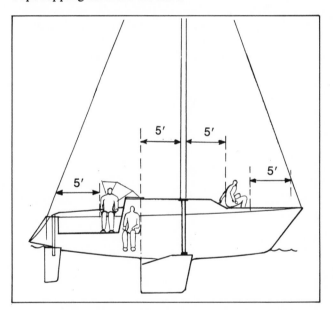

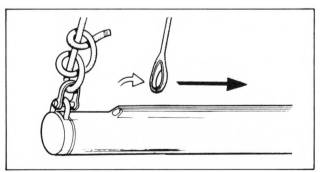

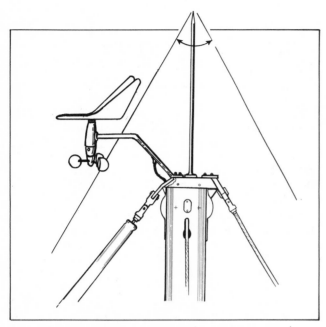

A lightning rod at the masthead will give protection below within an included angle of 60 degrees. This includes the vessel and crew, if it is high enough. Even in this case you must ensure electrical continuity via the mast to the keelbolts or grounding plate on the hull.

Anyone who tries to haul his anchor chain during a thunderstorm is gambling with his life! The lightning — or at least a portion of its potential — takes the direct path down the forestay and the anchor chain to the water and the man on the foredeck connects himself to the circuit the instant he touches the windlass lever. If you absolutely must work the windlass, at the very least wear rubber-soled boots (which serve as electrical insulators) and insulating clothing as well. Still, the general rule remains: No anchor work during a thunderstorm!

The Rudder Is Broken— What Do I Do?

With respect to rudder installations in pleasure craft, the most remarkable mistakes are constantly repeated. Designers and builders economize in the wrong way, or perhaps they underestimate the forces that act upon the rudder assembly, including wear and tear, which are continuously at work.

Above all, the vogue of the freestanding spade rudder has spawned many serious incidents. A freestanding rudder has no support at its lower edge, so that the shaft, blade and bearing have to take the entire load. Regular inspections of all possible weak points in every rudder system are most important.

Concerted maintenance is of special value in the case of pedestal wheel and cable steering systems. Nevertheless, these systems have generally stood the test in yachts. Hydraulic installations, initially subject to leakage problems in the distribution system, are now relatively free of such difficulties due to technical improvements.

Defects in Pedestal Steering

Out of ignorance, many a steering cable has been overstressed in an attempt to eliminate all play at the wheel. This can lead to breaks in the cheeks of a sheave (1) so that the shaft and sheave pull right out. The mount or base may crack (2) as well.

If, on the other hand, the cable is too loose, there is considerable risk that the cable will jump the sheaves below the pedestal (3). Cable drives may break as a result of wear or chafe (4). Inspect at least yearly; this is important. Other causes of failure in pedestal steering are unreliable sheave pivots (5), broken quadrants (6), cables that have jumped out of the groove in the quadrant due to loose tensioning (7), broken turnbuckles (8), or breakage of the segment that bolts the quadrant to the rudderstock (9).

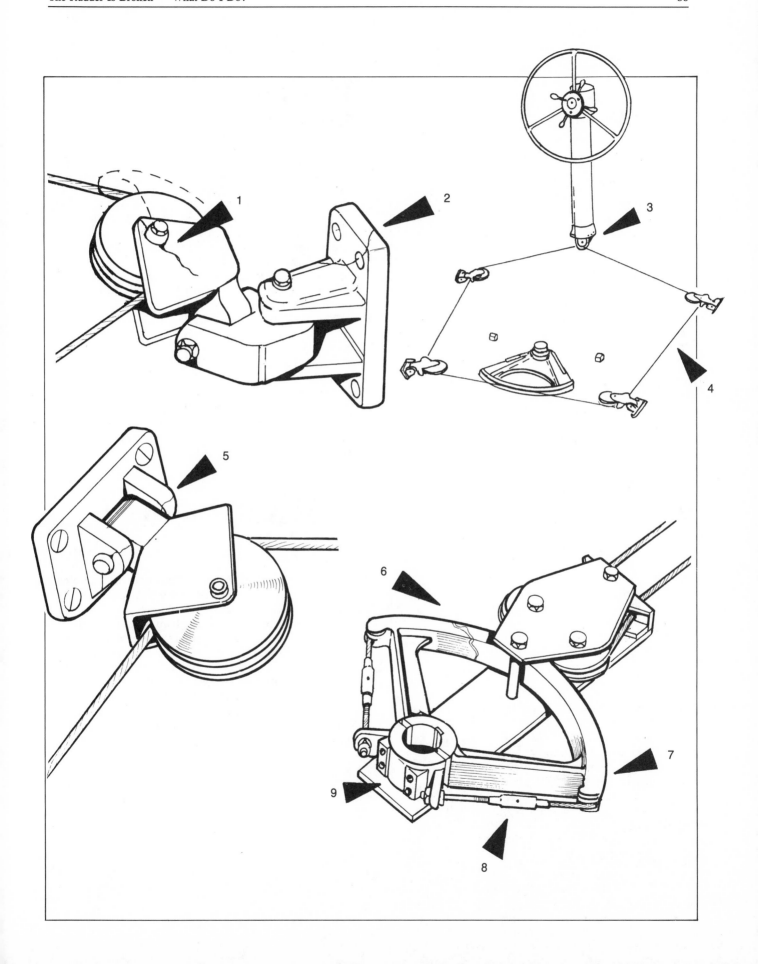

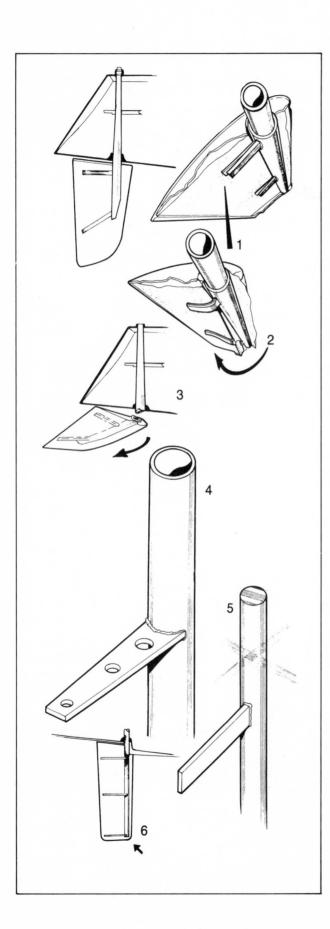

Poor Rudder Construction

Probably the most common cause of rudder damage is a deficient connection between the rudder blade, the steel reinforcing bars and the stock. Freestanding rudders are particularly prone to this hazard. Usually the rudder blade consists of two half-shells laminated over the reinforcing bars and the shaft, and then filled with foam. This operation is difficult and requires considerable technical know-how if it is to be carried out without defects. As a result of faulty workmanship, delamination of the fiberglass shells occurs or even the loss of whole pieces (1).

This kind of trouble can arise, too, if the horizontal reinforcing bars, which may be made of a relatively soft vanadium steel of inadequate strength, bend under a side load (2). Finally, the rudderstock itself may be undersized for economy's sake, leading to a break where it exits the hull (3).

Horizontal bars welded to the shaft (4) are much stronger than those set on edge (5). The latter is in much greater danger of bending. And the rudderstock should run all the way to the lower edge of the rudder (6).

The Lifting Outboard Rudder

The lifting rudders that are mounted on the transoms of many smaller boats are at particularly high risk. The pivots and the lower edges of the rudderhead assembly (1) are often quite high above the water, which leads to an increase in the transverse stress (2). If the rudder blade is constructed of marine plywood, only half of the veneers are load bearing because every other one has its grain parallel to the edges of a potential break. This is the reason that so many rudders break off at the lower edge of the head assembly (3). Faired metal rudder blades have stood up best but are used mostly on small boats. Next come wooden blades built up of hardwood staves, glued lengthwise with grain opposed (4). Delamination is a major problem. Fiberglass outboard rudders have the same problems as freestanding inboard spade rudders; still, they are very strong, provided that the laminated construction is skillfully carried out.

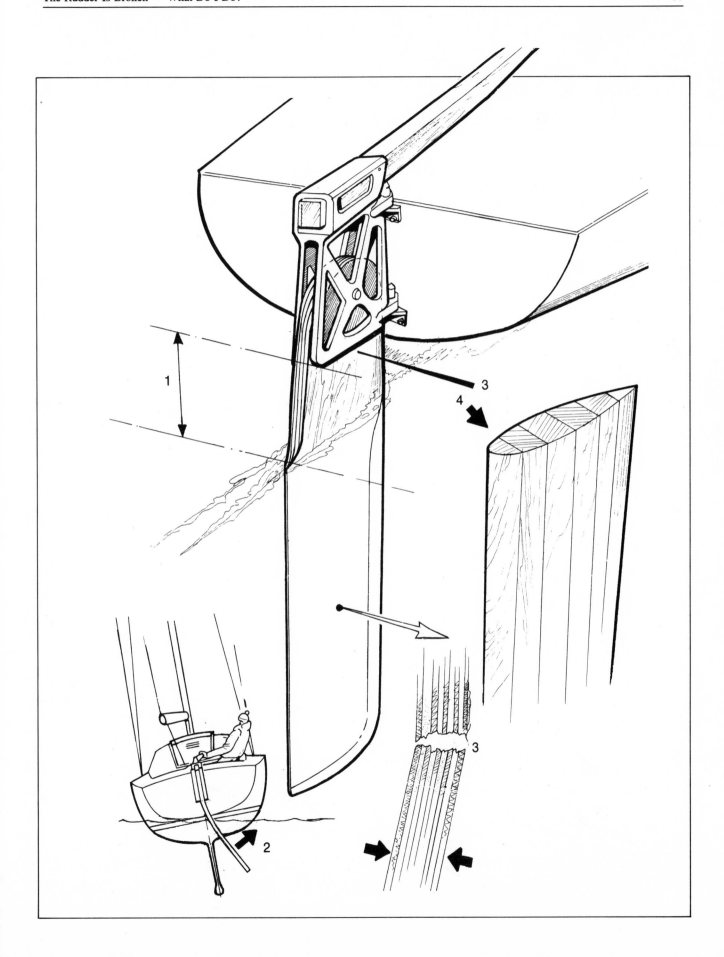

Breaking the Rudder While Surfing

The rudder blades of fast yachts can break while surfing down the face of a sea. As a result of the high speed, even a small rudder angle can cause very high stresses on the rudder blade **(1)**. A similar effect occurs in racing yachts under spinnaker, when the boat luffs up **(2)**.

Long-distance cruisers on an extended passage may incur damage because the rudder moves continuously. The bearings develop flats and the reinforced plastic joints deteriorate.

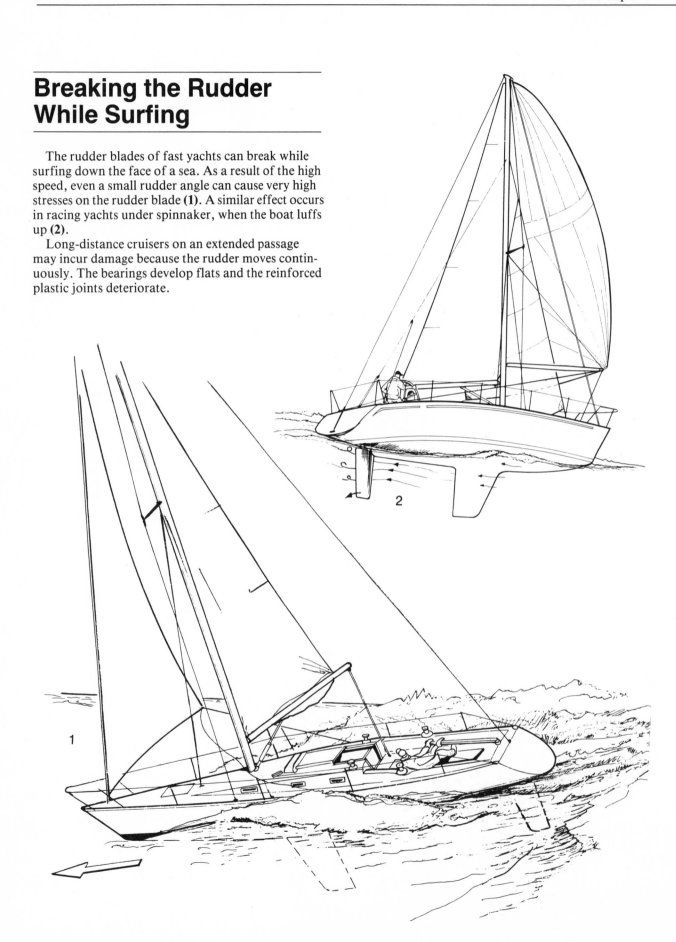

Attention When Going Astern!

Likewise, rudders are vulnerable when powering astern. At higher speeds, the tiller can be torn right out of your hands. The rudder turns athwartships and breaks off in a forward direction. In this case, too, the freestanding rudder is at special risk. And it goes without saying that even a rudder hung from the keel, and therefore more rugged, has to be built with this kind of treatment in mind. Actually, one should calmly risk a test during builder's trials and set the rudder athwartships at full speed astern. If no harm is done, then it is not likely that anything serious will happen at sea.

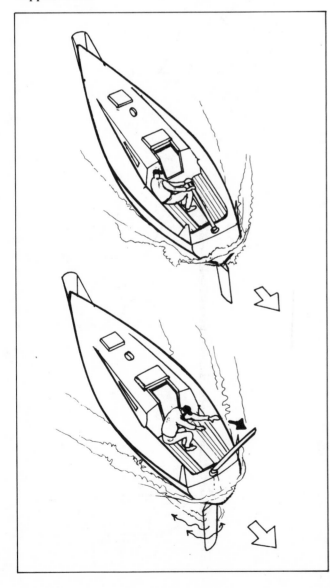

Watch Out When Tying Up to a Quay

Rudders that slope aft so that they extend beyond the edge of the transom are at risk if the boat has to lie stern to at a berth along a quay. An outboard rudder can hit the quay even more easily still. So you have to be careful that the anchor chain or the forward mooring lines are set out far enough that even with heavy wind or swell in the harbor you cannot be driven down toward the quay.

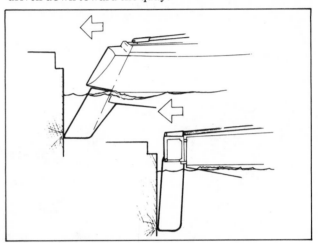

Setting the Rudder at an Angle

Among racing one-designs, a common cause of rudder breakage is due to a blade that is not quite vertical. Even a slight tilt aft causes a substantial increase in transverse stress, which the man at the tiller notices as increased rudder pressure for which he must duly compensate. If the rudder blade snaps upward at higher speeds, breakage is virtually a mathematical certainty.

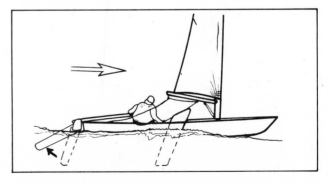

Dragging a Drogue

Before you call "Mayday" because your rudder has been damaged, consider the chances of remedying the situation. Even after total loss of the rudder, most yachts can usually make the next harbor with the resources on board, or at least be kept on course until another vessel can be asked for help. Most important: In the open sea you will generally not meet serious danger to ship or crew. Indeed you may well find that quite simple means will get you out of trouble when the rudder has mutinied.

You can, for example, steer the boat with an improvised drogue. The drogue is towed with two lines paid out over the stern. Haul on the port-side line and the boat will veer to port (1). Ease off the port-side line and the boat will veer to starboard (2). As a drogue you might use a fender with an anchor added to increase weight or a bucket or a coil of rope (3). Larger boats, power or sail, naturally call for greater water resistance in the tow. An inflatable or hard tender, half-filled with water, will give you the desired steering effect. Be aware that there is a risk of tearing out the towing eye, so use the lowest possible speed (4).

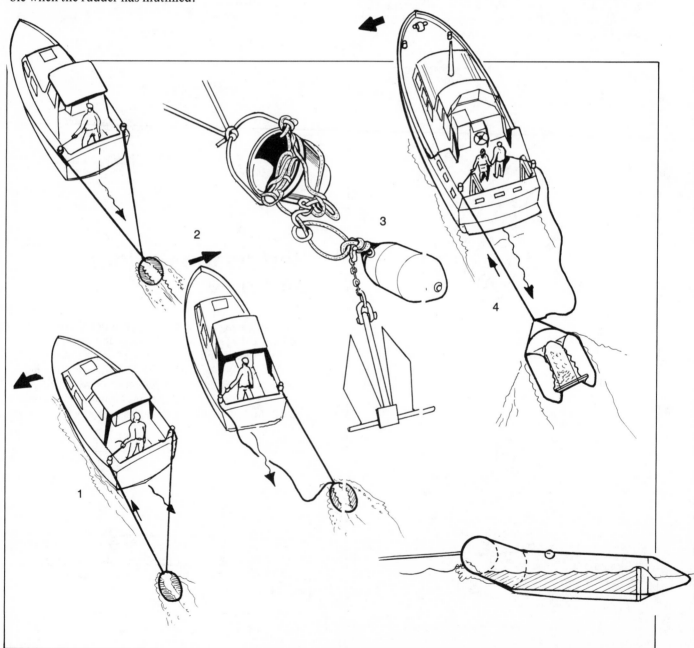

The Emergency Tiller

It should be obvious by now that every boat — motor and sail — with wheel steering should have an emergency tiller. Many builders include this essential emergency equipment, but how does it work in practice?

The emergency tiller is sometimes fitted belowdeck, buried somewhere deep under bunk upholstery and hatch lids. In such installations, one cannot usually steer from the cockpit, which is of course ridiculous. Try it sometime!

Much better is an emergency tiller arrangement on deck (1), or directly under the opening of a watertight deck plate (2). In any case, one must be able to handle the emergency tiller from the cockpit. In larger boats with aft cabins and center cockpits, this calls for a long, heavy pipe, perhaps with extensions.

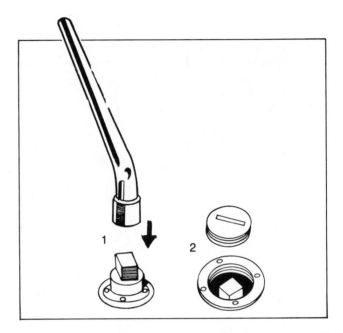

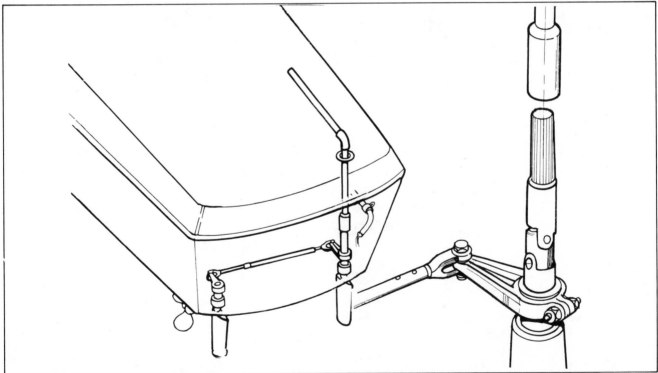

It is widely perceived that emergency steering is unnecessary on twin-screw boats; the designers maintain they can be properly steered with the engines. This seems correct, but is merely hypothetical. Anyone who has gone through the difficulty of steering a motorboat over long distances by simply varying propeller rpm will plead for an emergency tiller. Best is a coupling that has been retrofitted to one of the rudderstocks.

One of the simplest and most rapidly installed steering devices is a pair of auxiliary steering lines mounted near the trailing edge of the rudder (see drawing, next page). Voyaging yachts commonly have a fitting (e.g., a pair of eyes bolted to the two sides of the rudder) to which lines may be attached. Better still, the lines can be shackled on before the start of the trip.

If there are no eyes, you can use a screw clamp, but be sure to secure it with a light line to prevent loss. The drawing shows how this steering rig is installed. You could also lead the lines to the winches through a pair of auxiliary blocks.

If your boat has an outboard rudder, it may be possible to devise an emergency tiller in a pinch. This is done by lashing a couple of long battens to both sides of the rudderhead. You can crudely fashion the necessary pieces of wood by using hatchet and saw on the interior accommodations or cockpit grating. Better still, carry along suitable battens; they may be useful in repairing other kinds of damage, too. Sometimes a shortened spinnaker pole can be used for the same purpose, provided its diameter is not too great. It is lashed along one side of the rudderhead.

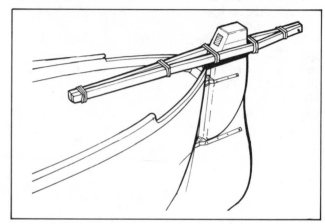

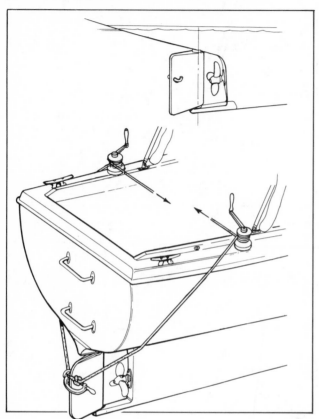

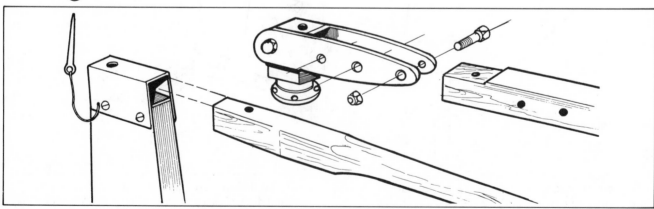

It's a good idea to carry a simple wooden tiller as a spare even on small yachts. On such boats tillers are not usually broken by undue rudder pressure, but rather as a result of inattention by a crewmember who inadvertently stumbles or falls on it. It is important that the fittings at the rudderhead be so built that it is easy to reach the bolts or screws to change tillers.

Jury Rudders

A good jury rudder can be fashioned from a spinnaker pole and two boards — companionway boards,
locker lids, floorboards or the like. However, it is
always better to take along a pair of special boards
and suitable bolts for the specific purpose of con-
structing a jury rudder **(1)**. The spinnaker pole is
lashed down at its midpoint to the backstay fittings.
A tackle is attached to the backstay with a rolling
hitch; it holds the inboard end of the pole up, which
keeps the rudder down at the desired depth. You steer
with two control lines fastened to the rudder and led
to the winches on either side. With good sail trim, a
rudder area of about five square feet will steer a
yacht of up to about eight tons displacement.

It is relatively easy to rig a jury rudder on a light-
displacement yacht. First, fasten a board to the spinnaker pole with hose clamps or lashings. Then, to
keep the rudder from riding up in the water while
under way, shackle an anchor and chain to the lower
edge of the rudder. You could also use a tackle on the
backstay, as mentioned above. Steer with a jury-rigged
tiller lashed through the end fitting of the pole **(2)**.

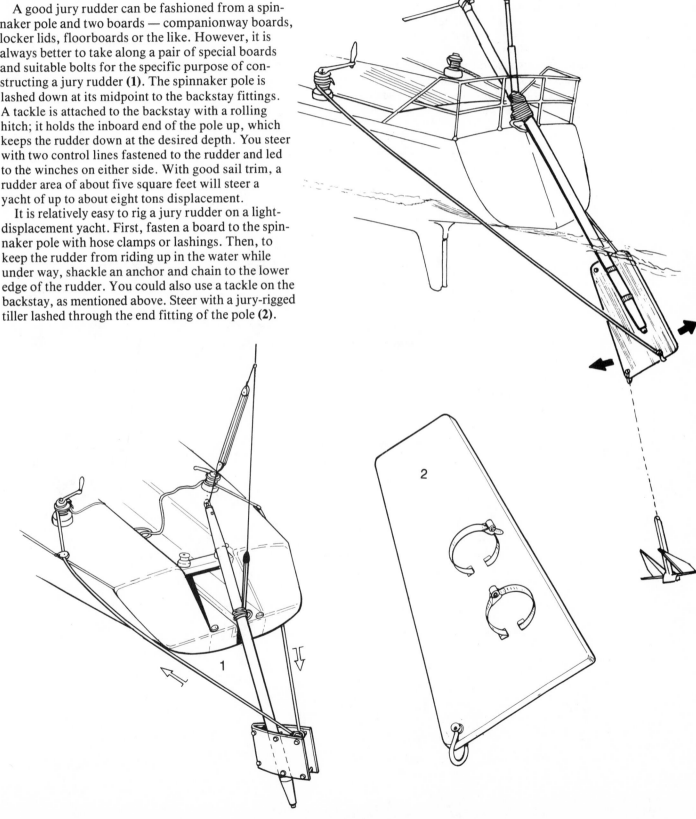

Grounding and Stranding

Nothing scares a sailor more than grounding on a lee shore (a shore without shelter from an onshore wind). If you cannot get off immediately after touching, under your own power, a stranding is likely to follow. While in earlier times large ships could not beat out against heavy winds and high seas, strandings of modern yachts have commonly resulted from inattention on the part of the helmsman, who approaches too close to the shore in difficult conditions or during anchoring.

Danger from Wind Shifts

With an offshore wind, the skipper may regard it as safe to anchor in a cove or off a beach, but this may be particularly dangerous. With a sudden shift in wind, a narrow cove may turn into a lee shore from which one cannot escape if the anchor drags or the boat touches bottom. In such wind conditions, the waves run into the shoal waters of the cove, changing to short breaking seas whose drive shoreward will break out almost any anchor. And often the crew, gone ashore, doesn't notice the wind shift.

Clawing Off a Lee Shore

The skipper often fails in his efforts to claw off a lee shore or bight. While the powerful, short, high seas, breaking at the shoreline, set the boat strongly to leeward, the skipper, afraid of excessive heeling, sets too little sail, sometimes only the jib.

Moreover, the sails may not be hardened in enough. As a result, the boat does not make enough headway and cannot compensate for leeway and set. Yet in most cases one can get out of the situation under flattened storm jib and trysail or heavily reefed and tightly trimmed mainsail.

Force 8

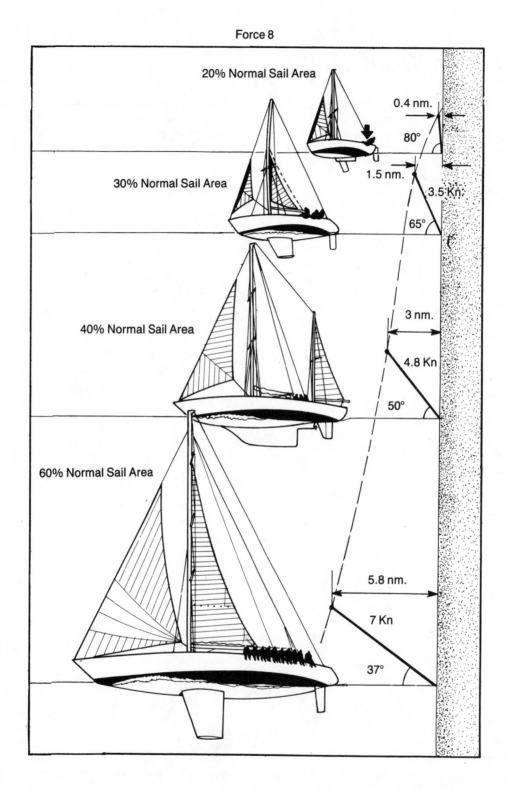

20% Normal Sail Area

0.4 nm.

80°

1.5 nm.

3.5 Kn.

30% Normal Sail Area

65°

3 nm.

40% Normal Sail Area

4.8 Kn

50°

60% Normal Sail Area

5.8 nm.

7 Kn

37°

Worry over reefing often causes a delay in reefing the main when in difficulty. The skipper has to ease the main, which, being hard on the wind, starts to flog very severely. This causes eddies and vibration that brake the boat so strongly that it can make no more headway to windward under the jib alone.

The graph shows the theoretical chances for four yachts of very different types to claw off a lee shore in a Force 8 wind — officially a gale. Basically, this depends on the sail-carrying ability of the particular boat.

The upper diagram shows a small keel-centerboard cruiser about 16 feet LOA. It can carry only about 20 percent of its normal working sail. Under small jib, it reaches a speed of about two knots and, set to leeward by wind and wave, makes good a course of about 80 degrees off the true wind. Even though the boat be optimally sailed, a stranding may not be preventable because it can barely make good any ground to windward and may, at times, be set to leeward. The second boat is a coastal cruiser of about 23 feet LOA. She carries a storm jib and trysail totalling about 30 percent of normal working area. On a course made good of at most 65 degrees off the wind, this vessel does 3.5 knots, making good 1.5 knots to windward.

The third boat is a blue-water voyaging ketch, 41 feet LOA. In this Force 8 wind, she is still carrying her #2 cruising jib and mizzen, about 40 percent of standard. Her course made good is about 50 degrees off the true wind, and making 4.8 knots she can pretty safely and surely make good about three miles off the lee shore each hour.

The bottom example is a modern maxi-racer, 78 feet LOA. She is carrying a #4 genoa and a double-reefed main, 60 percent of normal. She makes good a calculated angle of 37 degrees off the wind at a speed of seven knots. The vessel can work free of the coast at a rate of 5.8 knots.

Use the Bow Anchor

When the engine fails, a motorboat generally drifts bow first before the wind, because the rudder acts as a lateral underwater surface resisting drift while the topsides constitute a "sail area." This misleads the skipper to drop a stern anchor in expectation of a stranding. Wrong! The broad stern gives the seas a good grip. Under these conditions, the anchor will probably not hold. Consequently, always use the bower anchor and pay out as much line and/or chain as you have on board!

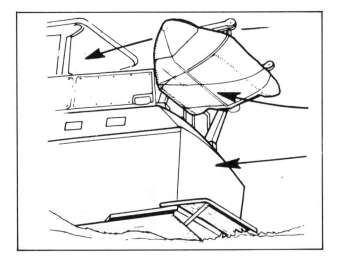

Grounding Through Navigational Error

Navigational errors are common causes of stranding. Capes, for example, often have off-lying shoals that are not marked. In poor visibility it's difficult to estimate your true distance off. Skippers who do not take soundings run the risk of going aground.

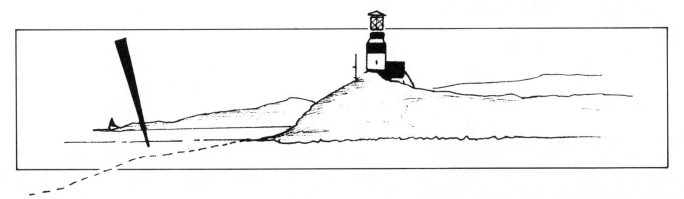

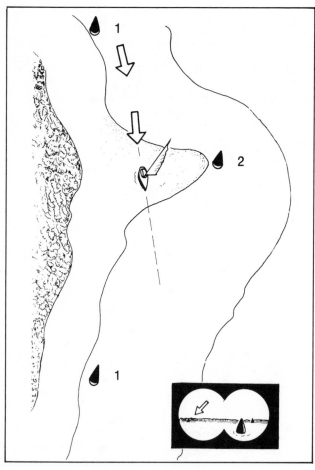

out of the water with every sea, so no headway can be made. Good seamanship dictates that under these conditions, small yachts always leave harbor with sails set. The amount of sail area should be chosen so that the boat is assured of being able to beat out to windward. If the boat cannot beat out of harbor under sail alone, don't try to leave!

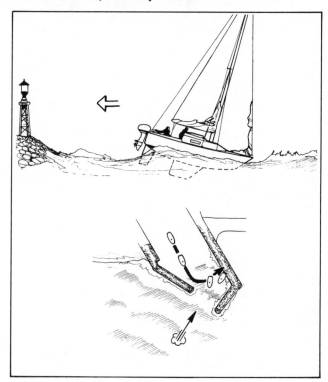

When running along a coastal channel, one often relies entirely on the channel markers, some of which may lie far to one side in the field of vision, and with apparent logic lay out a course to keep off the shore without checking the chart (1). In this way it's easy to overlook a marker farther offshore that shows the boundary of a shoal (2).

When the Outboard Keeps Coming Out

Coming out of a narrow harbor entrance against heavy incoming seas and an onshore wind, light displacement boats with outboard engines may be set down upon the stone jetty to one side or the other. This happens because the outboard's propeller comes

Dangerous Shores

Skippers often underestimate the power of breaking or meeting seas off a shelving shore. Such seas become very steep as they approach the shoaling bottom and can bring a tacking boat to a complete standstill, causing a quick set to leeward. So when beating, keep a good offing from moles, slopes and steep coasts.

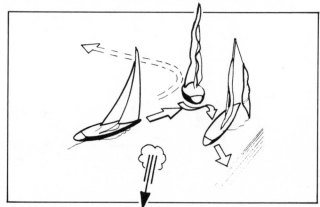

The Stranding of the *Ouwe Reus*

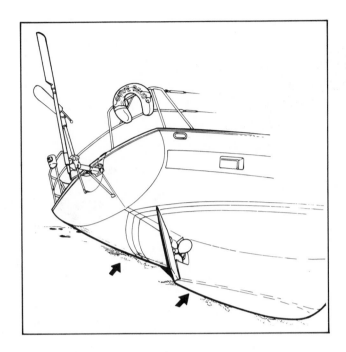

When the steel Dutch yacht *Ouwe Reus* stranded on a reef in the Pacific, the skipper acted with great foresight. As soon as she touched, he set the tiller to leeward so that the rudder was canted upward and could not be damaged. Next he hauled up the pendulum of the self-steering. In general, these measures should be taken whenever a stranding is expected. The *Ouwe Reus* was, in fact, freed from the reef to continue her circumnavigation. The steel hull was dented, but developed no leak.

Analysis of many strandings has shown that steel boats generally withstand such accidents better than wooden or fiberglass boats. Fiberglass hulls resist damage from rocks or coral heads less than any other kind of hull because the material is very sensitive to point loading.

When a Sailboat Is Stranded. . . . .

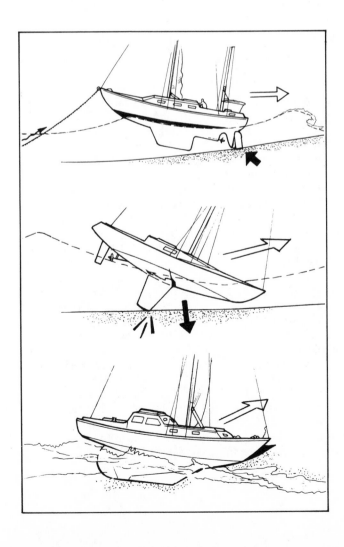

1. If a sailboat lies to a dragging anchor, it drives aground stern first. The rudder hits first and in a seaway can sustain crippling damage. Freestanding rudders are instantly bent or broken away.

2. When a sailboat drives ashore under bare poles, she strikes stern to the wind with her bow pitched down to the slope of the bottom. In the trough of a wave, the keel hits bottom first. Boats with narrow, deep keels spring leaks around the keel, more often forward than aft of the keel itself.

3. Long-keeled boats withstand the initial contact better, whether they have bolted-on, externally ballasted keels or encapsulated keels.

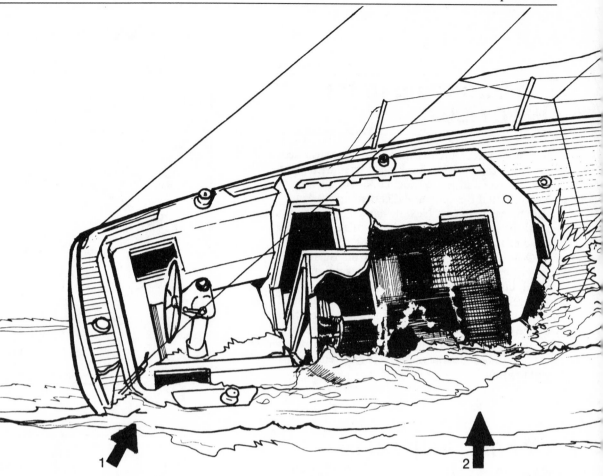

Stranding can have a variety of results, depending on the configuration of the shore and the respective effects of wind and sea. Yet there is a fairly general sequence of events when a shallow-draft cruising boat grounds on a steeply sloping, sandy shore: The boat is driven on the beach in such a way that she heels to windward, presenting the deck to the in-rolling breakers. This is due to the fact that the keel is very soon washed in on the shore, while the powerful undertow tries to suck the boat out again. Since the keel is held fast, the greatly feared knockdown to windward follows.

An example of this sequence of events is given by the stranding of Bernard Moitessier's legendary *Joshua* on the Baja California coast in 1983, following a sudden wind shift. Twenty-six other boats were caught the same way and most ended up mast-to-seaward on the beach.

The results of this kind of stranding are nearly always fatal to the vessel. The deck and deckhouse, unprotected, become prey to the breaking seas. The cockpit and lazarette locker lids and the hatches are soon broken off **(1)** and the boat fills. Even the deckhouse cannot survive the waves as the impact of the breakers soon smashes it to bits **(2)**.

Other behaviors are possible. Stranded in shoal water, a keel yacht may be carried so far up the beach and heeled so far to leeward that the topsides touch the ground. Each breaker lifts the boat and lets it fall, lee bow first, so that the hull soon starts to break up. The final phase of this kind of stranding is usually the total loss of the boat. Cases are known in which only fragments of the hull remained after just a few hours. This is especially true of fiberglass boats.

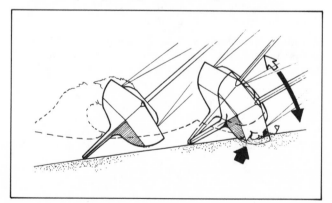

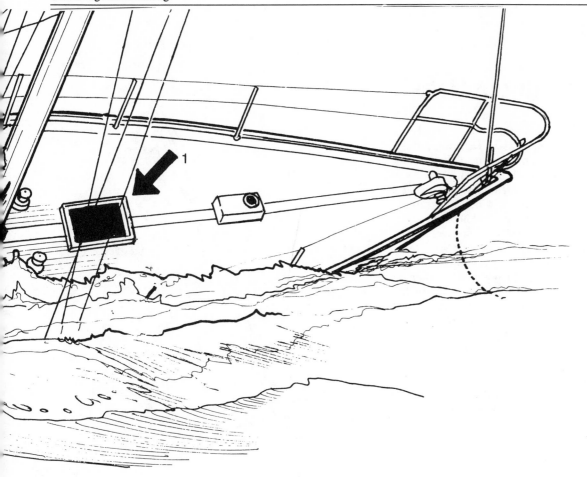

Stranding of a Motorboat

When a motorboat having little draft runs onto a lee shore bow first, she immediately grounds on the beach. Damage in the bow area is to be expected, but in the first phase of the mishap, it is not usually too serious **(1).** In the second stage, the vessel is quickly broached and then driven higher up the beach by each successive wave; the rudder, propeller and shaft are severely damaged. Cabin windows are stove in. More severe hull damage occurs only in the final phase, when the hull is lifted to windward by the back of each wave and then toppled to leeward. As time goes on, the boat breaks up at the turn of the bilge — if built of wood or fiberglass. Steel vessels have a chance of coming out of the situation merely with dented topsides, without developing leaks **(2).**

Getting Off without Help

To free a stranded boat without outside help calls for great experience as a seaman, as well as good judgment. Certain rules are basic and must be observed:

Do not simply lay the bow anchor out with the tender. Rather, having set it out on a long rode, bring it amidships and lead it to the anchor windlass through a heavy turning block. If you do this and heel the boat while carrying out all of the other steps necessary to free the boat, you most likely will succeed. To heel the boat, start by attaching a halyard with an eye on the end to the anchor rode, on which you have taken a good strain. Now haul the halyard tight with its winch **(1)**. The greater the angle that the halyard makes with the mast, the easier it is to heel the boat over **(2)**. Then haul in the anchor line (which, remember, is amidships) using a sheet winch and a turning block **(3)**; the boat may come free. Under the load, the eye will work its way toward the boat and the heel will grow correspondingly less, so the procedure may have to be repeated several times depending on circumstances.

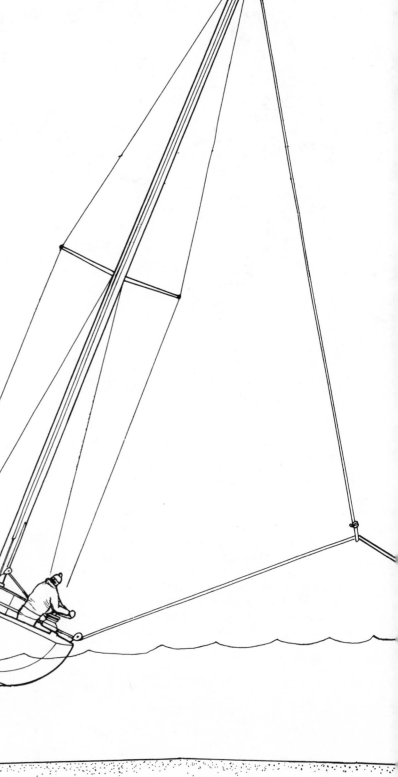

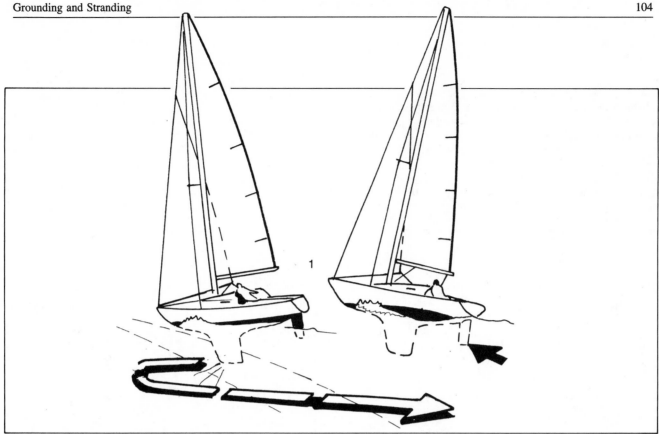

It is axiomatic that you will leave on a course reciprocal to the one that grounded you in the first place. This is the only way to be sure of reaching deeper water in the shortest possible time (1).

It is easier to get off if two or three crewmembers mount the boom which you then swing out. But take care! A rope topping lift has to be reinforced with the main halyard or it may break, dropping the boom to the deck and injuring the crew (2).

The heel can also be increased by having a man climb the mast and sit on the spreaders. The crew on deck can then get a good heel with a slight change in trim. Of course, this method will work only on smaller boats and, besides, you have to consider the danger to the man on the mast. No one should climb the mast without a life jacket or without being secured with main or jib halyard (3)!

In the case of bilge-keeled boats, a grounding while on the wind is usually less dramatic. When the boat is heeled, only the leeward keel is stuck and easing or trimming the sails generally suffices to make the boat more upright, so that its draft is reduced (4). Bilge-keelers are in greater trouble if they drive aground before the wind; on this point of sail they scarcely heel at all. You cannot heel them farther as described above as you would a single-keeled boat (5).

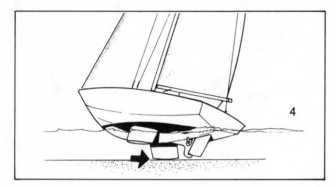

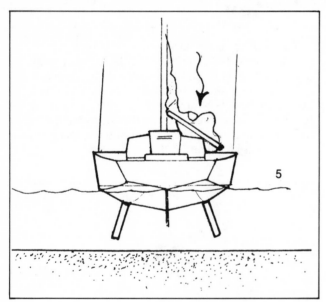

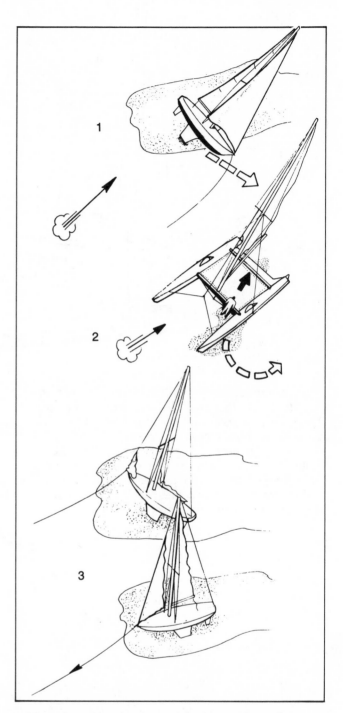

If you have just about crossed a bar and have discovered that you cannot turn the boat toward deeper water by use of a backed jib (1), the boathook, spinnaker pole or muscle power (2), try the anchor (3).

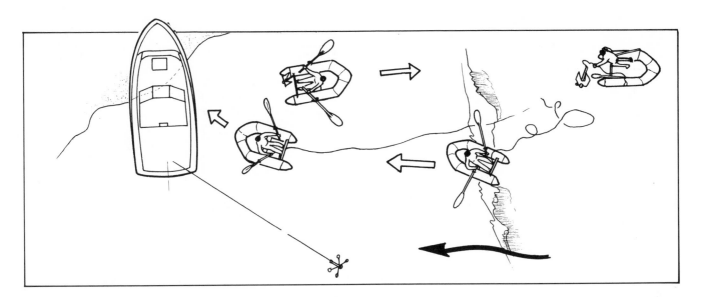

Laying Out an Anchor

As shown in the illustration, an anchor set out in deeper water is often the best way to get the vessel afloat again without outside help. The anchor must be set out as far as possible toward the deep channel using the tender. Put the anchor and plenty of anchor line in the dinghy. Be sure the end of the anchor line is made fast on the boat. Now row up to windward and drop the anchor at least 10 boat lengths upwind or upcurrent of the stranded yacht. Naturally, this procedure can be used only when the wind is not too strong. In order for this method to work smoothly and without fraying the nerves, it is important that the anchor, chain and the whole length of the line be run over the dinghy's side without fouling. The whole fall of the line is laid in the stern of the dinghy in big open coils. The chain is laid on top of the coil and the anchor is hung over the stern, secured with a lanyard (1) in such a way that it can be released very quickly and easily from the rower's position (2).

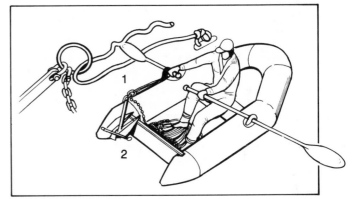

Getting Off the Ground— But How?

From the standpoint of the skipper coming to the rescue, many a grounding seems harmless and freeing the boat a simple job. As a result, he often misjudges the necessary precautions and makes elementary mistakes that can lead the would-be rescuer into danger himself. Many well-meaning attempts to help have, through the ignorance of the rescuer, resulted only in greater damage to the grounded boat.

Approach from Leeward

A common error is to fail to heed the direction of the wind and sea. An attempt to approach downwind or with a following sea nearly always results in a collision (1). If the water depth is sufficient, the correct method is to approach the stranded boat at an acute angle to the wind or even directly against it (2). Generally speaking, keelboats have a draft of about 4½ to six feet, while motorboats often draw less than three feet.

It's common enough to approach dismasted and drifting yachts from the wrong direction also, i.e., from upwind (illustration below). In these cases, there is the danger that the damaged boat's mast, lines and parts of its rigging are adrift, too. They can easily be caught in the propeller of the rescue vessel so that she in turn becomes a casualty. For these reasons the towing ship should always come up on the distressed boat from leeward.

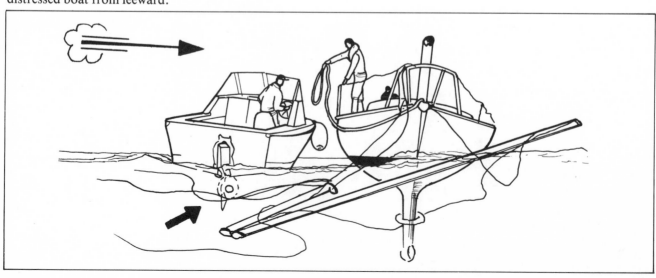

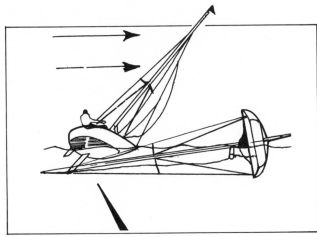

This applies also to the small boat sailor who wants to come to the aid of a capsized friend. If he approaches from the windward side, he will inevitably be set down on the capsized boat by the wind and the seas, so that he collides with its mast and/or its sails — if indeed he is not himself capsized. In fact, he may be expected to capsize with the next puff anyway, his mast and sails coming down on the original victim.

Hauling Off

A sailor trying, under sail alone, to free a boat aground on a lee shore quite often underestimates the potential dangers. As a rule, he approached downwind and then maneuvers to come closer on a beam reach before heaving a coiled, weighted towline to the stranded boat (1). At this point the would-be rescuer drifts to leeward, unable to gain headway because of the pull of the tow (2). The result is inevitably a grounding near the vessel in distress (3).

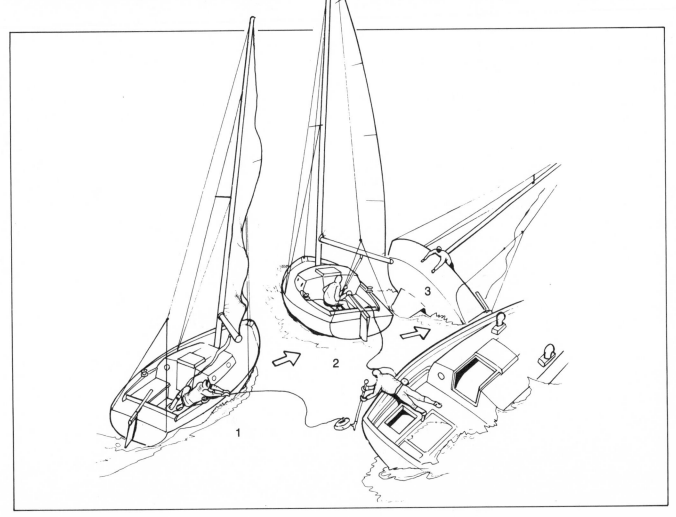

Freeing a yacht aground on a lee shore is a difficult
and dangerous operation. It can succeed only when
both parties exercise all the care that the situation
demands. The rescuer must turn to windward and hold
his position upwind of the grounded boat against

wind and sea. Have the helmsman keep an eye constantly on the depth-sounder (1). Let another crew (2) stream a long light line (the messenger) aft from the stern (3). To this is attached a life ring (4). The foredeck crew on the grounded boat should wear a life jacket and be secured with a safety harness (5) throughout this operation. It's a must that the distressed vessel prepare a towing hawser in advance (see ''Towing with Understanding'') by making it fast to the mast or the winches—to the mast only if keel stepped. (6). It's best then to pass it to the rescue boat with the light messenger line. Now tow under half power. If you cannot budge the boat, you will have to stop so as not to endanger your own boat.

A motorboat can get itself into trouble when it tries to haul off a boat that has been driven upon a submerged jetty in a current. In this case, the special factors to be watched are the direction and speed of the current and the corresponding safe offing that must be maintained. Too short a distance would make it likely that the rescuer would drift down on the jetty while passing the towline, with the result that he would himself go aground. Then he would either be unable to get off under his own power or suffer damage (1).

Always pay close attention to the current in the vicinity of a grounded boat in tidal or river waters. Approach against the current, with one exception: If a boat has gone aground on a jetty with the current, never try to tow it free down-current, as you would merely drag the distressed boat farther up the jetty. Instead, pull at an angle against the stream toward deeper water (2).

Under some conditions, even a powerful motorboat might struggle fruitlessly to tow a sailboat off; first try heeling it over farther. This can best be accomplished with an anchor as previously described, but when circumstances demand, it can be achieved by fastening the towline around the mast with a bowline and hoisting it to the spreaders or to the shroud tangs using the jib or main halyard. The rescuer can then pull off to the side with great care—too much power and he might break the mast and damage the rig (3). A downhaul must be rigged to the towline's eye to keep it from damaging the shrouds and spreaders.

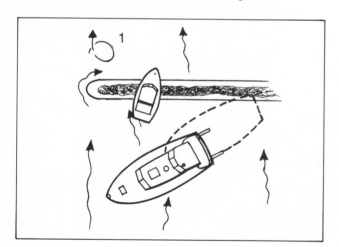

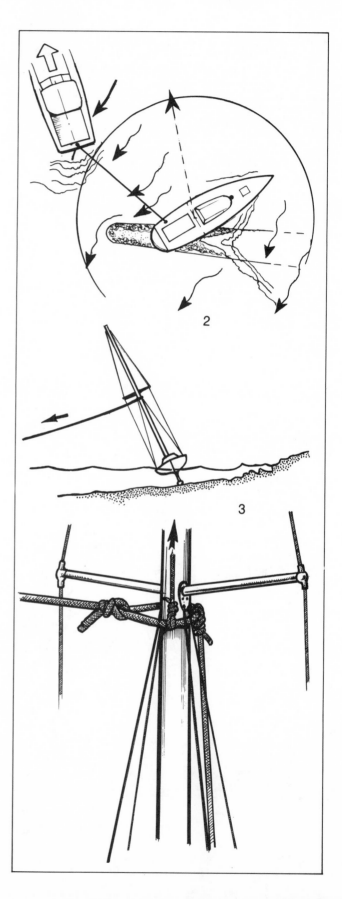

Righting a Centerboarder

A fully capsized centerboard boat must be righted before towing. In this case, the rescue boat comes up carefully from the leeward side of the drifting boat and makes fast a towline to the chain plate of the lee shroud. At the same time, it attaches a light control line to the rudder fittings **(1)**.

With both lines paid out, the rescuer then maneuvers around the casualty and takes a position to windward **(2)**. When the tow begins, the crew governs the attitude of the boat with the control line, keeping it crosswise to the direction of pull **(3)**.

The towing vessel should stop even before the capsized boat is fully upright, otherwise it may capsize to the other side **(4)**. After being righted, the centerboarder is made fast alongside the rescue boat and bailed out. Then, before it is towed off, its sails must be lowered, board raised and rudder taken inboard **(5)**.

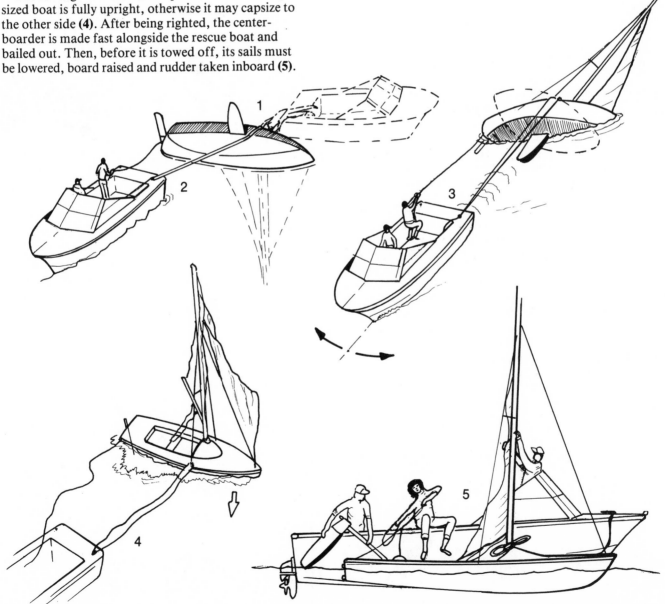

Rescuing the People

When the rescuer comes right up to a yacht stranded on a lee shore to take off its crew, there can be dangerous consequences, illustrated by the case of the *Cormoran*.

It happened in the Adriatic Sea. The yacht *Cormoran* was stranded, jammed between rocks and helpless prey to the incoming rollers. The hull developed severe leaks and sank. A fisherman maneuvered right up to the wreck to take off the skipper and his wife. The lady was caught between the hull of the wreck and the side of the fishing boat, suffering crushing injuries to both legs. The skipper jumped down to help her and broke both feet. In spite of these injuries the couple were saved. The rescue of persons who are essentially helpless is particularly hazardous when it must be carried out in a seaway. To effect the transfer, the boats must of necessity be kept only a short distance apart, but during the operation the weight of the unfortunate crew being taken across tends to pull the boats closer together. Thus the people being rescued could be drawn between the hulls, suffering severe — even fatal — injuries. If no other course of action is possible, the rescue boat must be securely made fast to the wreck and fendered with special care, even if this is expected to cause damage to both boats.

In the event that a crewmember has been severely injured or shows symptoms of being seriously ill, the wisest course is to call a fast motorboat for help by radio or emergency signal to get the patient to a hospital as quickly as possible. To begin the transfer at sea, the sailboat approaches the motorboat's lee quarter — the latter cannot maneuver as precisely as required, especially at low speed in a seaway. The sailboat's bow area is carefully fendered **(1)**. As soon as the bow overlaps the stern of the motorboat, it is made fast. In a sea of any size, it is not wise to go fully alongside for fear of damage to both boats. Now, with the lines made fast, it is possible to transfer crew to the cockpit of the motorboat with the aid of crew on the foredeck **(2)**.

1

2

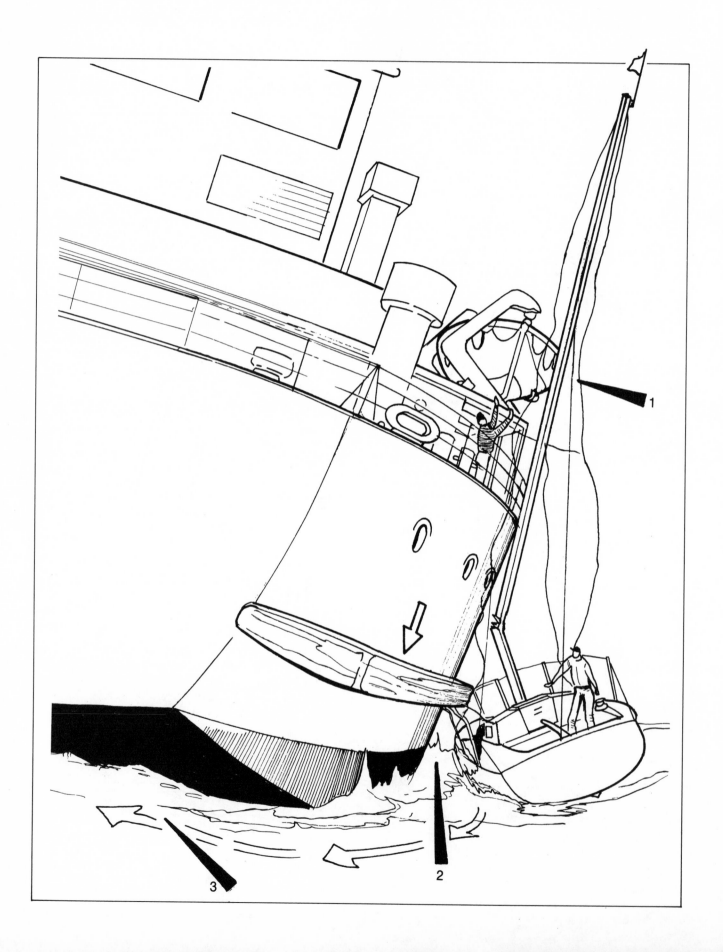

Towing and Rescue by Commercial Vessel

The result of a towing attempt in the North Sea is shown in the drawing. The skipper of a sailboat, disabled by heavy seas with rudder damage, radioed a passing freighter for a tow. The vessel stopped at once and let the damaged boat drift down upon her. The storm blew the boat broadside against the stern of the ship, where a lifeboat, hung outboard, swept the entire rig off the boat at the first contact (1). Then the heavy rubbing strake on the ship's stern punched the stanchions right down through the deck (2). The yacht struck the broad stern several times so hard (3) that it sank in a few minutes. The crew was saved but the boat was lost.

Here is another authenticated rescue attempt, this time on the East Coast of the United States. During a storm, the containership *Paul Getty* attempted to make a lee for the capsized trimaran *Gonzo* and to take her three crew aboard. Since the big ship lay across the wind and sea to windward of the yacht, it started to drift down upon it at a speed of several knots. The shock at the moment of contact was so great that it flung the three sailors into the water, where they were in imminent danger of being washed under the huge ship. By good luck, the skipper, Walter Greene, and his two shipmates were able to drag themselves back aboard the capsized trimaran. Efforts at rescue were terminated and the ship went on its way.

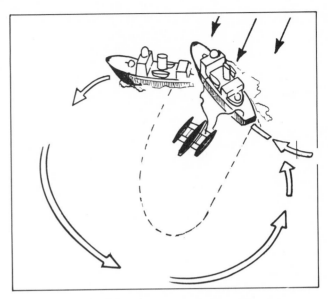

Later a Coast Guard cutter hurried to the scene and completed the rescue. The crew of this vessel first brought the cutter to windward of the casualty so as to estimate the state of wind and sea as well as the drift. Then they made a large circle around the capsized cat, finally taking up a position somewhat to windward to make a lee (dashed line). There they stopped, thus preventing any contact between the two hulls in this first stage of the rescue. They then drifted two light lines down to the cat. The trimaran was then very carefully hauled in with these lines until its crew was able to climb up nets to safety. A smaller cutter was subsequently able to tow the trimaran into harbor almost undamaged.

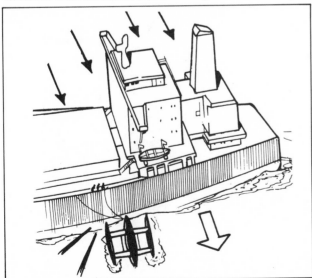

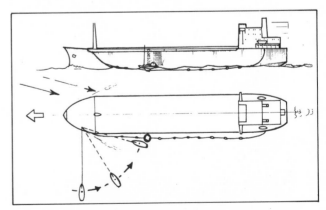

Here is perhaps the best way that a large freighter can rescue the crew of a disabled yacht. The rescuer steams up at an angle some 20 degrees off the wind, to windward of the yacht. She then heaves over a messenger line from her bow. This is then used to haul the towline over.

After passing the towline, the ship maintains just enough headway to ensure maneuverability (1). The yacht swings sideways toward the ship, which has in the meantime run a "boat rope" alongside to protect the boat from damage (2). As soon as enough towing hawser (3) has been paid out to let the yacht reach a

position suitable for the transfer of the crew, the latter places the life raft between the boat and the ship to act as a large fender. This is particularly important in an open sea. The freighter's crew then lowers a climbing net from the deck (4). The yacht crew, now in the life raft, takes a good grip on the net and climbs up. Before starting the climb each crewmember should have an additional safety line well secured.

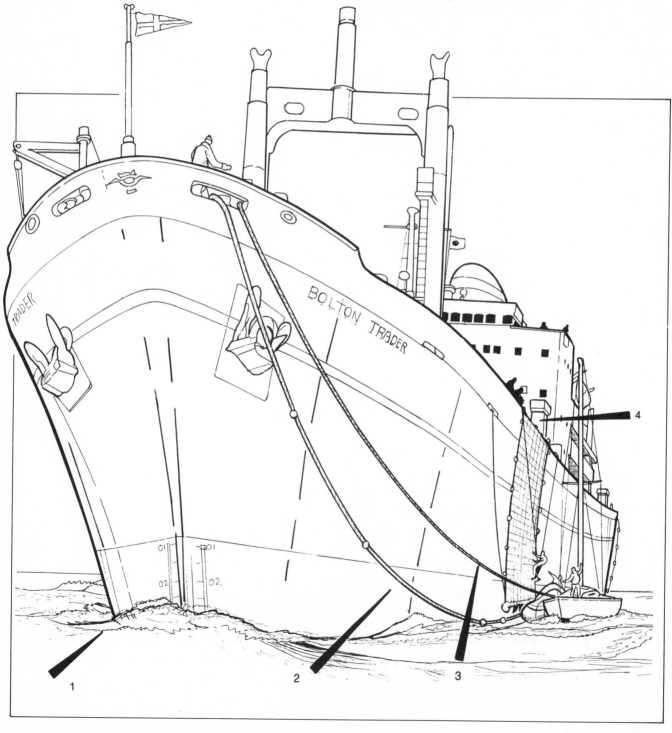

Rescue by Helicopter

The successful rescue of a patient from a yacht by SAR (Search and Rescue) helicopter demands both caution and the proper steps on the part of the rest of the crew. A hovering helicopter develops a downwash —a stream of air of storm strength forced downward by the rotor blades (1). Therefore you must remove all sails, or at least make them solidly fast. The helicopter will first approach to ascertain just what the state of affairs and the position may be and will then turn away before returning for the actual rescue. Don't become panicky when the rescuer appears to fly away at first. Meanwhile, proceed under power directly to windward on a steady course.

Use hand signals to indicate which side is best for the rescue (2). If your rig is still standing, the helicopter will have to take a position to one side. Therefore, remove the topping lift and lash the boom down on the other side (3). Remove the backstay, too. While hovering, the helicopter will be kept exactly in position by its crew in the entry hatch, who will then lower the steel winch cable or a messenger line to the water (4). This grounds out any electrical potential. Otherwise the man on the sailboat might get a shock, although a harmless one.

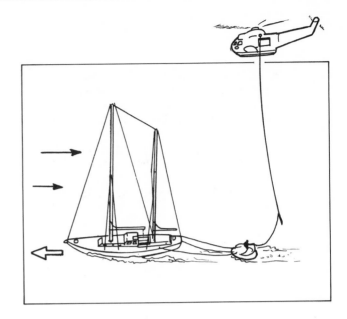

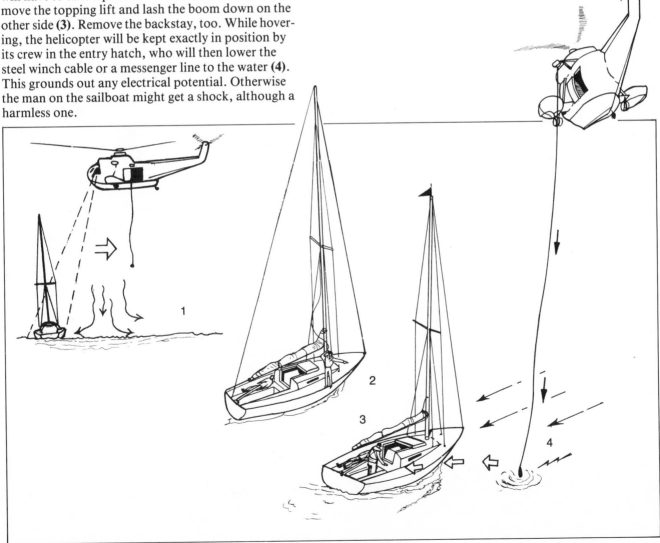

If the yacht has a mizzensail, taking a person directly off the boat is difficult. In this case, it is better to let the patient drift astern in the tender. If you don't have one, use your inflated life raft, towed astern on a line. In either case, the patient must get into the boat or the raft before the helicopter starts to hover over it, for the powerful downwash will at once blow these light craft hither and yon. During this procedure, keep the boat motoring slowly into the wind, to the extent allowed by the tow.

When rescuing a person from the water or a raft, a two-man winching procedure is used. The helicopter crew lowers a man who fastens the rescue sling around the injured person in precisely the right way and sees to it that his or her body remains in the correct attitude. Thus, even a helpless person is hoisted safely into the aircraft.

To take a helpless crewmember off the yacht itself calls for a different technique. A carrying basket or stretcher is used; the patient is placed in it and well strapped down. Of course, the stretcher is merely set down on the deck and never made fast. Generally, the helicopter will lower a man first to give expert supervision.

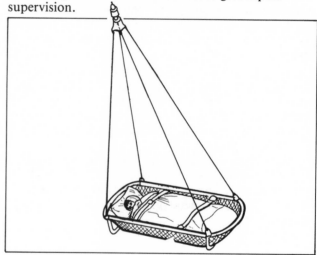

So Don't . . .

. . . ever snap the winch cable to anything on board. A cable made fast could cause serious difficulties for the helicopter, whose winch-protection system would let go. In the final analysis, the helicopter might have to jettison the cable and with it all chance of rescue.

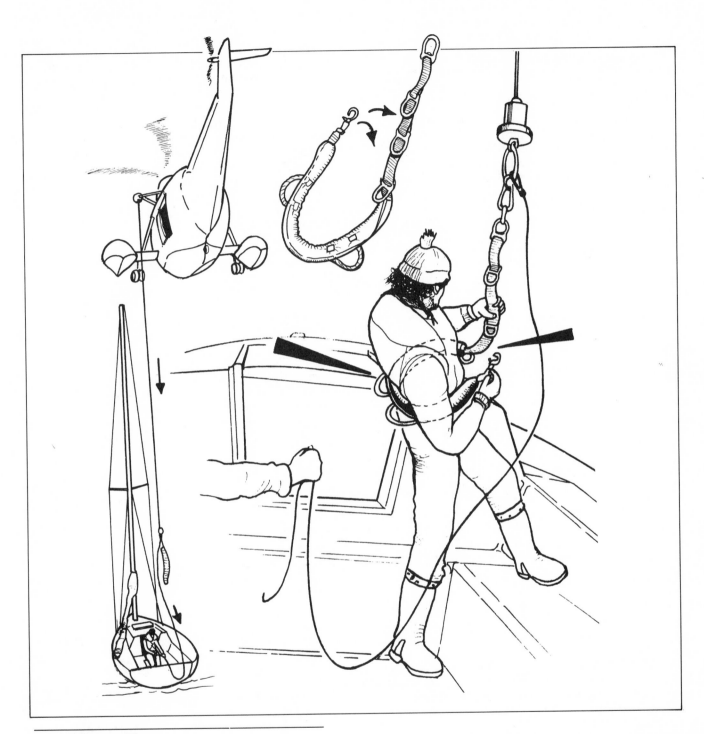

. . . But Do

. . . follow the winching-up procedure correctly on your boat! As soon as you have grasped the messenger line, haul in the winch cable and rescue sling. If possible, have a crewmember hold onto it by hand. *Now pass the sling under the armpits and around the body from back to front, fastening it in front of the*

chest with one of its locking snaps. This is the only way to ensure that you will not slip out of the sling while being winched up. (Note: The sling in use in Britain differs somewhat from the one shown in the illustrations.)

Rescue from the Land

When it appears impossible to get a yacht off a lee shore, its people must be taken off from the land. The crew of the stranded yacht starts by drifting a long light floating line, well buoyed (with fenders, for example) through the breakers to the land (1). This is then used to haul over a stronger hawser and made fast either to the ground itself or a car (2). Near its eye, the yacht's crew has rove it through a block with a becket (3). To the becket a long line has been bent, which is attached to the yacht at its bitter end (3). The method of use is as follows: The messenger line — the one that went ashore first — is used to haul the block to shore, riding on the hawser; the line to the boat is used to pull the block back to the yacht (4). With the help of this system, every member of the boat's crew can be hauled through the surf to safety (5).

This is the only way to overcome the greatly feared undertow of the breakers which has so often sucked out to sea those who attempted to swim ashore through the surf.

Practical Seamanship Illustrated

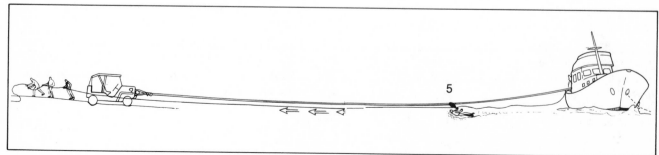

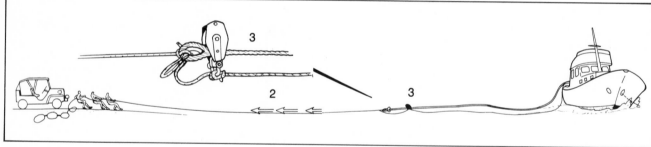

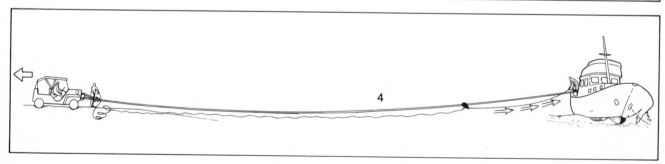

Help — Water in the Boat!

Every responsible skipper fears a leak. This includes entry of water after a collision or a grounding. More often the cause is to be sought in material fatigue, non-watertight thru-hulls, poor hull-to-deck joints or the defective mounting of fittings. Such leaks are not irremediably life threatening to boat or crew, but they can be very irritating because they may be difficult or impossible to locate.

A sailboat traveling at speed can scarcely hope to avoid leaks if it collides with a heavy object. The most common causes of these serious collisions are containers, barrels, baulks of timber from various sources including the decks of freighters, channel buoys and—more often than stated—sleeping whales. Except for the buoys, all this flotsam lies low in the water so that it is hard to make out at twilight, in poor visibility or at night.

A yacht with low-cut sails is in special danger because of restricted vision on the lee side.

The "Blind" Helmsman

This drawing shows the angle of vision of a helmsman on a racing yacht. The genoa, usually cut low, obscures most of his field of view to leeward. The helmsman sees scarcely better to windward, because generally several members of the crew are sitting out on the rail to help balance the boat. The field of view forward is thus reduced to about 10 degrees. This demands that the crew sitting on deck keep a most careful lookout in bad weather and at night. In addition, the watch to leeward should be assigned to one man as a specific duty.

It is even more difficult to keep a good watch on downwind courses. Spinnakers, other light sails and the mainsail combine to obscure the course ahead.

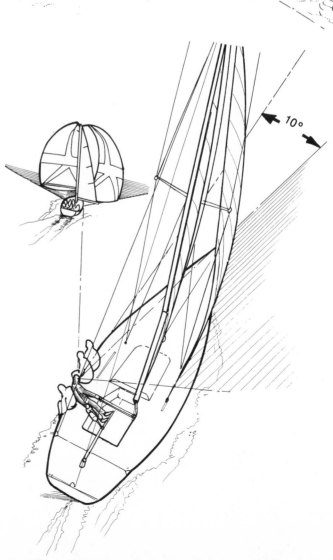

Danger Points on Sailboats

Leaks can be due to the most varied causes. The illustration shows the places where leaks most often occur.

1. In numerous cases the chain plates are poorly anchored to the hull, with the result that the hull-to-deck joint opens up. Although such leaks do not usually admit a great deal of water, on a long passage they can soak everything below.

2. The bow area is at risk from collisions with flotsam.

3. Also in danger through collision with flotsam are both sides of the vessel forward.

4. Tears in the laminate and even complete breaks causing localized leaks have occurred in the area of the mast step. These result, as a rule, from design errors or overloading.

5 and **6.** Equally at risk are the stern tube and the strut fastenings. Vibration of the propeller and/or the shaft (due to imbalance) can lead to cracks in the laminate.

7. Freestanding rudders are in extreme peril from collisions with submerged flotsam or simply from sheer overloading. Cracks or breaks in the hull can result.

8. Grounding is almost always the cause of leaks around a bolted-on keel, mostly in the area near the trailing edge. The problem is rarer when the keel is part of the laminated structure of the hull and the ballast is inside. Still, the danger is just as real if an internally ballasted hull strikes stones or rocky out-

croppings. In this case, the leak at the bottom of the keel allows water to enter into the ballast cavity. It will not enter the boat's interior so long as the ballast has been glassed over.

9. The dangerous areas in a day sailer are the trailing edge of the centerboard trunk and/or the part of the hull abaft the slot.

Danger Points on Motorboats

If a collision occurs in a motorboat, the higher speed nearly always results in total hull failure and correspondingly heavy water intake.

1. The main collision point with flotsam is right at the stem.

2. Still, flotsam can damage a motorboat's skin, usually near the waterline.

3 and **4.** Grounding usually damages the keel shoe, the lower edge of the keel and keel-to-hull joint (if separate pieces as in a wooden boat) all at the same time.

5. The propeller area is very subject to damage from flotsam as is the rudderstock and tube when a free-standing rudder is used.

6. In high-speed planing boats, the V-shaped underbody is at serious risk from floating objects.

7. Bottom leaks in the area of the engine mounts can arise through material fatigue, design errors or overpowering.

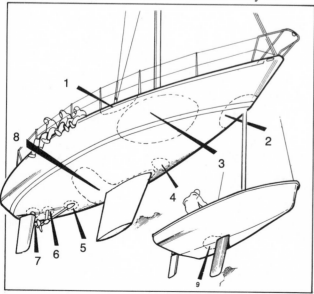

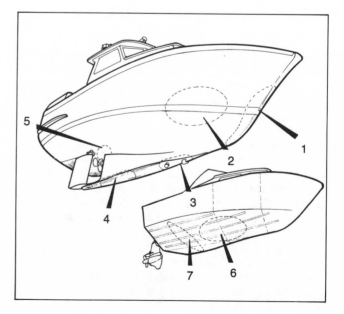

Leaks around Thru-hulls

1. Thru-hulls below the waterline are hard to inspect, but they can potentially develop small leaks. Later, sitting in harbor between weekends, the boat slowly fills.

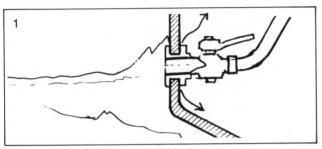

2. Human errors can cause leaks, too, such as by breaking off the knotmeter impeller's thru-hull by a careless step when cleaning the bilge. One must take precautions even when merely removing the impeller, unless there is an automatic shut-off. Before one has laid hands on the cap, a good deal of water can pour in. (At least in this case one knows exactly where the leak is!)

3. Many hand-pump heads are poorly installed so that when the boat is heeled, water overflows the rim of the bowl and gets into the boat. On long cruises this can lead to real complications, especially in foul weather and heavy seas.

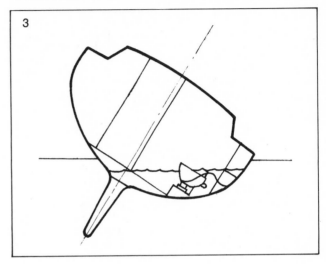

4. Leaks at the head can occur under power as well. If there is a considerable leak at the shaft stuffing box, the inflowing water will sink the boat deeper in the water. Often only a couple of inches are needed to bring the edge of the bowl below the waterline. Therefore: *Always keep the toilet sea cock closed.* This goes for the wash basin, too.

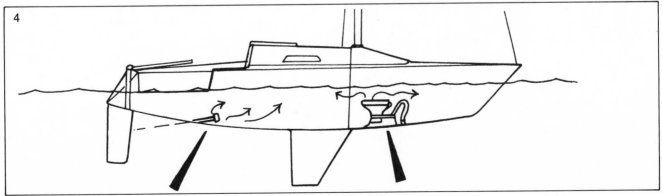

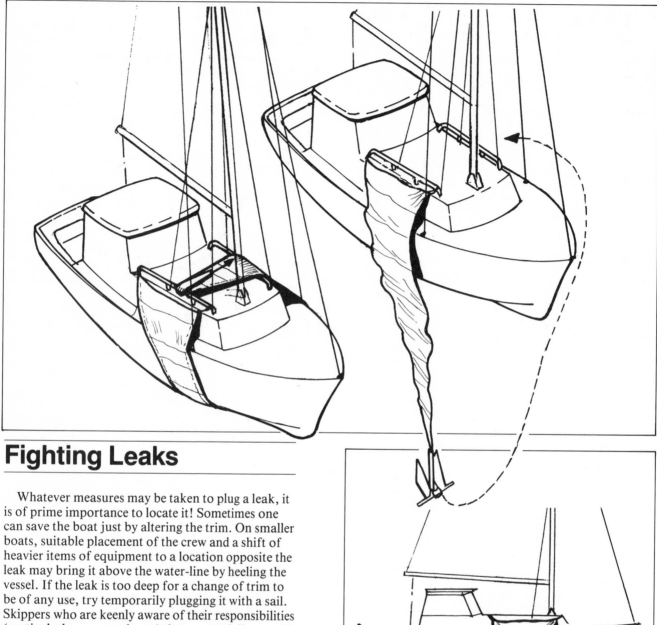

Fighting Leaks

Whatever measures may be taken to plug a leak, it is of prime importance to locate it! Sometimes one can save the boat just by altering the trim. On smaller boats, suitable placement of the crew and a shift of heavier items of equipment to a location opposite the leak may bring it above the water-line by heeling the vessel. If the leak is too deep for a change of trim to be of any use, try temporarily plugging it with a sail. Skippers who are keenly aware of their responsibilities (particularly on motorboats), keep a specially cut sail or piece of fabric on board for this purpose; it is provided with its own lines. This sail is attached at its bottom or foot to the toe rail, grab rail or other convenient spot. At the head of the sail there is a line long enough to circle the hull and a light anchor. The line is taken over the bow or stern down and around to the other side of the boat where it is hauled tight and made fast. Then there is usually enough time to do a more thorough job of plugging the hole from inside the vessel.

A cushion or life jacket will generally serve to stem a leak below the waterline at the bow. This kind of material usually doesn't conform too well to the shape of the bow so it is pressed against the hole in the hull with suitably rigged lines. It is advisable to fasten the pad to the lines beforehand with short strops to keep it from slipping. The lines are fastened to the bow pulpit and the necessary tension developed with a Spanish windlass (see illustration).

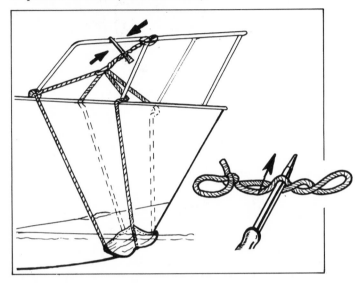

Broken-off sea cocks, transducers and other thru-hull fittings can be made nearly watertight with the handle of a tool such as a screwdriver, for example, wrapped with a rag to make it fit the diameter of the pipe. By screwing it in tightly, against the direction of wrap, you can overcome the water pressure. It's a good idea to carry soft, wooden, tapered plugs just for this purpose.

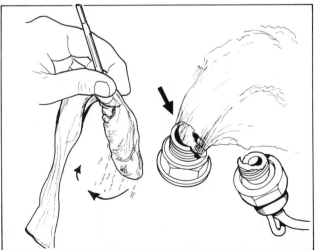

Leaks at the Skeg

The skeg has to be strong enough to resist all the stresses generated by the rudder. On long trips, material fatigue has been known to cause leaks at the lower gudgeon or the shoe. The only way to deal with a leak in this difficult area while under way is by means of a jib or piece of fabric as described earlier. It is much the same with a leak at the lower edge of the keel. One thing is certain: A diver will be needed to guide the sail into position. This task is made easier if one provides, in advance, a line with a series of bights in it along the luff of the sail. These are easily grasped by the diver. Signals to the winch man are best given by means of a small fender on the end of a line. It can be pulled under the surface once for "Haul in," and several times for "Ease off." Before attempting to use the "leak sail," however, it is worthwhile to start with a tube of underwater epoxy, which is available in stores. Many a yacht has been brought safely to harbor after application of such a "bandage."

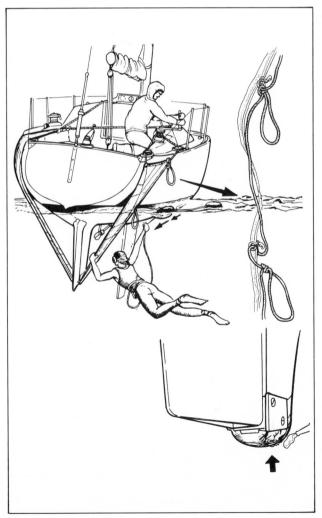

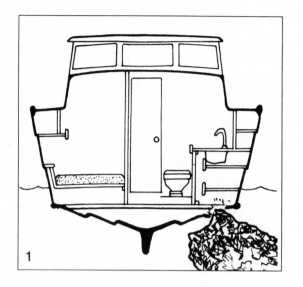

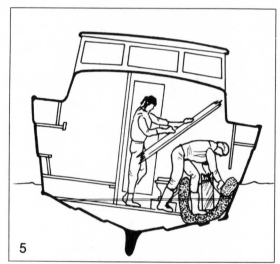

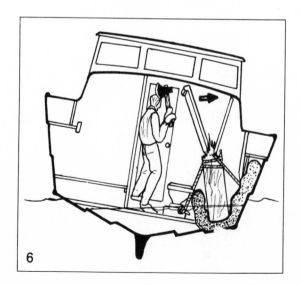

Stopping a Leak

This series of drawings shows how to carry out a successful damage control operation.

1. The hull of a fiberglass motorboat has hit a projecting rock. Water is pouring into the boat through a foot-size leak beneath the lockers in the head compartment.

2. The measures that must be taken at once require that you overcome a natural antipathy toward destruction. But such destruction can decisively affect the result, because if the leak is inaccessible it cannot be repaired and the crew must at once abandon ship.

3. The frayed and splintered edges of the leak are hammered down as flat as possible, to enable the stuffing material to fit well.

4. Now a cushion is stuffed into the hole. Usually the intake of water can be virtually stopped under foot pressure alone.

5 and **6.** Another crewmember now has time to devise a "shore" out of the chopped-away joiner work. This is held in place with lashings.

7. A chunk of wood, thrust between two of the lines, forms a Spanish windlass with which the necessary tension is developed by twisting. Only now does one begin to bail.

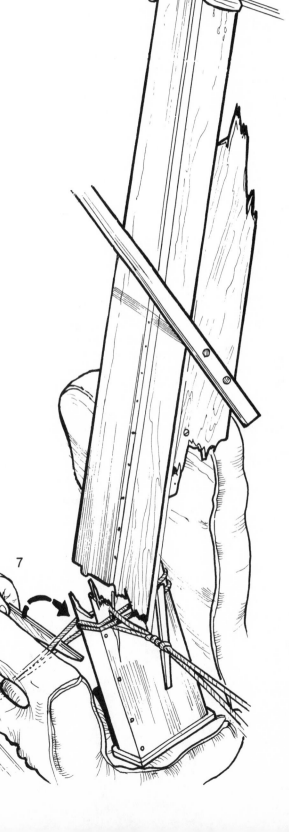

7

The Leak Umbrella

The Leak Umbrella is a commercial device. It comes folded up, to be thrust out through the hole **(1)** then, with a light pull, it opens up like an umbrella **(2)**. Water pressure holds the fabric against the outside of the hull, largely stopping the leak **(3)**. This device has proven effective in actual use. Of course, one must take further steps because a certain amount of water will still get through **(4)**. Also, the leak must be easily accessible from inside the boat and not near the keel or the device will not work.

The Leak Kit

On long-distance cruisers, a leak kit is recommended without reservation; it is used for those first measures that are so critical. It should be kept in a bracket near the companionway or upright in a nearby locker and instantly accessible. It should consist of an ax, leak umbrella and a leak sail with suitable lines. Absolutely essential on board is an ax; it should never be treated as a toy. Its handle must be at least two feet long and it should have a head weighing about six to seven pounds.

Often the first few seconds after a collision determine whether a boat will be saved or lost. During a long search for the right gadget, the boat may take on so much water that the leak can no longer be found.

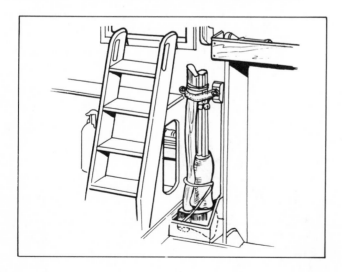

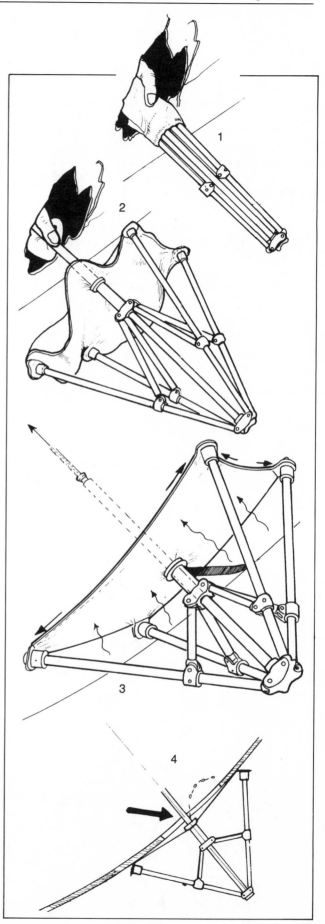

Fire on Board

Fire breaking out on board a yacht need not necessarily lead to its total loss. Preventive fitting out, precautions in dealing with flammable materials and — if a fire should occur — appropriate and decisive firefighting usually avert truly serious damage. The following paragraphs will show you what you can do in case of fire on board.

The Fire-Safe Motorboat

This illustration shows how to make a motorboat fire safe.

1. Large hatches in both the main and the fore cabin allow quick escape.

2. Place your propane gas cylinders in a separate compartment with an overboard drain.

3. For fire safety in the engine room, install a diesel.

4. Isolate the engine room from the rest of the boat with a solid bulkhead.

5 and **6.** Isolate your fuel tanks from the engine room by means of a bulkhead covered with a fire-retardant material.

7. Make sure there is no connection between the boat's main bilge and that of the engine room.

8. If you have a gas-operated refrigerator be sure that it is equipped with a fire protection system so that, if the flame goes out, the gas valve will be automatically closed.

9. Install an easily reached fire extinguisher in the forecabin, too.

10. Use only fire-retardant materials for wall covering and upholstery.

11. Equip your stove with fire protection and an auxiliary main gas cut-off valve.

12. Place a second fire extinguisher in the second most important spot — at the companionway to the galley and forecabin.

13. Locate the battery high in the boat (in case water comes aboard) under the helmsman's seat where it's away from the engine room but easily accessible.

14. Fit the roof of the pilothouse with an escape hatch.

15. Make sure your curtains can be instantly snatched away from the danger zone.

16. Run your main air induction for the engine through the cabin ceiling.

17. Install a fire extinguisher at the outside steering station so that you can fight a belowdeck fire from the outside.

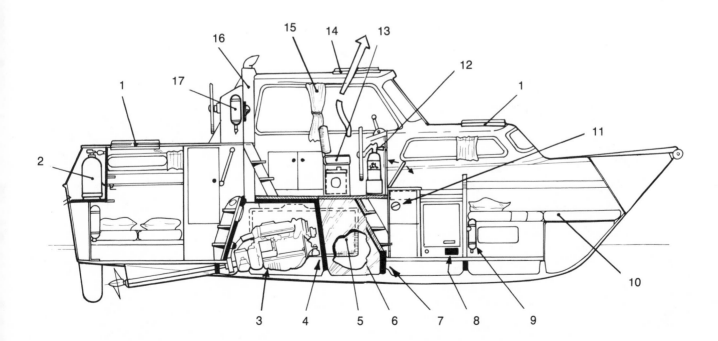

Propane on Board

This is how a propane gas cylinder compartment should be made: The storage space must have no openings that will allow gas to get to the rest of the boat. Use rubber ferrules where the line from the gas cylinder to the stove passes through the wall of the compartment to make it vapor proof (1). Use copper tubing where the lines pass through bulkheads; this prevents chafe (2). Further safety assurance is provided by the use of a pressure-regulating valve at the cylinder (3) and by strapping the cylinder firmly to standoffs or retaining brackets. This prevents it from slamming back and forth (4). It is helpful to stand the cylinder on blocks so that any water condensing due to the cooling effect of gas expansion cannot cause rusting on the bottom of the cylinder (5).

Since the gas is heavier than air, it sinks to the bottom of the compartment. The gas outlet must be right at the bottom, leading overboard in such a way that no water can remain standing in bends or sags in tubing (6). On older boats, one constantly finds gas installations with connections between copper tubing and flexible hose using only hose clamps. These are dangerous in the highest degree and unreliable in that the copper tubing can easily slip out. The illustration shows commercially available flare-type connectors that are easy to install.

If you detect an odor of gas, immediately test all lines and connections. Dab the hose and connections with a soapy solution. If you see bubbles you have a gas leak. *Never use a flame or a burning match to test for gas!*

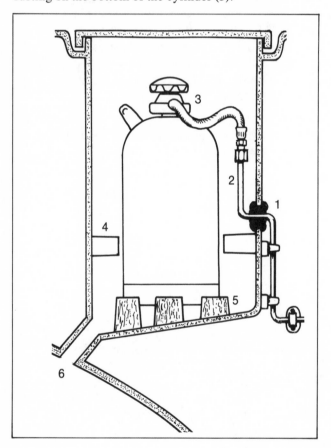

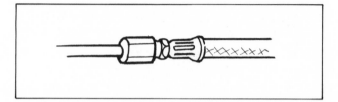

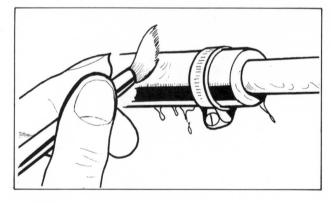

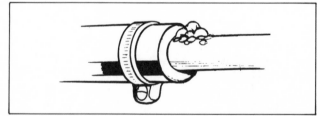

Tank Vents

Gasoline vapors can settle below into the bilge because of defective installation of a tank vent. Vapors absolutely must be led outside the hull, the usual thru-hull location being in the transom or topsides aft. The vent must be located and configured so that it will not take in water, and the vent thru-hull must be fitted with a flame arrestor (not shown in the drawings below).

You can also vent the tank with a gooseneck at the deck. The gooseneck must be placed well above the level of the fill plate so that, should the tank be overfilled, gasoline cannot overflow onto the deck.

All fuel lines and fuel-consuming devices must be examined for leaks, just like the tanks themselves. In addition, the seam welds of metal tanks should be examined from time to time.

Risks When Filling Up

Most fires in motorboats with gasoline engines are caused by improper practices when fueling. The greatest care is needed with gasoline engines because an explosive gasoline vapor-air mixture can be formed inside the boat; spilled gasoline vaporizes belowdeck.

If possible, tie up bow to the wind. While fueling, close all hatches and windows.

Engine off, no smoking, operate no electrical switches.

No boarding and leaving the boat.

Make sure there is metal-to-metal contact between the nozzle and the fill plate.

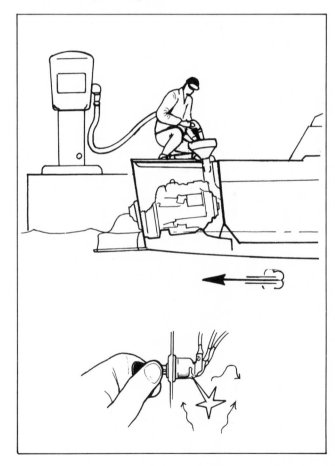

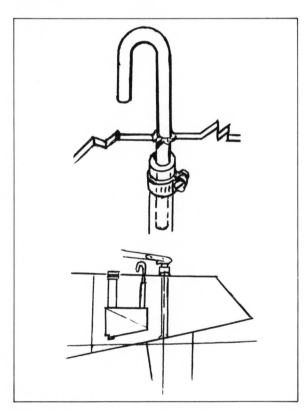

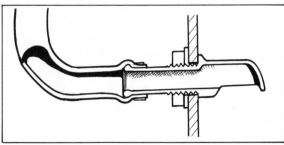

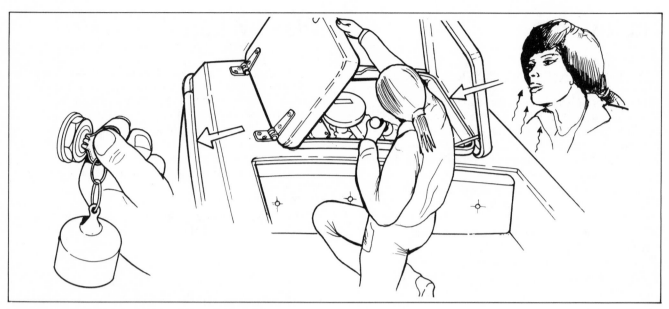

Merely turning the ignition key can cause an explosion. Therefore, plan for enough time, after filling up, to ventilate the boat thoroughly by opening hatches and operating the engine room or bilge blower until there is no odor of gasoline. The most effective and the simplest test before starting a gasoline engine is the sniff test. Even before the blower is turned on, stick your nose into the engine compartment and sniff for any noticeable odor of gasoline. If you do smell it, find the cause at once. And don't turn on any electrical device.

Tiny leaks sometimes develop in metal tanks through electrolysis or defective seam welds. These leaks are noticed only when a tank is filled to overflowing (1), so that a column of liquid (2) is formed in the fill pipe. This causes extra pressure in the fuel tank. If you have an overfill, check below for gasoline odor and/or leakage at hose clamps and seams (3).

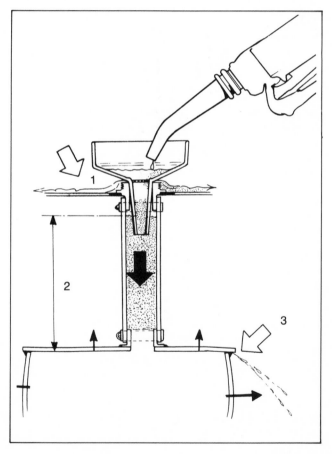

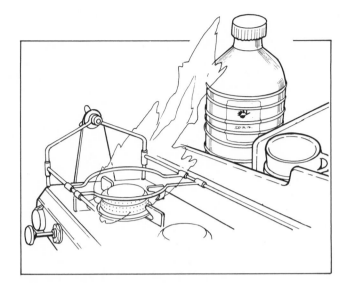

Dangers at the Stove

Using the stove has often caused fires on board. Some people believe that gas stoves are very dangerous, while kerosene and alcohol stoves are safe. Insurance statistics indicate that this is not so. Far more fires result from badly handled alcohol and kerosene stoves which, due to inadequate priming, can develop a serious flare-up that ignites curtains and countertops. Regardless of the stove and fuel system, overheated fat ignited by the surrounding cooking flame can flare up. Even pressurized alcohol stoves can suddenly do it. As alcohol is very easily ignited, the alcohol supply tank should not be kept near the stove. In some countries, alcohol is often sold in thin-walled plastic containers. Even a small flare-up can set the container and contents afire. Any significant quantity of burning alcohol is hard to extinguish and develops such a high temperature that it can ignite the joiner work in a very short time.

To use a charcoal grill in the cockpit of a yacht is foolish. Aside from the fact that smoke and odors can annoy the neighbors, there is the danger that plastic or wooden gratings may catch fire. This can easily happen if the barbecue is knocked over through carelessness. One cannot remove the glowing coals from the cockpit sole quickly enough. And, if a bottle of lighter fluid — the starting aid — is nearby, an almost uncontrollable fire may result.

Care with Solvents

Many a sailor has thoughtlessly set his boat afire. Very flammable vapors are formed when one uses a solvent such as acetone for cleaning. Belowdeck, a glowing cigarette then suffices to cause a flash of flame which can start a fire. No smoking and no open flames when working with solvents!

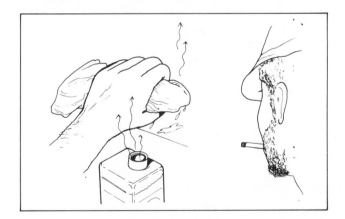

The Fate of the *Elia*

The *Elia* was on a trip from England to southern Norway. The crew was able to lay the intended harbor on one long port tack and, since the weather was worsening, they stayed on deck during the approach. Consequently, no one noticed the odor of gasoline that was increasing as a result of leakage through a loose connection in the fuel line. In this case, a solid tubing outlet without a shutoff was secured to the rest of the fuel line with just a hose clamp. The leaked gasoline was distributed over the insides of the vessel by the sloshing of the bilge water and there it remained, presenting a large surface when the yacht came upright in the calm waters of the harbor.

Since the crew was waiting for customs, they did not go below after tying up. Meanwhile, the explosive gasoline vapor continued to build. When an attempt was made to start the engine a short time later an explosion occurred, killing one man and badly injuring the other. The fire that ensued destroyed the boat completely.

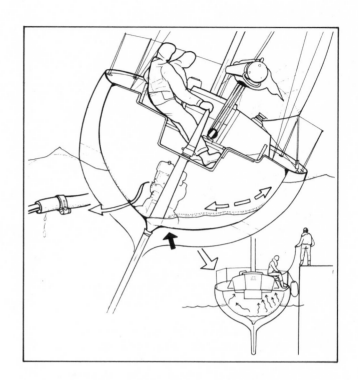

Damage Control

A small powerboat was filling up at a marina near Cannes when it caught fire; apparently the ignition had not been shut off. The owner wanted to attack the fire at once with a nearby fire extinguisher, but the attendant yanked him back and forced him out of the danger zone, which cost valuable time (1). However, it was possible to cut the stern line, whereupon the boat drifted stern first away from the gasoline pump (2). As a result, the fire at the stern could not spread and was extinguished (3).

The effects of a shipboard fire depend on its type and size. The boat need not necessarily be abandoned instantly because of a fire below. If the fire is still under some degree of control, get all sail off immediately and, if the water depth allows, anchor. This will keep the bow to the wind and the crew will have a smoke-free place where they can hold out until a rescuer comes along. If possible, haul the mainsail and the boom out of the danger zone and close all hatches. If a yacht catches fire in harbor take the following steps: First, use your fire extinguisher (1). Have a second person bring up the extinguisher from the pier (2). Fight the fire from the pier (3). If the fire extinguisher is no longer effective, you have to protect the neighboring boat (4). Cut your lines (5) and let her drift (6). If nearby boats are not in danger, use the mobile fire equipment (7) from the pier (8). If nothing helps, tow the burning boat away (9).

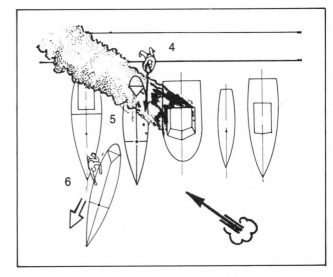

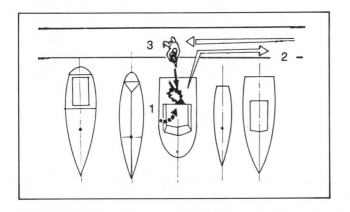

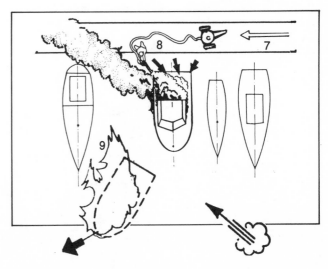

If the fire is the result of an explosion, or if it has spread so quickly belowdeck that it seems useless to fight it, the crew must at once put on their life jackets and jump overboard or get into the tender or life raft. To make this possible, it is essential that the life jackets not be stowed below but in a cockpit locker.

Fire Aboard a Big Boat

When a fire breaks out on a large yacht with several cabins, it may be extremely difficult to orient yourself because of heavy smoke. Lives may be saved if, before a long voyage, the skipper gives the crew exact instructions including the locations of fire extinguishers. Everyone on board should know how many doors there are between his cabin and the companionway. Thus you can feel your way to the exit even when there is no more visibility. Under these conditions, it is best to tie a wet cloth around your mouth and nose and crawl out.

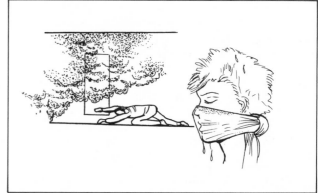

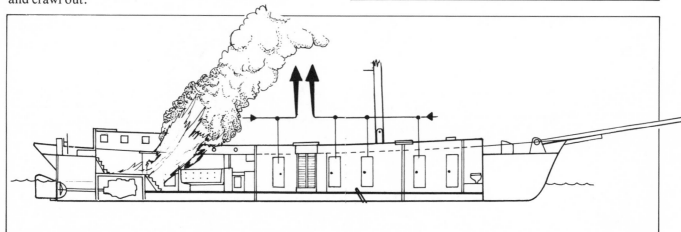

Flooding Through Melted Hose

Frequently a boat will sink shortly after a fire in the engine room. Nearly always the cause is the melting of plastic hose connections between the cockpit drains and the sea cocks. It is well worthwhile to extend the metal piping from the sea cock above the waterline.

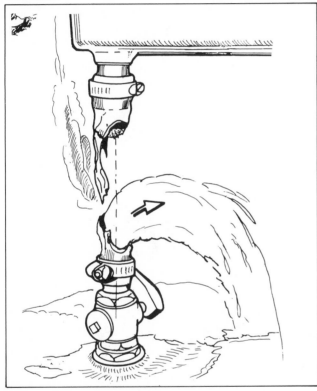

Fire Extinguishers

Hand fire extinguishers are the simplest fire-fighting equipment on board a boat. They can be placed anywhere, each being a self-contained unit. The United States Coast Guard requires fire extinguishers on every boat with an engine and enclosed spaces such as cabins or cuddies.

Types of Fires and Extinguishers

Fires are classified by the type of material being burned. Each is given a letter designation; the same letter is used to specify fire extinguishers appropriate for that type of fire. The size of the extinguisher is denoted by a Roman numeral (I, II, etc.) based on the weight of extinguishing agent contained.

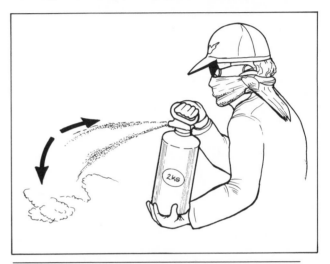

Types of Fires

A — Ordinary combustible materials such as wood, natural fibers, plastics

B — Fuels and other flammable liquids, oils, greases.

C — Electrical

Type B extinguishers are designed to combat Type B fires, but many are more broadly suitable and may be used on Type A or Type C fires. Carbon dioxide (CO_2) or "dry chemical" is effective against electrical fires because it is non-conductive. Foam is suitable for Type A. (But remember that plain water is even more appropriate on burning paper, wood and the like). The Coast Guard makes a further breakdown by weight required for a given size of boat.

Class	Foam gal.	CO$_2$ lb.	Dry lb.	Halon lb.
B-I	1.25	4	2	2.5
B-II	2.5	15	10	10

1. Boats less than 26 feet in length but possessing an engine and enclosed spaces such as a cabin or cuddy must carry at least one B-I extinguisher (if they have no built-in system). If you have provided a built-in system in your engine room, you need not carry a portable extinguisher, too.

2. Boats 26 to less than 40 feet in length must carry at least two B-I units or one B-II: If there is a built-in system, only one B-I is required.

3. Boats 40 feet to no more than 65 feet long must carry at least three B-Is or one Type B-I and one Type B-II. Again, the presence of a fixed installation reduces the number of B-Is by one unit.

Fire extinguishers have to be inspected periodically; just how the inspection is done depends on the kind of unit. Carbon dioxide extinguishers are weighed every six months. Dry chemical types have their gauges examined.

These inspections should be carried out by a professional and each unit tagged with his name and date. It's good practice to enter these in the log as well, both as a reminder and as a legal safeguard in case of insurance problems later on. Another good practice with dry-chemical types is to take them out of their brackets every few weeks and give them a good shake to make sure that the effective material is not all caked in the bottom.

Foam units are rarely used in boats — they are heavy and very messy. Carbon dioxide and Halon types are very effective and leave no residue, but one must be aware that even in some seven to 10 percent concentration, they cause breathing troubles that could be serious. Dry-type extinguishers turn out to be the most popular in actual practice.

Just about all fire extinguishers must be used from a distance of only three feet or so, the stream being directed at the base of the flames in Class A fires and sprayed from above on Class B.

Firefighting

Tips on firefighting:
- Use your extinguisher with the wind.
- Hold the extinguisher upright and shoot short bursts on various parts of the fire.
- The effective duration of the extinguisher is no more than about 10 seconds.
- Work on the fire from bottom to top and from outside in.
- Don't use up all the extinguishant at once — flames may flicker up again.
- Get as close as you can to the burning material, so as to give the extinguishant the best possible chance.
- First priority goes to saving people and putting out flames on their clothing. A damp cloth around mouth and nose, as well as goggles, will give you short-term protection against smoke and heat.

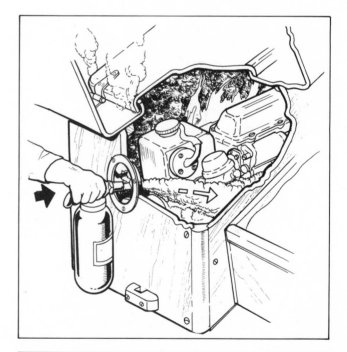

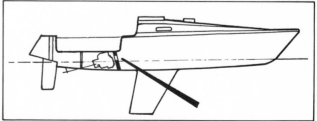

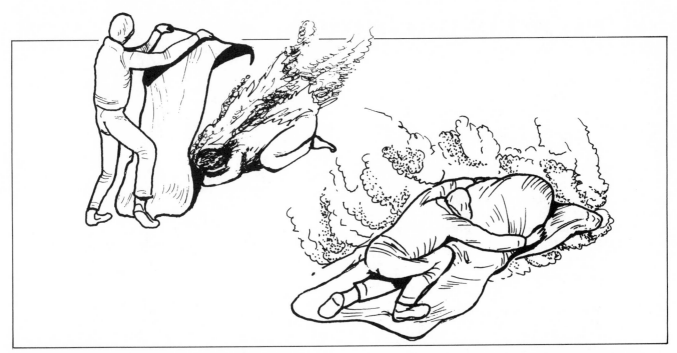

Attention: If plastics such as the hull structure are on fire and producing heavy smoke, keep out of the cabin! Extremely poisonous fumes are formed when these materials burn; they can render you unconscious in a few seconds. If wooden parts are on fire, such as gratings or parts of the cabin accommodation, you can put the fire out with water or sand quite satisfactorily. Burning plastics are another matter. On these you must use foam, dry powder or Halon. And use Type B extinguishers on fuel fires.

Oxygen from the air must be kept away from a fire in the engine compartment. Don't open the hatch! It's a very good idea to install an automatic Halon extinguisher inside, which will be activated if a preset temperature is reached in the engine room.

Another good installation is a fireproof breakable port sealing off the engine compartment from the rest of the boat. A combination of this device with a Halon extinguishing system (opposite top) would enable you to fight the fire without ingress of oxygen while permitting the extinguishant to reach the heart of the fire. The lower drawing shows a suggested installation; the upper one a concept of how it's used.

Do not use a fire extinguisher on a person whose clothes are on fire. If the boat is in harbor, have him jump overboard at once. But if there are burns, symptoms of smoke inhalation poisoning, or unconsciousness, lay the victim down and smother the flames with a woolen blanket. Work downward from windward of the person or from the head downward so that the fire cannot spread to the eyes. It is most important to keep oxygen away for at least 60 seconds. Thus you must press the blanket close around the person and to the floor. You can free the head after this length of time.

On no account use a plastic blanket or awning; these materials are flammable and endanger the rest of the crew by rapidly intensifying the fire, thus virtually welding burning fragments to the skin.

Stove fires, too, are most conveniently and quickly extinguished with a blanket or better yet with an asbestos mat. Hold the blanket at the lower edge of the stove and throw it over the whole burning area from bottom to top. The blanketing method is particularly good on early fires that have not yet developed a very high temperature, for even a short burst of dry chemical extinguishant makes a big mess in the boat. Keep an asbestos fire-fighting mat handy in the galley of your boat.

After a Dismasting

Dismasting is still the commonest cause of distress
among sailboats, despite the use of modern materials.
The most usual victims are racing boats because, in
order to save weight and permit better trim, designers
use the lightest and most flexible extrusions possible.
Besides, during a race, these boats are sailed to the
limits of the rig's load-bearing capacity. Near the
coast, a dismasting does not always present an over-
whelming danger to boat and crew, but in the open
sea far from any harbor, it's quite another matter.

Modern aluminum masts are enormously strong
and when they do break it is very often because of
some defect in the rigging.

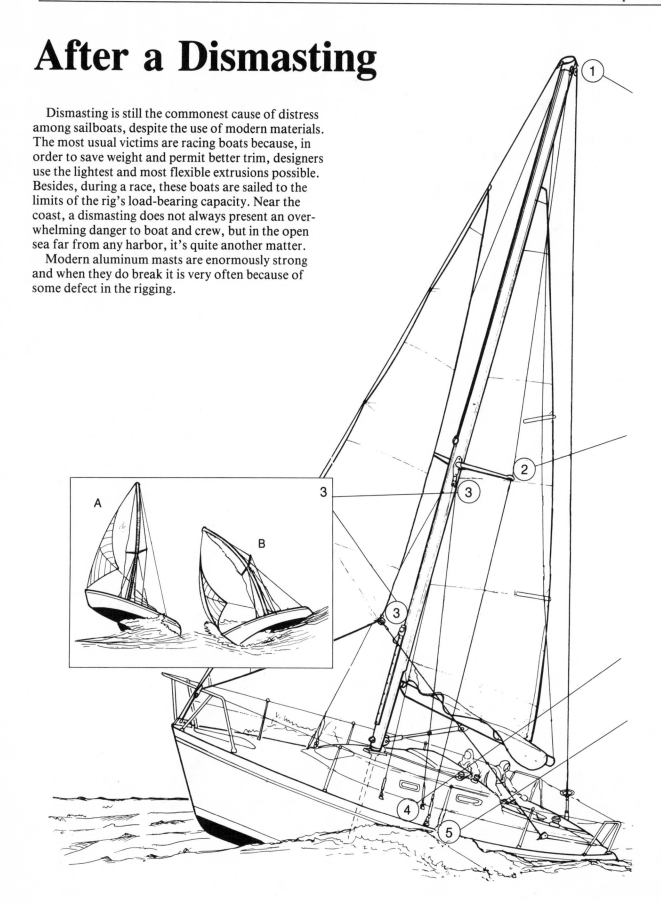

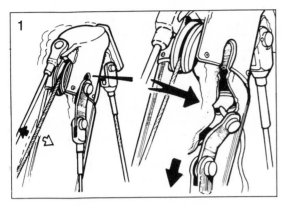

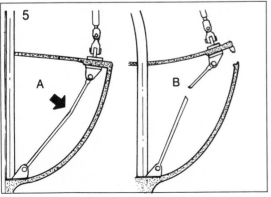

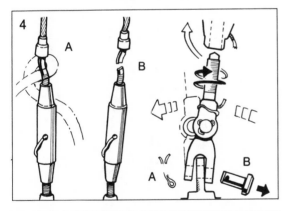

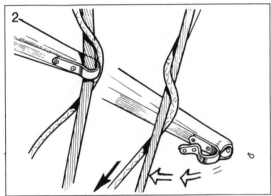

1. If the shrouds and stays are too loose, the masthead can whip about. The extrusion becomes brittle so that the upper shroud tangs break out. Inspect your masthead fittings every winter during layup.

2. The spreaders are another weak point. Inspect wooden spreaders every year for any sign of rot. Another cause of mast failure is a halyard fouled around the end of the spreader. Hauling tight on the halyard can tear the shroud out of the spreader's end fitting.

3. The lower shrouds are left too slack. When beating under heavily reefed main and genoa, the mast bows aft in the middle; this is furthered by a slack backstay which allows the masthead to bend forward (**A**). Then, when the bow slams into a trough, the impact overloads the system. The spreaders bow forward and break (**B**).

4. Damaged turnbuckles can cause a mast to break. A bend in a turnbuckle spells danger. It may lose up to 40 percent of its strength (**A** and **B**). In time, a leeward shroud whipping about can break the cotter pins or rings (**A**). A clevis pin could then fall out (**B**). Or a turnbuckle could unscrew itself unnoticed. If your masthead fittings are not pop riveted but bolted on, use only self-locking nuts with plastic inserts.

5. In modern racing boats, the chain plates are connected to the hull with tie rods, which a heavy object flung about can easily deform (**A**). This can lead to a break later on, as a consequence of which the hull-to-deck joint is opened up (**B**).

Cracking Due to the Spinnaker Pole

Another cause of dismastings in racing boats with keel-stepped masts is the constant thrust of the spinnaker pole **(A)**, which causes severe bending stress on the mast where it comes through the deck. This ultimately leads to a crack in the extrusion **(B)**. Many masts were lost in the 1978 Whitbread Round-The-World Race because the spinnakers were flown most of the time.

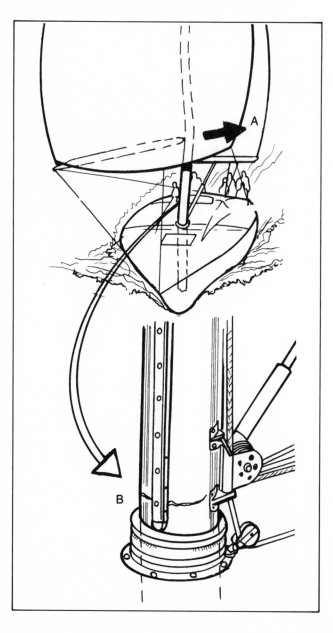

How the *Incredible* Lost Her Mast

These three sketches show how the *Incredible* lost her mast in the 1978 Trans-Pac race. She was running under storm spinnaker in a Force 8 (34 to 40 knots) wind **(A)**. In these conditions the spinnaker pole had to be carried fairly high up the mast **(B)**. The main was trimmed flat **(C)** by hauling down hard on the vang, which reduced the boom end's clearance above the water **(D)**. This sail arrangement **(2)** caused a

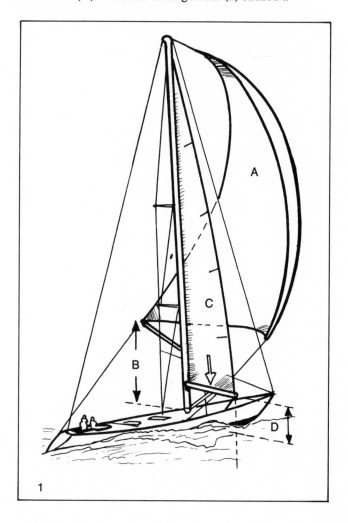

1

heavy compressive stress in the mast extrusion **(G)**, while the tension of the backstay **(F)** compensated for the forward pull of the spinnaker and main **(E)**. As the *Incredible* was forced down into the trough by a particularly high following sea, this is what happened: The end of the boom went underwater to leeward **(3)**,

suddenly increasing the pressure at the foot of the mast while the preventer held the boom in place. The boat's way was abruptly braked. Under the increased pressure of the spinnaker pole, the lower part of the mast went out of column **(H)**. In this situation, the pull of the spinnaker was greatly increased **(I)**, which in turn led to more thrust **(G)**. The extrusion could no longer sustain the load and snapped. The ultimate cause? The crew had too much sail up as well as a dangerous trim.

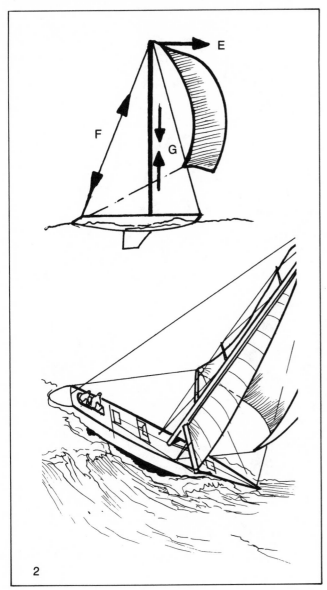

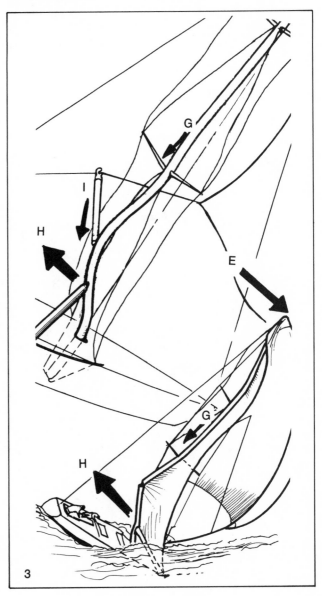

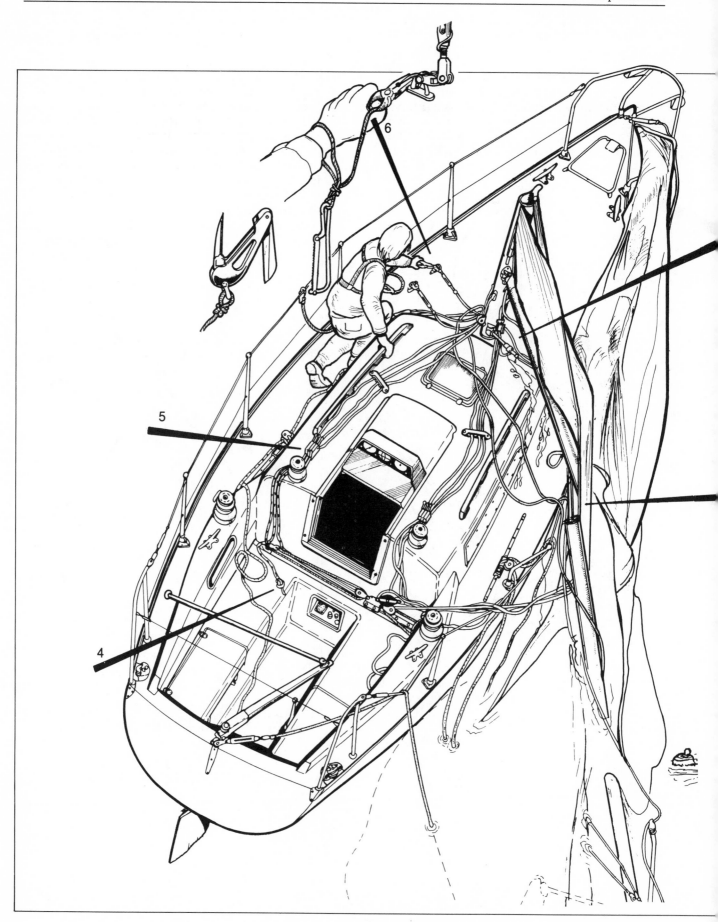

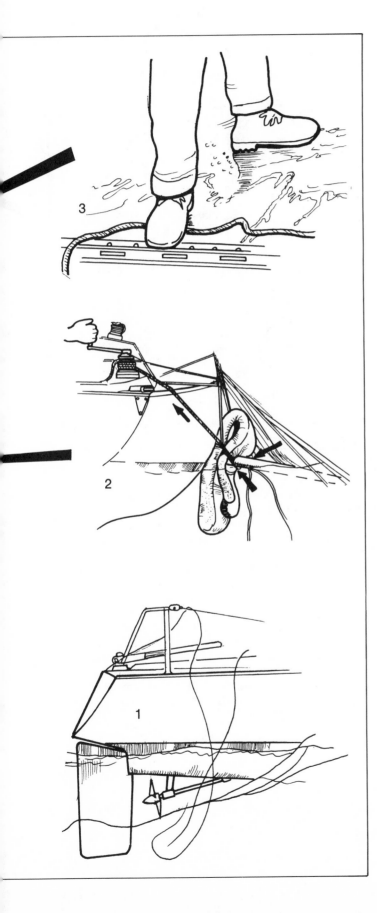

The real danger for the boat begins after the mast has been broken and is overboard. In a seaway, the consequences are often more serious than the loss of the mast itself and demand quick but careful response on the part of the crew.

To salvage the mast or not? In this situation every skipper is confronted with the same question. He must figure out what the results will be, taking into account the weather and the sea conditions. He must also figure out how long it will take to make the next harbor under power. Many a dismasting has had fatal results because the crew were unable to free the boat from the damaged rigging. This can be done only when such an accident has been foreseen and the necessary tools and equipment are on board and ready to hand.

You have to decide whether it is absolutely vital to fire a red flare, the internationally recognized distress signal. Very often the boat can be made seaworthy again so that it can proceed under power if the parts of the broken mast can be removed with the vessel's own resources. Fire the flare only if stranding is imminent, the boat is taking on water, a man is overboard or someone has been badly hurt.

1. Most important: Don't start the engine! You have to reckon that loose gear and halyards can become fouled in the propeller.

2. The greatest danger to the boat is that a piece of the mast or the boom may soon hole it under the action of the seas. Winch the parts of the mast that have gone overboard as tight as you can with the halyards or other lines, taking out any slack that would allow the wreckage to pound the boat. Jam bunk cushions between the wreckage and the hull.

3. Move about on deck only with great care! You could slip and fall by stepping on a loose rope. And if there is fluid from a hydraulic boom vang on deck it could be as slippery as an eel. Therefore, the second safety rule: Safety harnesses on the whole crew and use them.

4. Free all halyards, vangs and downhauls starting at the cockpit.

5. Open and free all sheet and halyard stoppers.

6. Before starting to free the wreckage, secure all tools with safety lanyards.

Work Lights

A source of light is often necessary after dark. A headlamp is best. A watertight flashlight can be inserted under your hood or hat and secured in place with adhesive tape by a shipmate (1). Various headlamps are available commercially. They are worn on the head and come complete with adjustable beam, battery box and elastic headband (2).

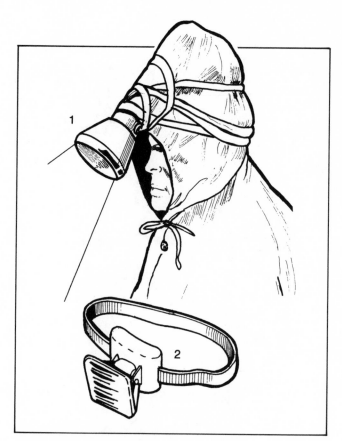

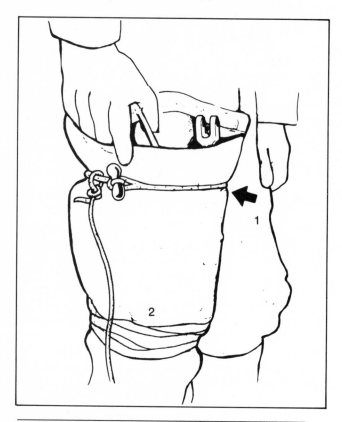

What to Do with Retrieved Fittings

Knee pockets on foul weather pants are a good place to put such parts. To prevent their falling out again, take a turn around the flap with a shock cord (1). Reinforce the bottom of the pocket with several turns of adhesive tape around the trouser leg (2).

Tools

The general anxiety and excitement following a dismasting make the preparation and placement of tools pretty difficult. Good seamanship demands that a dismasting kit be prepared in advance. It should contain: Two metal-cutting saws with spare blades, wire cutters, slip-joint pliers, rigger's knife, hammer and screwdriver, each equipped with a lanyard.

After a dismasting, a bolt cutter will surely be the most important tool. It will cut shrouds, stays and even turnbuckles up to nearly 3/8-inch diameter. Choose the right size for your own rig. There are even hydraulic cutters for rod rigging. These cutters are not cheap but must be on board nevertheless. The list of cutters is rounded out with a hacksaw, which can be used one-handed. It is essential for cutting pieces of a broken mast.

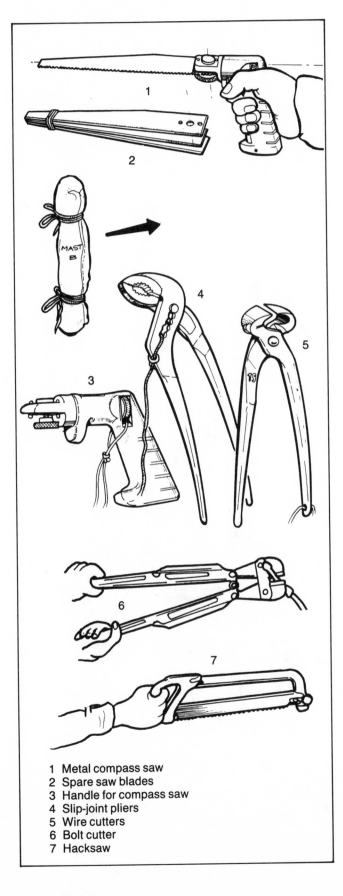

1 Metal compass saw
2 Spare saw blades
3 Handle for compass saw
4 Slip-joint pliers
5 Wire cutters
6 Bolt cutter
7 Hacksaw

Saving the Mast

1. Remove tape from turnbuckles.

2. Cut away cotter pins and/or rings.

3. Remove clevis pins.

4. Remove jammed clevis pins with a hammer or the emergency hatchet. A hatchet is important because it will cut broken pieces of aluminum masts, cable and halyards all at the same time. If heavy spars are full of water, their increased weight will make salvage much more difficult. Such a spar can be hauled up only step by step; each time the strop from the winch is eased by the movement of the hull in the seaway, the mast is hauled in a few more inches and snubbed until the next opportunity.

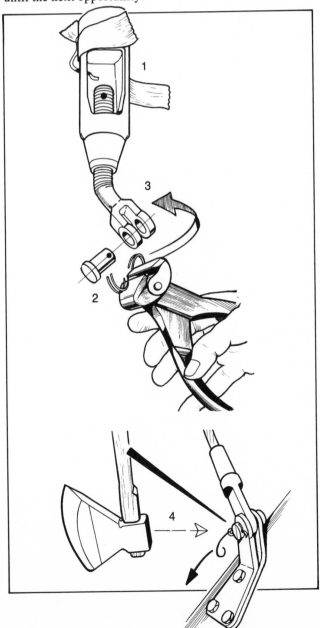

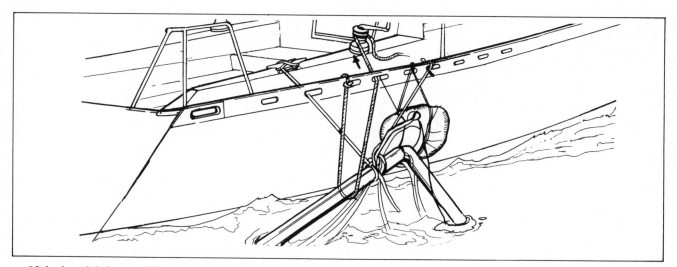

If the break is located farther up the mast and seas are high, it is best to cut loose all stays, shrouds and halyards, letting them go overboard. But if weather conditions allow, and the boat is far from the next harbor, one should save the stump and the halyards along with it. Secure it first and then after most of the rig has gone overboard, seize it to the toe rail (1) at such a height that you can carefully cut away the upper broken part of the mast. An auxiliary line led to the nearest winch and hauled tight will improve the security of the operation (2). Get the sail off the mast to the extent possible (3 and 4). Saw around the mast with care so as not to cut internal halyards—you will need them for the jury rig (5).

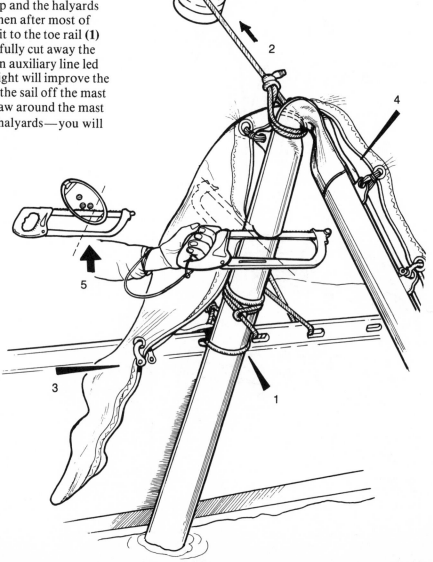

If the mast stump is very heavy, you will have to rig a tackle to get it up on deck. Mount the tackle on a stanchion base. Remove the other nearby stanchions. Make fast a line at the toe rail, bring it around the mast and heave it aboard.

You can set up an effective jury rig with the boom and spinnaker pole, which is your only choice when the entire mast has gone over the side and cannot be retrieved.

The boom is lashed at or near the step and held in place using the gooseneck fittings. The spinnaker pole can now be rigged to the mast stump to extend it. A turn is taken around the boom and through the spinnaker pole end fitting and the running end of the line rove through the bail or block of the boom's downhaul. This line serves to control the spinnaker pole (1). For the upper guide, a round turn is taken through the boom's end fitting and around the spinnaker pole. If the main outhaul leads through the boom it can be used as this line. Again, the running end is led to the deck. This permits control of the round turn after the spinnaker pole has been hoisted (2).

The "main shrouds" are fashioned from the flexible wire halyards. They are attached to the chain plates using wire rope clamps (3), which should be plentiful in the dismasting kit. To be able to hoist sail, one must remember to reeve a halyard through a block at the end of spinnaker pole (4).

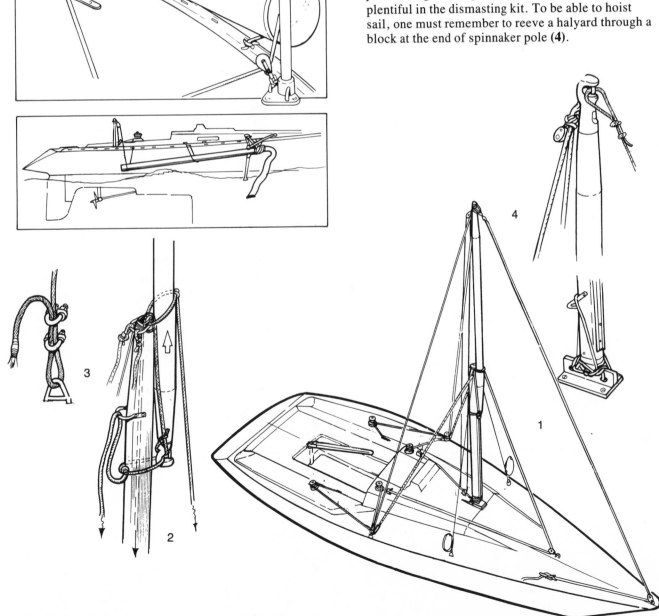

Dealing with Seasickness

Beginners and experienced seamen may suffer alike from seasickness; it depends on conditions and individual susceptibility. Many persons who claim they are never seasick learn the truth under extreme and unfamiliar conditions at sea. These conditions and the particular vessel on which one happens to be, can have a decisive influence on the onset of seasickness. Consequently it is important to know the factors that must be considered in taking steps to prevent it.

1. Seasickness is most quickly brought on while working inside the ship, especially by bending forward, head down as, for example, in an uncomfortable stowage space.

2. Rapid turning of the head speeds up the onset of the malady, as does the absence of a horizon; this could occur when a part of the sail hangs down in front of one after reefing **(3)**.

4. The absence of optical references exacerbates the disturbance of the body's balance center initially brought on by movement. Optical observation is lacking belowdeck and when you add to this the effect of cooking odors and the sight of the swinging stove, the steadfastness of the cook becomes questionable.

5. Movement is greatest in the bow and stern areas **(6)**. This is why the off watch gets sick more quickly in the forward cabin than amidships.

7. If, in addition, a crewmember has been drinking alcohol, smoking, is overtired or chilled, or if there is a musty odor in the cabin, the result is virtually preprogrammed.

8. A greatly feared troublemaker is the odor of diesel fuel often found sloshing back and forth in the bilge.

9. Fin keel sailboats have a short, sharp motion when running fast in a seaway. This can affect the body's balance centers, too.

10. Even a hardened old salt can get sick while repairing an engine at sea.

11. In heavy seas, freestanding rudders may turn the boat quickly, and this in turn leads to the kind of sharp motion mentioned above.

There are recognizable symptoms of seasickness in a crewmember. He becomes unusually quiet, loses interest and ceases to participate. In this state, both his ability to react and his coordination are reduced; he should not be allowed out of the cockpit to reef or change sails.

The victim of seasickness is pretty much indifferent to everything. Even mistakes in navigation arise from early seasickness; navigation should be the task of seasoned sailors only. Anyone in this stage of the malady needs help; he loses control over his movements and his willpower gradually disappears. It is even possible that the sufferer may vomit while lying on his back and could suffocate if he is unable to turn over.

Why Seasick Sailing Downwind?

Small boat sailors, running downwind in races close to shore, often get seasick. One might wonder why since the pitching motions are less abrupt than when hard on the wind. However, downwind the motion is combined with much rolling and yawing, which, being less constant than when beating, make it difficult for the helmsman to maintain his orientation to the true direction of the seas.

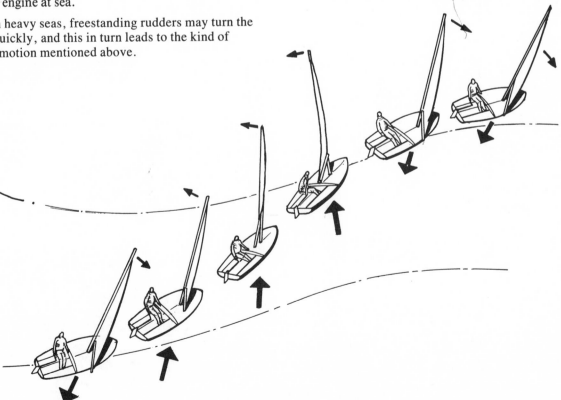

The Axes of Motion

The three axes of motion of a yacht (pitch, roll and yaw) are centered in an area roughly three-fifths of the boat's length from the bow. This is the most stable area in the boat; this is where the victim of seasickness should be placed if possible. Actually, it is not often possible — least of all in sailing yachts — because that is where the engine is usually installed and the quarter berth, which is also near this area, can be difficult to use.

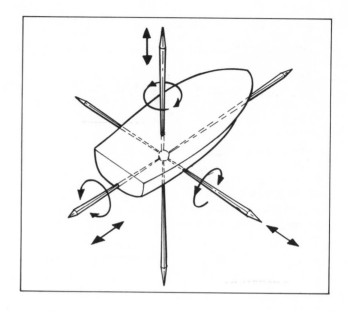

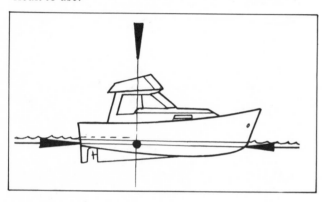

What to Do with a Seasick Sailor?

In the cockpit: If the length of the cockpit permits, lay the victim down on the leeward side of the sole and turn him sideways. If the cockpit has a high coaming, you can try laying him on the leeward seat and lashing him firmly in place. His head should point in the direction of motion. While he is vomiting (use a flat basin, even a cut-down plastic bucket), a shipmate should support his head and/or upper body and promptly clean out the container.

Belowdeck: Here the poor fellow is often left alone because the rest of the crew has to stay on deck to handle the boat and must remain fit. Yet belowdeck one generally gets seasick more rapidly than in the cockpit where there is fresh air and a view of the horizon. For this reason, it is unwise to simply leave the victim in the leeward bunk, because he may not be able to haul himself over the edge of the bunk to vomit. Better to lay him face down in the windward bunk safely secured with the lee cloth and the bucket lashed firmly near his head. In this case, too, the other crewmembers must keep a careful watch over him.

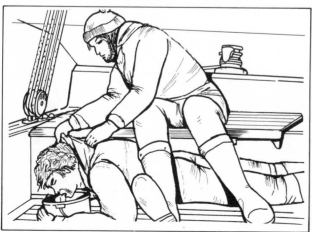

There is a whole series of factors and design details on a sailing yacht that can aid in preventing or at least minimizing seasickness. Do not underestimate psychological factors, either. A boat that sails more nearly upright has a calming effect on the crew: It eases tension to reef early (1).

Good circulation of air belowdeck maintains a pleasant atmosphere. Ensure this by having large watertight Dorade vents (2).

The navigator (3) is in special danger because he has to stay below much of the time. It is best if the navigation station is built fairly high and close to the companionway so that the navigator can have eye contact with the crew and a view of the horizon without turning his head.

The off watch too should sleep close to the center of rotation of the boat's lengthwise axis (4). It is important to have a strong, high lee cloth and a warm sleeping bag.

Frequently turning the head to and fro brings on seasickness, so it is best if all of the important navigation instruments can be seen by the helmsman at a single glance (5).

The spray hood or dodger serves not only to protect and soothe the crew but also tends to direct a supply of fresh air below (6). Before putting to sea, fill a Thermos with hot tea or broth and keep it in a bracket near the companionway (7).

The person least likely to get seasick is the helmsman because he can anticipate the movements of the boat and prepare himself accordingly. Moreover, he is almost constantly looking at the horizon. Concentration on handling the boat prevents incipient illness. It helps if he can take a position well forward in the cockpit (8). If possible, crewmembers who are fighting off seasickness should get a turn at the helm. A strong feeling of safety does a great deal of good! It has been shown that people who tend toward anxiety become seasick more rapidly than most. A deep cockpit with a high coaming is very good in this connection (9).

The most important items of equipment, including the storm sails, should be stowed in easily accessible lockers (10), never in a deep lazarette where they can be reached only by bending down head first.

Large cockpit drains also contribute to a feeling of safety by quickly freeing the cockpit of water that may come aboard (11).

Full keelboats with attached rudders are generally more agreeable in a seaway than fin keel boats. Thanks to their greater lateral surfaces, full keels tend to hold their courses better (12).

A safe companionway set at a good angle and fitted with handholds, makes it much easier for those who are only slightly ill to climb into and out of the cabin (13).

A separate bilge for the engine room is very desirable; if possible, it may even be separated by a bulkhead to keep the odor of diesel from spreading throughout the boat. A good measure against seasickness is to keep the engine room bilge clean at all times (14).

A bilge or sump for collecting leaked-in water ensures a dry ship (15).

A high ballast-to-displacement ratio allows the boat to sail more upright, though the righting motion

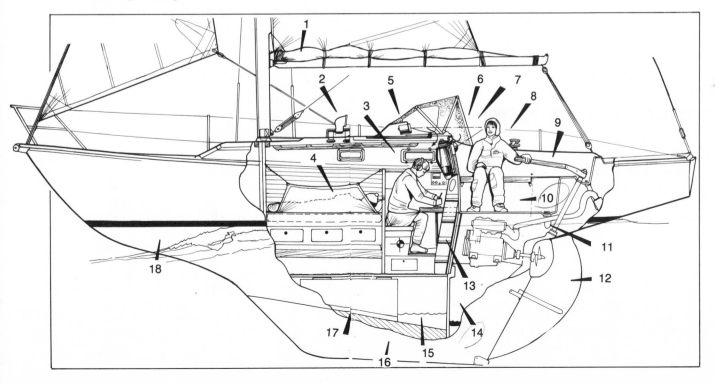

may be jerkier **(16)**.

Finally, an adequate supply of fresh water is necessary so that any sufferers on board can be taken care of and refreshed **(17)**.

Persons subject to seasickness should avoid the forward cabin altogether on high-seas passages **(18)**.

The Balance Centers

These are located on both sides of the head in the inner ear. They consist of three semi-circular canals **(1)** and saclike enlargements **(2)**. These little sacs are lined with sensory cells. The canals and sacs lie in the three principal planes of space and are filled with liquid. They respond to movements in pitch, roll and yaw, sending impulses from the sensors via the equilibrium nerves to the brain **(3)**. If the balance centers are overloaded, seasickness results.

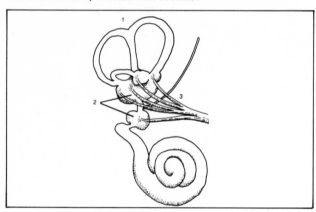

Seasickness Remedies

Today we have effective anti-seasickness medications, but one should be aware of their side effects. Antihistamines may cause significant sedative effects, especially when combined with alcohol. Some of these are prescription drugs; in any case, it would be wise to see a physician before taking any of them because some of them may cause fatigue and/or disturbances of vision. On the other hand, some have a soothing effect and to some extent relieve anxiety among those unaccustomed to the sea. These remedies come as tablets, capsules and suppositories.

In recent years, adhesive patches containing the medication in an inactive matrix (e.g., Transderm Scop®) have been introduced. These products work by slowly releasing scopolamine at the surface of the skin. The scopolamine diffuses through the structure of the skin into the bloodstream, obviating any effect on the gastrointestinal tract. This is a real advantage in practical use. The pad is stuck to the skin behind the ear not far from the balance center. The medication reaches full effectiveness in a short time and lasts about 72 hours. The possibility of undesirable side effects from adhesive patches is still being investigated. (Note: the RNLI has abandoned tests with adhesive patches.)

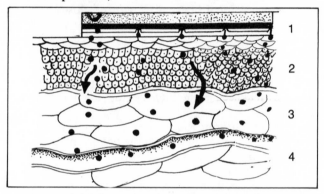

The scopolamine in its matrix **(1)** diffuses through the outer layer of the skin first **(2)**, and then through the deeper layers **(3)**, finally reaching the blood vessels **(4)**. The blood conveys the active agent to the brain where it suppresses the response of the corresponding centers.

There is always a lapse of time before any of these remedies will start to work, hence they should be taken an hour or two before the need arises.

In cases where the medication cannot be tolerated, or if it causes undesirable side effects such as fatigue or disturbances of vision, acupressure has been used. To be sure, its calming effect is less than that of more conventional medications and many physicians doubt its effect on seasickness altogether, but blue-water sailors have tried it with success.

Very possibly the placebo effect — the belief that a method will work — plays a role here. The simplest way to apply acupressure is with a little hemispherical knob on the inside of an elastic band. The pressure point lies some two inches above the wrist, about where the pulse is felt. You can buy such straps in stores or simply cement a little knob inside your watch strap and place it over the spot.

Stereo music has been found to be an effective anti-seasickness measure especially for short trips. You might try listening to a portable radio with head phones. Not only are children and teenagers soothed by music but adults too recommend it. Distraction is the secret of this method. Similarly, community singing by the crew has been found useful in preventing the onset of seasickness — so long as they keep on singing!

Safely Through the Storm...

Chances of coming through a storm undamaged are always enhanced when boat and crew are thoroughly prepared in advance for the expected stresses, and everyone on board knows just what to do.

Preparations for the Storm . . . On Deck

Most precautions for storms have to be taken on deck. Many cockpit seat lockers and lazarettes don't have hasps or equivalent closures. They need to be tied down as securely as allowed by the resources on board — a suitable improvisation is shown (1).

At least one solid horseshoe-type flotation device should be hung at the stern (2). The crew should put on foul weather gear, life jackets and safety harnesses (3). Tighten up the topping lift until it forms an additional support for the boom (4). Tight lines can be rigged in the cockpit so that one can safely get to the side decks (5).

The main should be deep-reefed while the wind is moderate. Reefing during a storm does not usually result in the best set, whereas unreefing is very much easier. A smoothly set mainsail sheeted in flat is a basic requirement for satisfactorily enduring a storm (6).

If you have a storm trysail on board, tie it to the foot of the mast so that it can be set instantly (7).

Correct tensioning of shrouds and stays is very important under storm conditions. They must be just tight enough. Above all, the forward lower shrouds and/or the baby stay (8) must be under strong tension to prevent the mast from bowing aft. The storm jib is

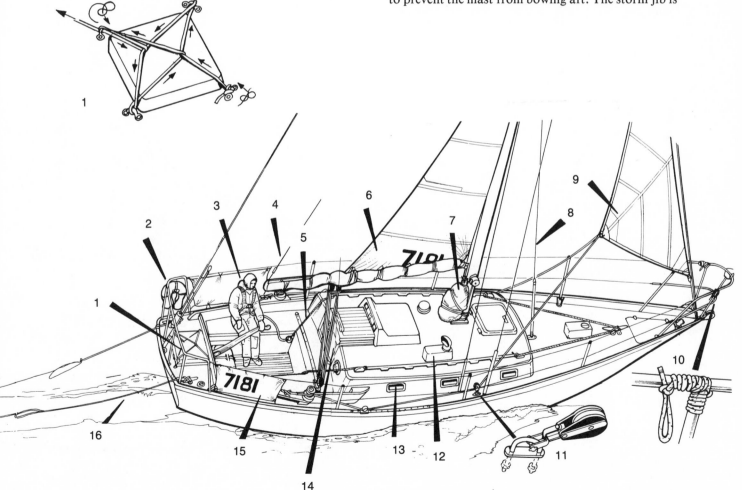

trimmed in tight with the leeward sheet. And trim the windward sheet good and tight so that when tacking it will not flog **(9)**.

Seize some short strops to the bow pulpit so that during a sail change you can quickly tie off the jib to one side **(10)**. A well fitted-out yacht will have thru-bolted lead blocks for the storm jib sheets **(11)**. If your boat does not have them, lash emergency blocks to the chain plates.

Turn all Dorade ventilators to face away from the wind. Tightly close all mushroom ventilators and similar through-deck fittings **(12)**,

All opening ports and windows demand a rigorous inspection below **(13)**. Slide the companionway boards into place, and tie them down with a strop so they cannot float away if you are knocked down **(14)**.

It is a good idea to paint your hull, sail or race number on your weather cloths to aid a potential rescuer. These cloths take a heavy load during a storm and must be very solidly lashed in place **(15)**.

As a possible aid to a man overboard, tow a couple of lines with eyes in them for handholds **(16)**.

....and Belowdecks

Remove and bag all light-weather sails and stow them in the side lockers **(1)**.

Test the manual bilge pump; be sure it works **(2)**.

Near the companionway or in the quarter berth, stow all tools that might be needed in case of trouble — such as a dismasting or a broken tiller — plus the emergency tiller and distress signals **(3)**.

Have the cook prepare a good hearty soup and put it in a Thermos **(4)**.

Take a look at the bilge. Carefully get rid of all the water, dirt and motor oil that you can **(5)**.

Fit the bunks with their lee cloths or bunk boards so that the off watch will be able to rest undisturbed **(6)**.

Pump out the head and close its sea cock **(7)**.

Coil your long lines and stow them carefully in the lazarette so that they are instantly accessible for paying out a sea anchor or drogues when running before the storm **(8)**.

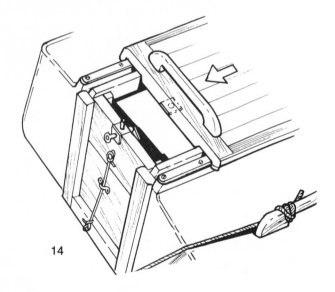

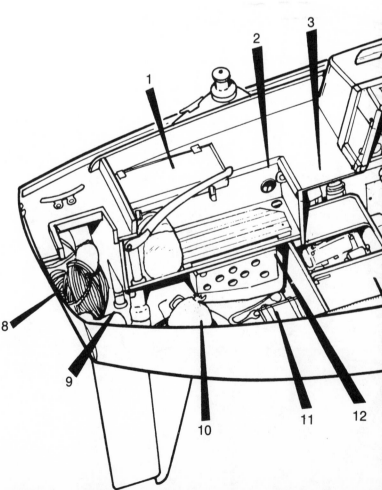

Clean out the cockpit drains **(9)**.

Stow all loose cabin gear in locked compartments or put them in seabags in the cockpit lockers **(10)**.

Liberally coat the battery terminals with protective grease **(11)**.

If you still have jerry cans of fuel on board, top up the tank with them **(12)**.

Close all sea cocks, even the engine cooling water intake **(13)**.

Have the navigator select the necessary charts and light lists and tape them to the chart table **(14)**. Write down the weather broadcast stations and their air times and assign someone as weather radio watch.

Rig the cook's and the navigator's safety belts at their stations, if possible. Remove and stow the cabin carpet **(15)**.

Stow and lash the Thermos of hot soup safely at the head of the off watch crewmember's bunk where he can easily grasp it **(16)**.

Check all lids and doors to ensure they are solidly closed. If necessary, tape them. Drawers will also have to be taped for security; they can jump out when the boat pounds in a seaway **(17)**.

While the weather is still good, have your two most experienced crew rest in their bunks; they will be under severe pressure when the storm hits **(18)**.

Place everything that might be damaged by water in plastic bags or containers and stow in the safest part of the ship. This includes food, changes of clothing, documents, etc. **(19)**.

If you have an inflatable, deflate, fold and stow it below where you also keep the life raft ready for use **(20)**.

Under the forward bunk stow a very small spare jib, fitted with its own sheets and ready for use **(21)**.

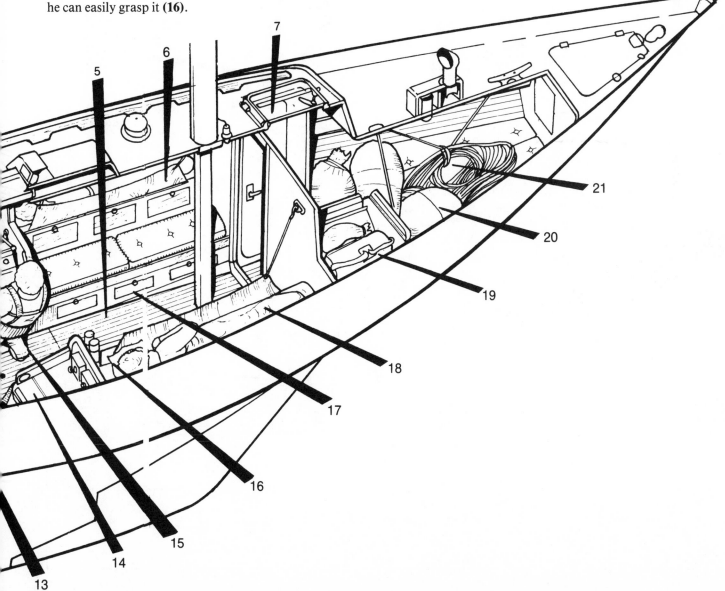

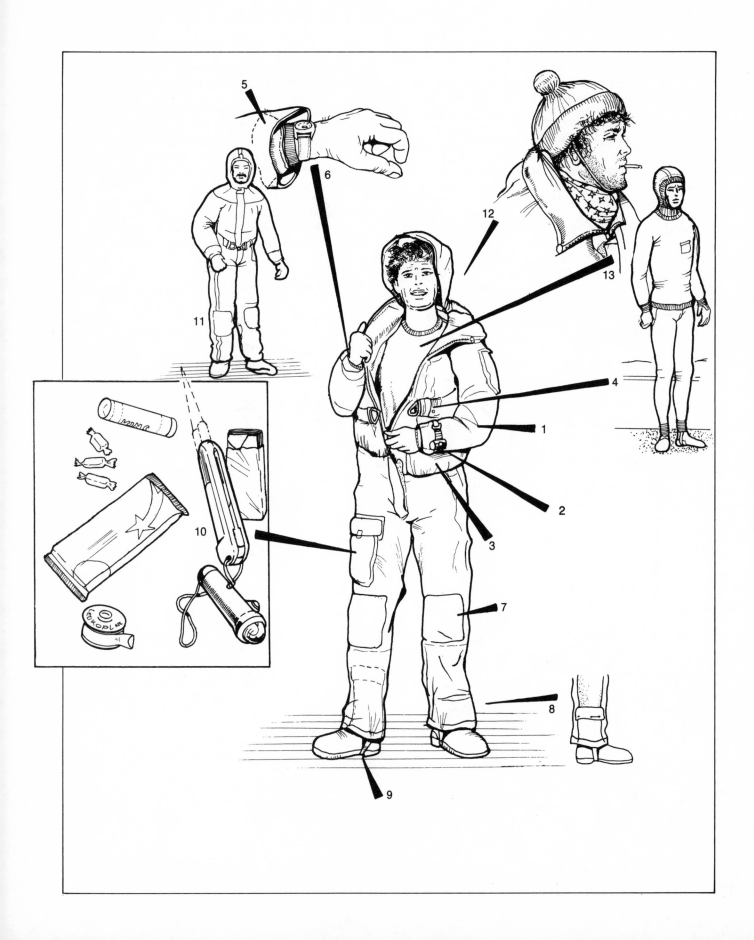

Preparing the Crew

The crew's clothing is of very great importance. The chandlery business offers special suits and heat-retaining underwear which slow the onset of hypothermia in colder regions.

1. Most important is a watertight, lined overall that keeps condensed water away from the body and warms the wearer at the same time.

2. A fixed light or a Cyalume chemical lightstick should be carried to help pinpoint a man overboard.

3. A self-inflating life jacket — the type that holds the head of an unconscious person out of water — is either a part of the overall or more commonly worn over it. This interferes very little with normal movements.

4. A safety harness is necessary, to which a safety line is clipped. It may be integral with the overall or life jacket or may be worn over these.

5. Watertight or water-resistant wristcuffs are a help.

6. A watertight wristwatch should be worn.

7. A good overall will be reinforced at the seat and knees.

8. Wear flexible rubber seaboots.

9. A rubber strap around the boot or a Velcro® closure at the trouser cuff reduces the chance of it catching on some fitting on deck.

10. The overall pockets, which should be as watertight as possible, should contain: adhesive tape, a small watertight flashlight, marlinspike, knife, paper towels, peppermint or other candies, chocolate bars or dextrose and glucose.

11. If the boat operates mainly in cold waters, an insulating suit should be worn, one specifically made for use in extreme conditions.

12. If this is not available, then the head at least must be protected with a warm cap and over it a hood which is attached to the overall. Thermal underwear and jackets and stockings should be worn under the overall **(13)**.

Sail Management

The table shows the correct sails to be carried under various wind conditions by yachts of about 35 feet LOA with a displacement of about eight tons. In a Force 6 wind, the sloop rig calls for one reef in the mainsail and the working jib; the cutter reefs the main and changes down to smaller headsails; the ketch changes down from genoa to working jib and takes the first reef in both main and mizzen. The schooner hands the fisherman and reduces the main with one reef.

In Force 8, the sloop has three reefs in the main and has changed down to the storm jib; the cutter is using only a pair of heavy-weather headsails; the ketch is down to storm jib and triple-reefed main and mizzen, although the latter might be furled altogether; the schooner is using only the sail on the forward mast and the storm headsail, while the main has been furled; at Force 9 and above, all boats heave to under storm jib and trysail. In the open sea beating is impossible under these conditions.

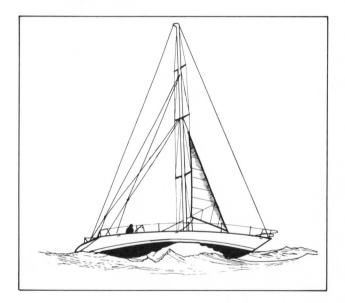

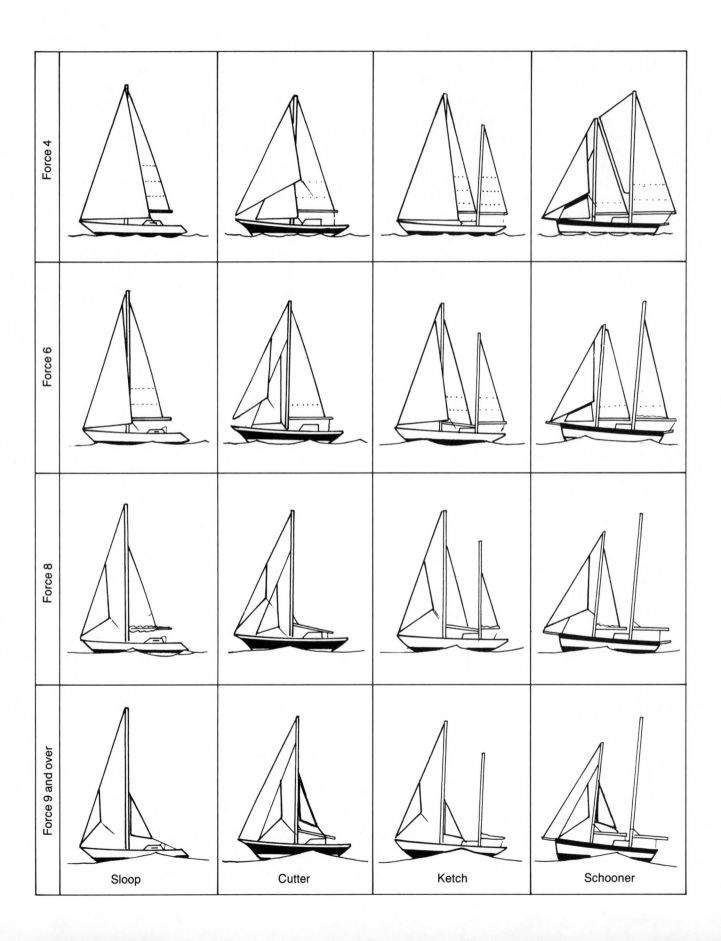

Racing yachts are often fitted with a baby stay, which runs from the middle of the mast to the foredeck. This is a good location for a storm jib and will aid steering.

The sail-carrying ability of a yacht is directly dependent on its size, ballast-to-displacement ratio and the inherent stability of the hull form. A 20-foot keelboat can carry only a storm jib in Force 7 winds; a 37-footer could carry a deeply reefed main and working jib; and an 80-foot maxi racer would be right in her element, really moving under No. 2 genoa and single-reefed main.

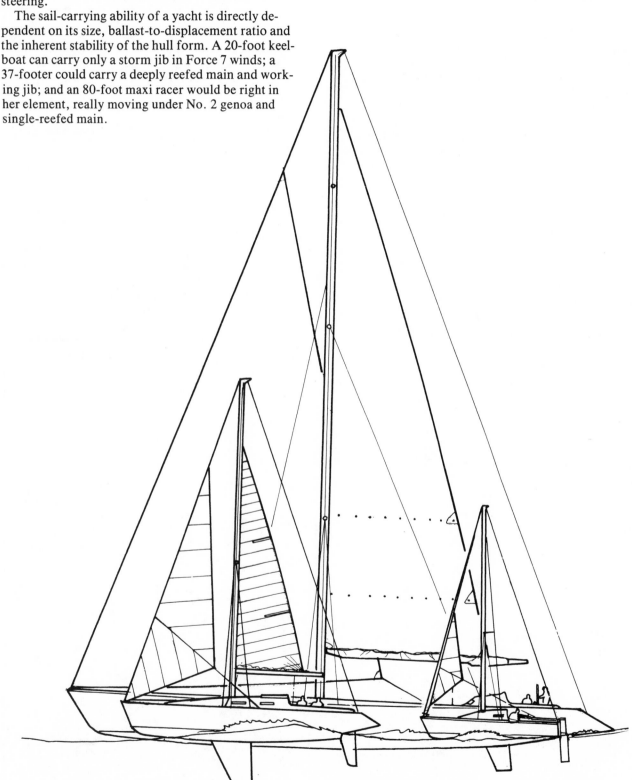

The Roller-Furling Jib as Storm Sail

The adequacy of roller-furlers as storm sails is doubtful, because when even partially rolled up they have a shape unsatisfactory for heavier winds and even tight sheeting does not flatten them enough. The main reason for this characteristic is that roller-furling genoas have an acute angle at the clew; leech and foot come together at an angle around 60 degrees. The leech and foot of a true storm jib form an angle of at least 120 degrees at the clew, as a result of which the sail may be trimmed extremely flat, a requirement for maximum drive and minimum heel.

Shortening Down with the Roller-Reefer

Roller reefing is scarcely installed any more on the boom because the rolled-down main does not have a good shape. The necessary flattening of the sail can be accomplished if towels or other pieces of cloth are inserted in the belly of the sail.

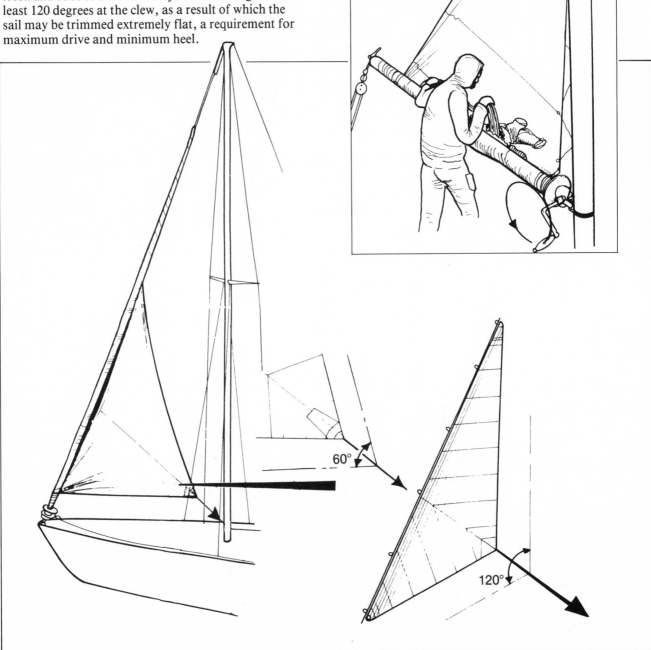

Shortening Down with the Jiffy Reef

There are several systems that enable the mainsail to be reefed from the cockpit using merely a reefing line — a jiffy reef.

1. In this arrangement, the jiffy reefing line is made fast at the side of the boom near its forward end. Then it runs upward through the luff cringle and back down to the boom where it is led aft. From the after end of the boom it then goes up again through the leech reefing cringle, back down to the other side of the boom, forward to a block near the gooseneck, down to a turning block at the base of the mast, then aft to a winch on the cabin top. Now, when the main halyard has been eased, the main can be reefed completely using only the winch. A disadvantage is that the system allows only one reef.

2. Small boats do well with the following system: The reefing line is dead-ended near the after end of the boom; from there it runs up through the leech reef cringle and back down to the side of the boom, where it is turned and led forward. It then runs through a turning block, up through the luff cringle and down to the foot of the mast. From there it is led aft to the winch on the cabin top. This system also allows complete reefing from the cockpit.

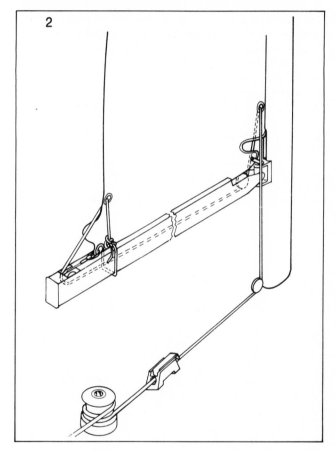

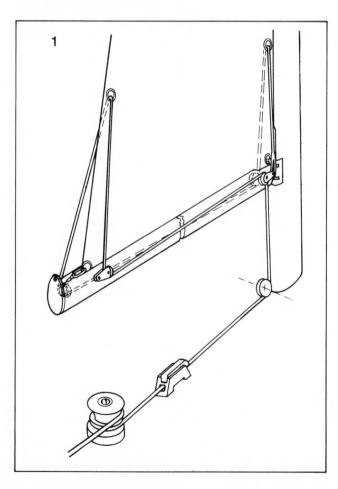

Reefing with Two Reefing Lines

3. On most large boats you will find a mainsail reefing system with two separate jiffy reefing lines. Dead-ended near the after end of the boom, each runs up to its leech reefing cringle, through it and back down again to the boom, forward inside the boom, exiting forward over a turning block near the gooseneck fittings. Modern booms include built-in stoppers which help to make fast the respective lines after reefing. Jiffy reefing lines can be hauled with a special winch on the underside of the boom. This system has the disadvantage that before reefing one must slack off the luff of the mainsail far enough so that the correct reef cringle may be placed over a hook at the gooseneck fitting, which requires the crew to leave the safety of the cockpit. After reefing, the halyard must be set up tight again. Still, this method is the one most used on voyaging yachts.

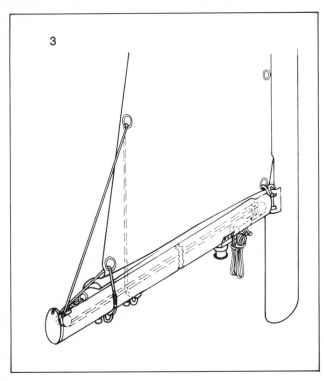

Roller Reefing Inside the Mast

Mainsail furling systems are being used on yachts in a wide range. In this system the sail is wound up on a stay within the mast; this is rotated by means of a gear drive at the foot of the mast. Either manual or electric power may be used. In this way the mainsail may be rolled up from the cockpit, without being slacked off and set up again with a halyard. Reefing does not proceed vertically downward from top to bottom, but at right angles to the mast. The disadvantage is that the traditional battens cannot be used; also, the leech must be cut holow. Recently introduced are vertically inserted battens, i.e., parallel to the mast.

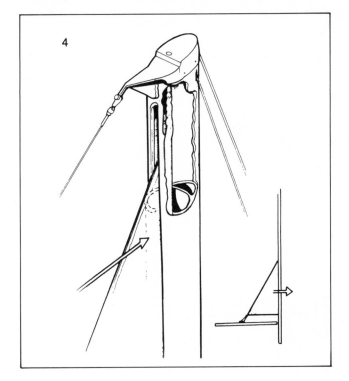

Reefing Aids

The old sailing ships were equipped with lazy jacks, auxiliary lines led from the mast to either side of the boom. These were essential to guide and support the huge gaff mainsail when it was being reefed or furled. The use of lazy jacks is appearing again on modern yachts as mainsails are getting bigger and bigger and harder to tame. Lazy jacks of the type shown are very useful in that they serve as additional topping lifts that hold the boom at a safe height while reefing. They are essential for fully battened sails.

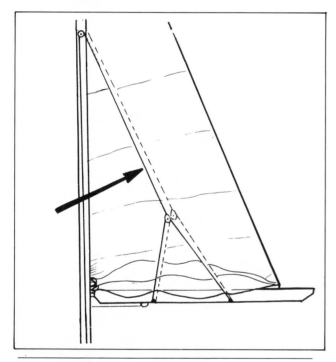

Handling a Yacht in a Storm

In many ways, the seakeeping ability of a boat depends on its hull form and construction. Let us consider three types of boats:

1. The classic full keel. This boat has the best tracking ability and may be expected to have the least tendency to broach.

2. The high freeboard, voyaging cruiser with split rig. She is harder to manage in storm conditions, especially when she has a high after cabin that offers considerable wind resistance.

3. The modern racing yacht. She stands up to storms if carefully managed because of a low profile and the low center of gravity of the ballast.

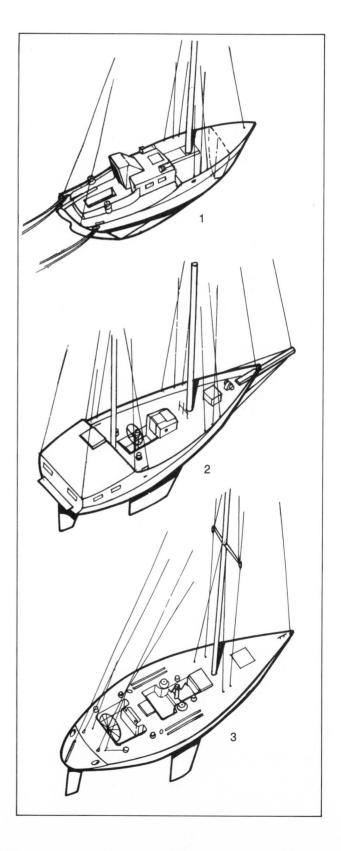

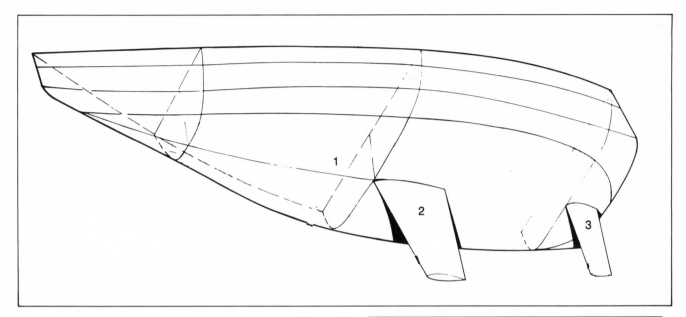

The drawing shows why light-displacement racing yachts are tricky in heavy weather: The underbody is extremely flat, which leads to pounding in a seaway (1). The keel usually has very narrow surfaces, which confer little course stability (2). Tracking is made worse by the freestanding balanced spade rudder whose angle must be precisely controlled with the tiller in a storm (3). Most helmsmen cannot keep this up very long so it is only a question of time before the yacht becomes very difficult to steer in the heavy seas.

Erroneous Estimation of Wave Height

One generally makes a false estimate of wave height from on board a boat. When the boat is running down the face of a sea before a crest, the sea *ahead* appears to be very high because of the angle of view. Similarly, when the boat is climbing the back of a wave, a sea *astern* seems very high, even gigantic. Don't let a glance at the heavy seas panic you because they are probably not as big as they seem.

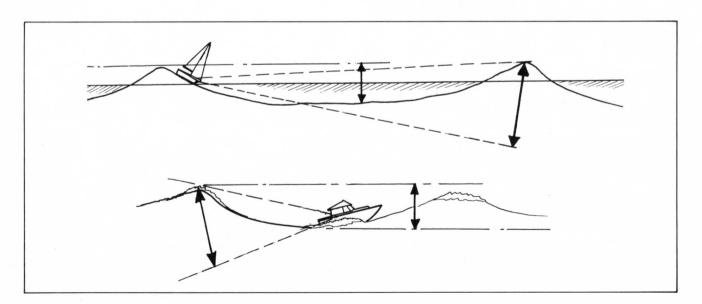

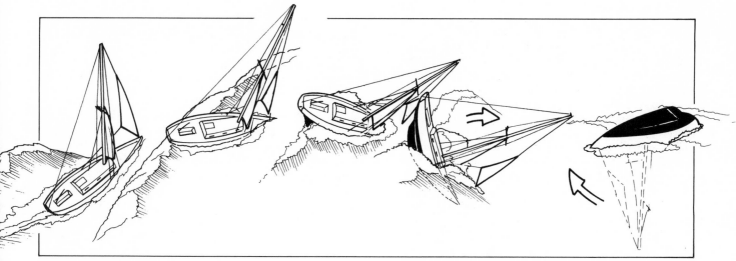

Capsizing

The heavy displacement of the classic full keel yacht is not always an advantage. The comfortable cruising yacht is not fast enough under storm jib and main when running before a storm. She is overtaken by the following seas. This is normal for the usual storm waves in the open sea and does not endanger the vessel. But the crest of a rogue wave can lift the after part of the boat; in a modern light-displacement yacht this merely leads to an increase in speed and surfing ahead of the crest. The heavy-displacement cruiser buries her bow. Her fate is sealed, for the following crest takes charge of the hull and pitch-poles her.

The generally accepted idea that heavy-displacement yachts can't be knocked down is basically false. There have been a great many misfortunes at sea in which voyaging yachts have rolled 180 degrees and even 360 degrees in a storm. But with proper sail management this is never due to the wind, but rather to the character of the seas and the orientation of the boat to their direction. There are various situations that can lead to a capsize. Among the most common occurs when the boat breaks through the crest of one wave and is broached by the following wave. The ultimate result is a knockdown with the mast in the water.

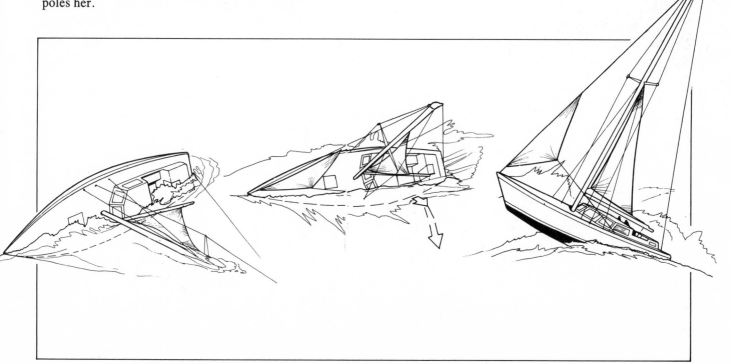

The crew of a large blue-water racing yacht will keep trying during a race to hold their course as long as possible in a storm, even when the course lies close to the wind. Under these conditions, some spectacular capsizes have occurred.

The boat no longer has enough headway to carry it through an unusually high wave crest. The bow is cast to leeward and the boat forced to make sternway. She becomes unsteerable and broaches. The action of the waves then knocks her down on her side until the mast goes into the water. A 360-degree roll follows.

Danger from Stove-in Windows

The drawings show why high cabin trunks with large unprotected windows are a potent source of danger on an oceangoing boat. When a boat is running under bare poles and has one side forced below the water by a great wave, the force can burst the panes. Windows set in rubber gaskets have proved to be particularly hazardous in such situations. The action of one single sea can break the windows, fill the cabins and quickly sink the boat.

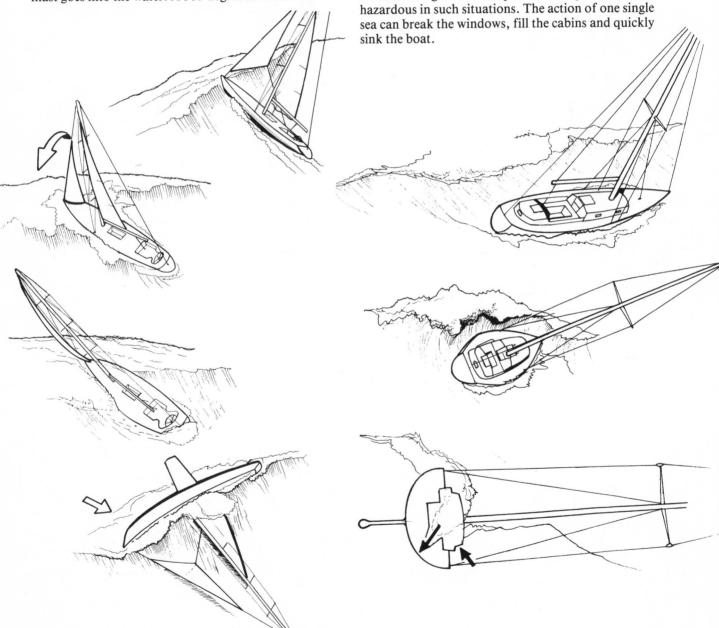

Cruising catamarans can also capsize; this puts them in very great danger because they cannot be righted.

Illustrated is a catamaran of the older type with covered deck, which some believe contributes to its undoing (1). Because of its shape, rather like that of a wing, the deck can provide lift in very strong winds; this could happen when the boat breaks through a high wave crest in a storm (2). Sail pressure, wave action and lift combine to raise the catamaran so that it turns over in the following trough and capsizes (3).

In the case of trimarans that do not have full decks (and therefore no aerodynamic lift), their great speed often leads to their undoing. They can reach excessive speed in a storm even when running under bare pole (1). When surfing before a following wave crest, it is dangerous to lose rudder control even for an instant lest the boat tend to broach. When this happens, the lee ama digs in at once, abruptly braking the speed on that side (2). The following crest completes the rollover and the lee ama goes completely under, acting as an auxiliary sea anchor (3). In a matter of seconds, the trimaran capsizes all the way (4).

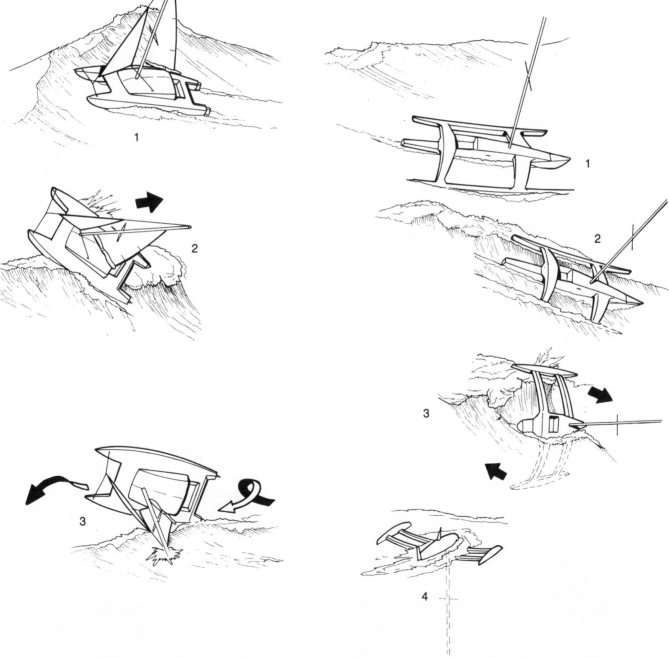

Running Before the Storm

How a sailboat best deals with a storm depends on its rig and hull design. Many types of boats safely come through a storm by running before it. Multihulls accomplish this by surfing down the waves. The only vital requirement is that the course be kept directly before the wind to prevent broaching.

Monohull passage makers whose maximum beam is not too far aft, but which have good buoyancy at both bow and stern, do well running before the wind. Double-enders are favored by some long-distance sailors **(1)**. It is a fallacy, though, that pointed sterns handle following seas better than other types. Transom sterns have shown themselves to be just as seaworthy, provided that they possess enough reserve buoyancy. Boats with full keels run off with the best course stability. Course stability can be further improved on any boat by towing warps astern.

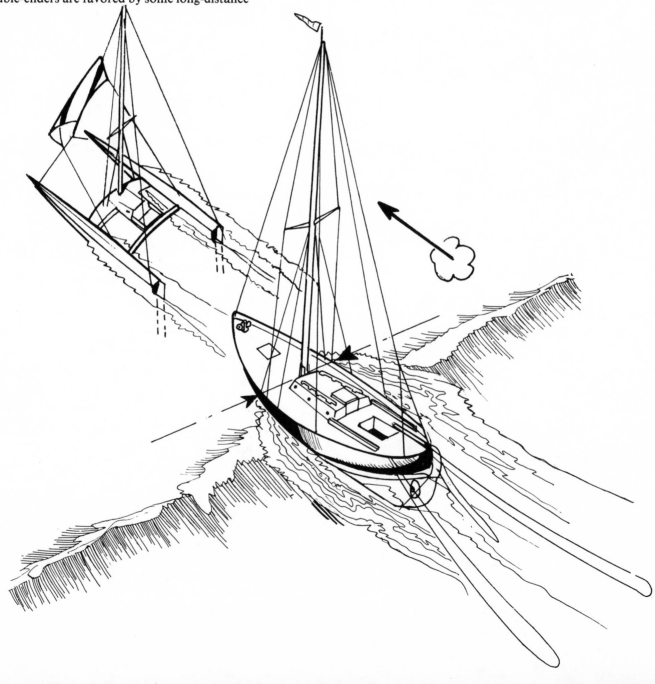

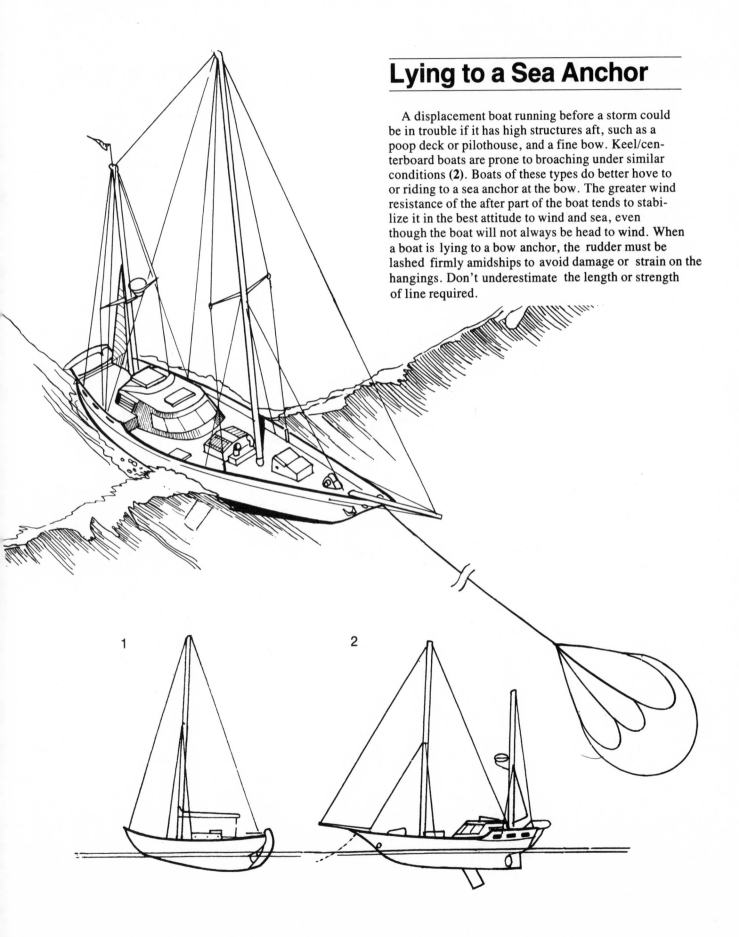

Lying to a Sea Anchor

A displacement boat running before a storm could be in trouble if it has high structures aft, such as a poop deck or pilothouse, and a fine bow. Keel/centerboard boats are prone to broaching under similar conditions (2). Boats of these types do better hove to or riding to a sea anchor at the bow. The greater wind resistance of the after part of the boat tends to stabilize it in the best attitude to wind and sea, even though the boat will not always be head to wind. When a boat is lying to a bow anchor, the rudder must be lashed firmly amidships to avoid damage or strain on the hangings. Don't underestimate the length or strength of line required.

1

2

Sailing to Windward

Light-displacement boats with fin keels and spade rudders do best combating storms if they can be sailed on the wind under storm sail. These are the tactics to be used in heavy seas. As you approach an oncoming sea, luff up as much as possible so that you head very close into the wind. On this heading you break through the crest. Fall off as you descend the other side of the wave to get up speed for the next cycle. This will ensure that you have steerage at all times, which greatly reduces the danger of being broached or rolled by a large wave.

This tactic is further illustrated by a cross-sectional view of a boat crossing such a wave. On the lowest third of the wave front, this small boat is almost on a beam reach. On the next third, the boat begins to luff up on the face of the wave so that it is hard on the wind when it goes through the crest (top third). The instant it goes through, a hard lee rudder brings the boat to a course of about 60 degrees to the direction of the seas, as it slides down the back of the wave.

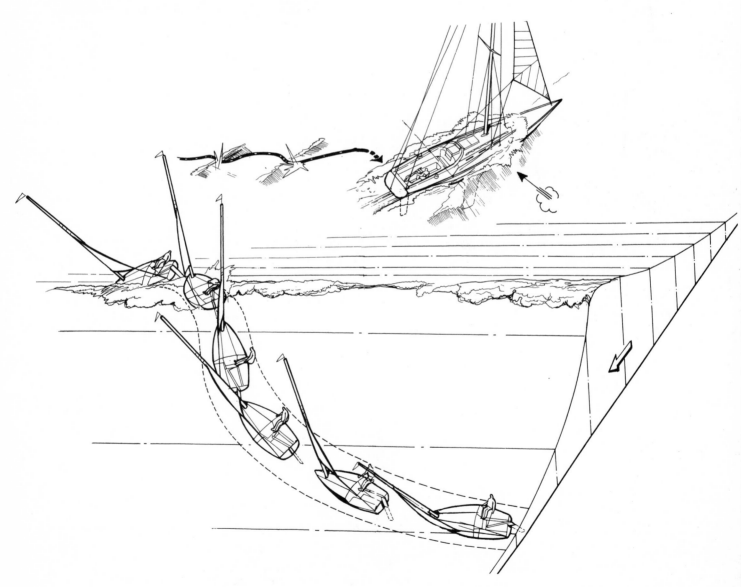

When the storm has reached such an intensity that you can no longer sail against it, even a racing yacht must run for it. An experienced crew will keep her safely on course before the seas by very careful steering. The sail area must be chosen so that the boat maintains steerage even in the surf of the breaking crests. This is the only way in which one can confidently prevent the dreaded broach.

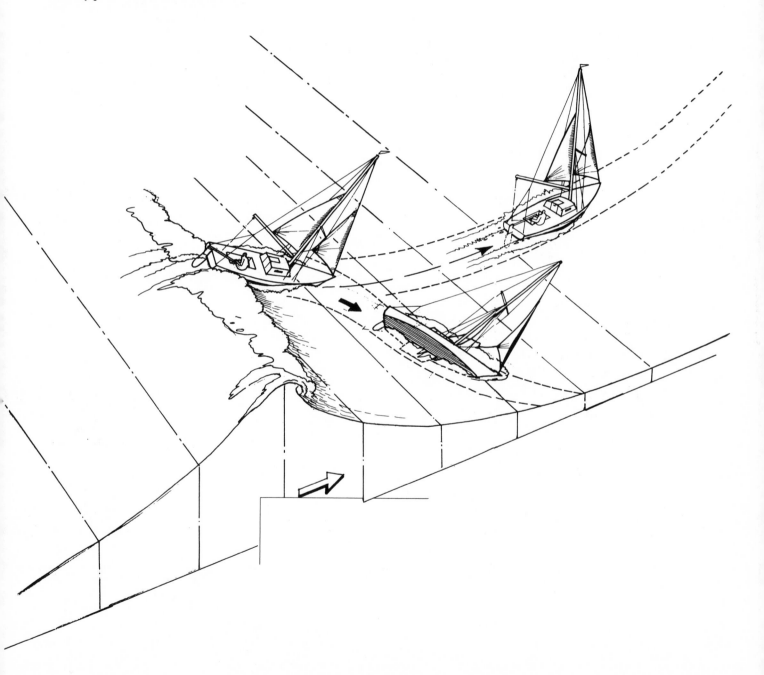

Running Off in a Motorboat

Small, half-decked motorboats of conventional displacement are in grave danger when running before heavy seas. Because of their low freeboard, an oncoming crest can break into the cockpit. In boats of this type the cabin is not, as a rule, truly bulkheaded off; hence the water that has come aboard is free to occupy every part of the hull. Consequently, the boat immediately sinks by the stern. This type of motorboat must be kept head to wind and/or sea if caught offshore in heavy weather.

Other motorboats, whether full displacement or semi-planing with high freeboard, have less of a problem with long following seas. Trouble arises only when the wave length is between one and two boat lengths and the height is greater than the freeboard. In such seas it is always safer to go slower than the waves. Otherwise, as the boat goes through the crest it tries to speed up, and the bow runs hard into the back of the wave ahead. This may lead to a broach. When the following sea is an unusually steep breaker, it is best to bring the boat around to a reciprocal course. It is wrong to slow down abruptly or to stop because the stern wave and the oncoming sea astern combine to overtake the boat. Above all, be careful not to ride the crests even for a few seconds, because this leads to the greatest risk of a capsize.

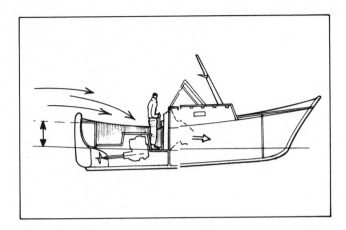

Below is an illustration of the best way for a motorboat to run off before wind and sea; keep a constant watch aft. When you see an especially steep breaking sea coming up astern, turn 180 degrees in the trough at low speed, keeping to this course until you have broken through the crest. Then in the following trough you can take up your regular down-wind course again. But don't initiate the maneuver too late or execute it on the crest or just below it—a broach will inevitably follow.

In less threatening seas, motor yachts can travel either bow to the waves or with waves abeam without too much danger.

Boats that can make 15 to 20 knots can ride across a bar into a harbor or river mouth on the back of the ground swell. You have to handle the throttle in such a way that you neither climb to the crest nor are sucked back into the trough. It is really safer not to try to enter harbor where you know there is a ground swell.

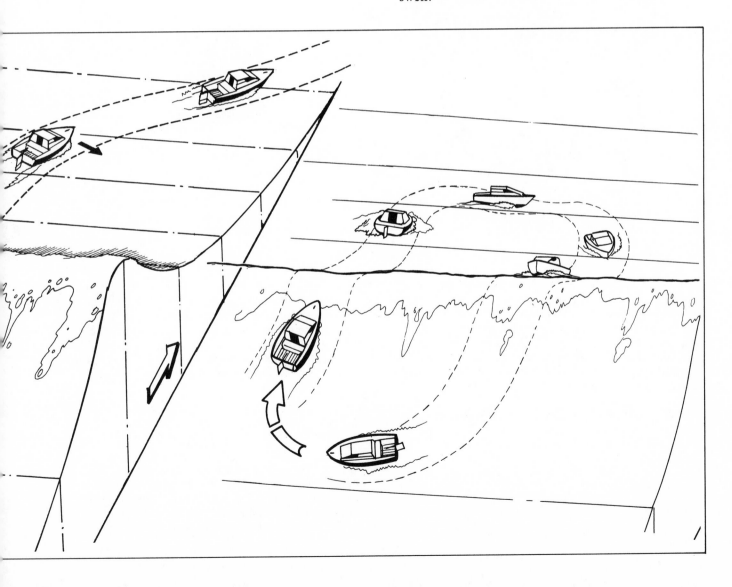

Overboard — and Saved

The worst experience for a small crew is to have a man go overboard. In many cases, it has proved impossible to recover the luckless person or sometimes even to find him. Often the crew still on board find it impossible to stage a recovery all by themselves. Therefore, one must know all the causes of a man-overboard emergency and take preventive steps well in advance. Safety can be calculated!

Hypothermia is the greatest problem. Many a sailor would be alive today if he had been wearing clothing suitable for the existing weather. Now you can buy insulating underwear that will keep your body warm even in the water. This underwear combined with a life jacket gives a much better chance of survival than light clothing that lets air and water through. The far-sighted skipper makes certain that his crew puts on warm clothing appropriate for the weather conditions, along with life jackets before leaving harbor.

Hazards

1. One cause of man-overboard situation is seasickness. It leads to a reduced ability to react and indeed to apathy. In one scenario, a victim of seasickness moves to leeward and vomits overboard. If at the same moment the boat pounds hard in a sea, the helmsman could be flung down from his seat on the windward side, hitting the man to leeward. The heel of the boat and/or the motion could send him sliding under the lifeline into the water.

2. A rope lying on deck is dangerous! So are sails. Ropes are rollers; synthetic sails are as slick as skating rinks. Hence the primary rule: Clear the decks after every maneuver. Sails not in use belong belowdeck. Halyards and sheets should be carefully coiled up.

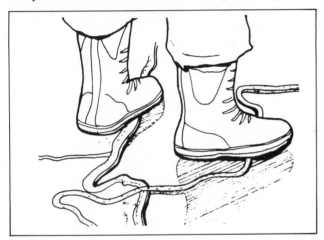

3. Another hazard occurs when the reef points are being tied. This requires both hands, so that one cannot observe the rule of "One hand for the ship and one for yourself." If the mainsheet is suddenly let go, the crew at the boom will surely go over the side.

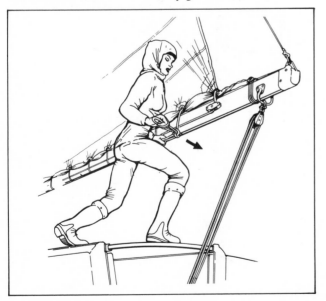

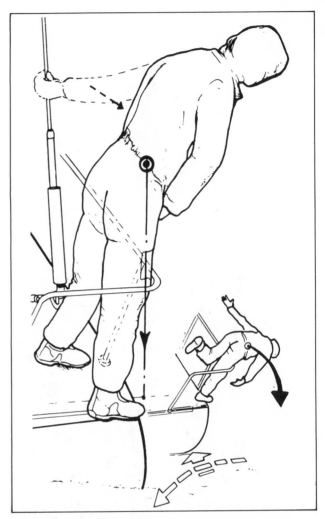

4. An untold number of man-overboard accidents have resulted from thoughtlessly seeking relief over the stern pulpit. The body is bent over the rail, when suddenly the stern makes a sharp heave and a yaw to windward — typical in a seaway — so that the man's center of gravity swings outboard. In heavy seas this movement can be so powerful that even a good grip on the backstay is not enough to keep his body aboard.

Rescue Equipment on Board

It is self-evident that every seagoing boat have these rescue items on board:

1. Man-overboard poles placed at the stern that can be thrown overboard with one hand. (This is a standard requirement for ocean racers of Classes I and II under the IOR rules.)

2. At least one — better two — life jackets and/or horse-shoe buoys bracketed on the stern pulpit, but not tied in any way.

3. At least one life ring equipped with a powerful light that is activated when afloat.

4. A long boarding ladder that can easily be unlatched; with the aid of a hanging line it is possible for a swimmer to unlatch it from the water **(5)**.

Consult various yachting associations for more detailed information on required safety equipment.

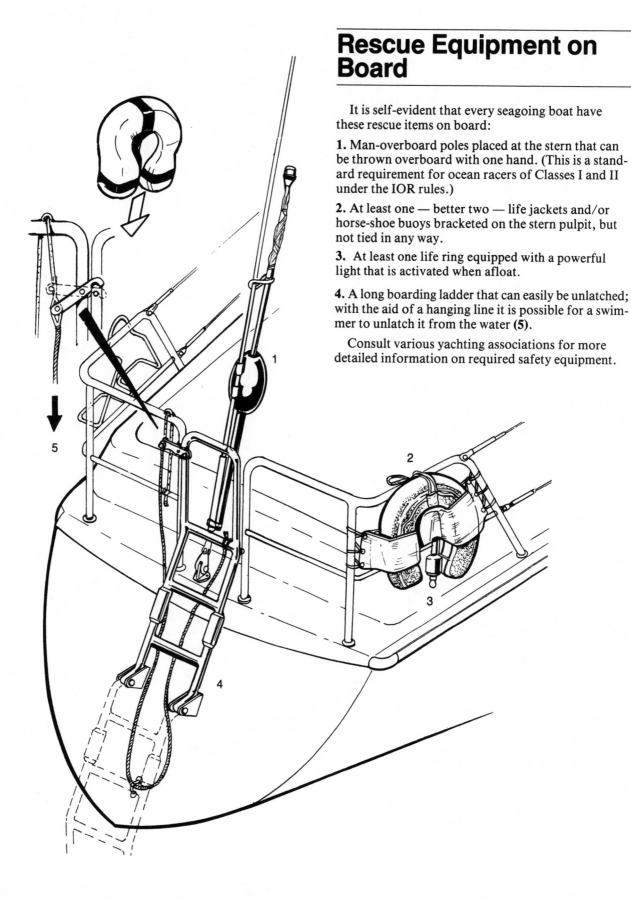

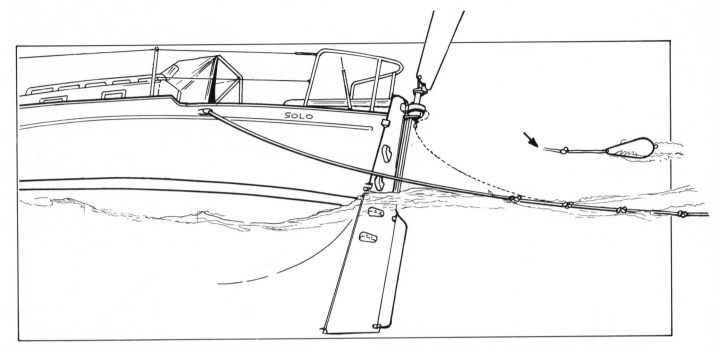

Overboard When Self-Steering

If a singlehander goes overboard when the self-steering is engaged, he has no chance of survival. Therefore he must always clip on a safety line when on deck. He possibly may be saved by a trailing line, say about 100 feet long, with a series of knots in it for handholds and a fender at the end for a still better grip. Chances are further improved if the trailing line carries a series of bowlines through which is led a trip line from the wind vane. This allows the vane steering to be disengaged from the water. Obviously this arrangement makes sense only if there are steps on the rudder or a boarding ladder that a swimmer can reach and thus climb back aboard. Without these aids a swimmer cannot get back aboard even if the boat's freeboard is very low.

Prevention of Hypothermia

Chances of survival in the water are directly dependent on the water temperature. Therefore it is vital to keep the body from rapidly cooling and to provide means for a speedy recovery.

The fetal position permits the greatest conservation of heat. Press the arms and legs close to the body and make no unnecessary movements. The good old watch cap does its job even in the water (1); a bare head dissipates as much as 40 percent of the body's heat. Provide a whistle on every life jacket (2). Use only those life jackets that are suitable for an unconscious person (U.S. Coast Guard Type 1) (3). This is the only type that permits the fetal position. Wear

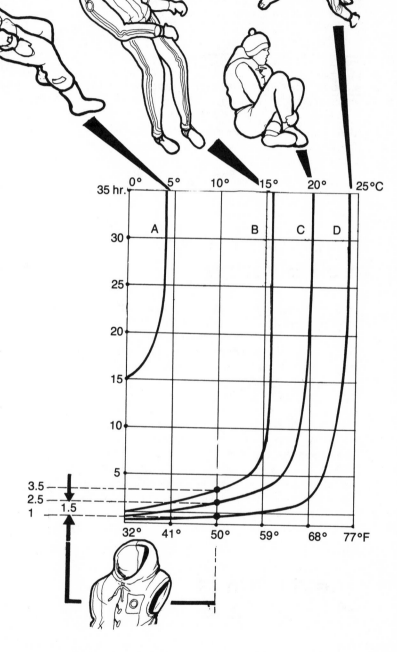

only well fitted, lightweight footgear (**4**). The line attached to the man-overboard pole can be wrapped around the legs to help you maintain the fetal position. This pole should be thrown over the instant "Man overboard" is heard. It is usually attached to the horseshoe on a line. Very often the victim will be able to swim to it, a task made easier if he is wearing close fitting pants (**6**). The pole must carry a bright flag at the top (**7**); fluorescent orange is favored, as is the flag for the letter "O" (for "Man overboard" in the International Code of Signals) a rectangle diagonally divided into red and yellow triangles. Also at the top there should be an automatically activated light (**8**).

Chances of Survival in the Water

The table gives data on the chance of survival depending on the water temperature and the clothing worn. The horizontal scale shows the temperature of the water in degrees Celsius (upper) and Fahrenheit (lower). The vertical scale shows the probable survival time in hours. Curve (**A**) shows that a man in a modern survival suit has a chance of being saved after as much as 25 to 30 hours in 40-degree water. Even a wet suit combined with a Type I life jacket may suffice for 10 hours in 60-degree water (**B**). Curve (**C**) shows one's prospects using the fetal position. Curve (**D**) gives an idea of the outlook for a person falling into the water unprotected by either life jacket or oilskins. The lower drawing shows the additional time afforded by the use of a life jacket or laced-up swim vest.

Man-Overboard Maneuvers

There are several options in a man-overboard situation. The drawing summarizes the possibilities within a visual circle about 200 yards in diameter.

In average weather, the best thing to do is to start the engine, turn into the wind and get the sails down **(1)**, which an experienced crew can do in about 30 seconds. Then you power over to the person in the water, reaching him in about 1½ minutes **(2)**.

Under sail, you use the second method, which is quick and positive. Immediately after the alarm "Man overboard," tack. As soon as the boat is on the other tack **(3)**, fall off to a beam reach and continue for about 30 seconds **(4)**. Then jibe — the jibe should be

complete at point **(5)**. Take a windward course toward the swimmer with sails luffing. Thus you will be able to trim in if you need a little more speed to shoot up to your target. Even heavy-displacement boats should be able to reach the person in the water in about 2½ minutes **(6)**. A jibe **(7,8,9)** is the quickest way for an experienced crew to get to the unlucky one. Under spinnaker, come a bit to windward and start a jibe **(10)**, take the spinnaker down **(11)** and start the engine. You can then motor sail using only the main very close to the wind right up to the person in the water **(12)**. Motorboats make a full circle **(13)** and, with their easy handling, reach their target in about 30 seconds.

For this diagram we have assumed a speed of four knots, a boat length of about 35 to 40 feet (10 to 12 meters) and moderate wind and visibility.

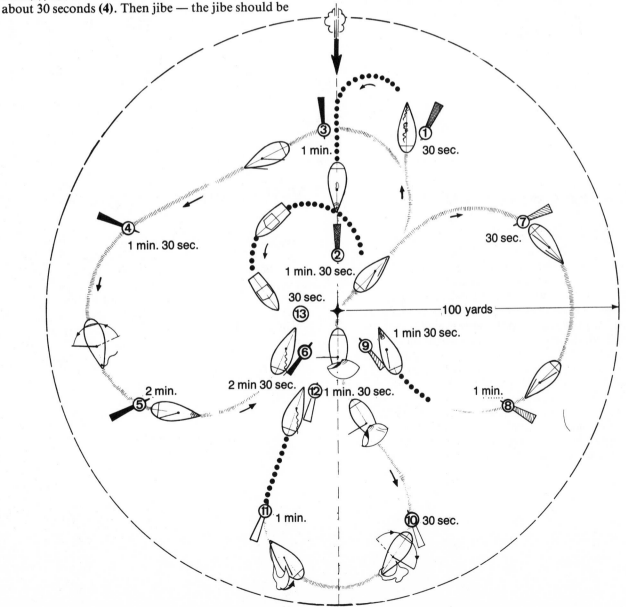

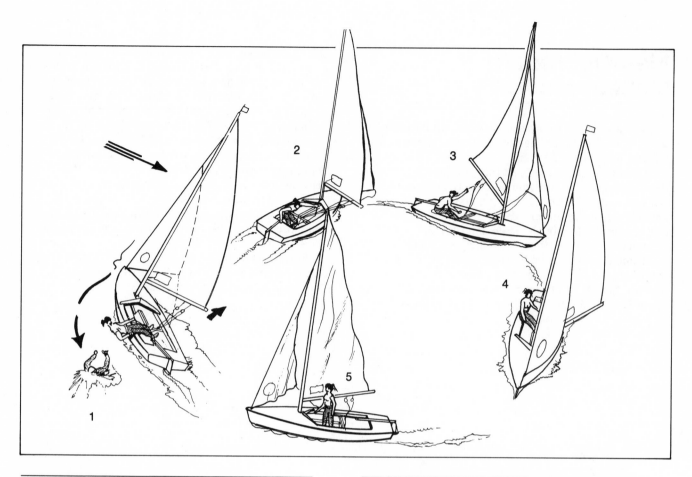

Small Boat Rescues

The jibe is normally the best way to fish up the person who has gone over the side (1). In the illustration, the lady at the helm instinctively corrects the trim for the missing man's weight by hiking out, hauls the tiller to windward and eases the mainsheet. This prevents a capsize. At (2) she starts a jibe and at (3) she has jibed and at (4) she comes on the wind again. At position (5) she has eased off all sail. Now she stands up for a better view and steers with the tiller extension. The boat shoots slowly up to leeward of the man, close enough for him to grasp the gunwale and hold on.

Many sailing schools teach this maneuver without easing the mainsheet before the jibe. This method is faster and leads to a smaller turning circle, but it involves a greater risk of capsize.

Motorboat Maneuvers

An approach from the windward direction is recommended for larger motorboats and sailboats under power because it's easy to heave lines and other means of rescue to leeward. However, one must prevent the boat from drifting over the victim and possibly putting him in even greater danger by drawing him under the hull.

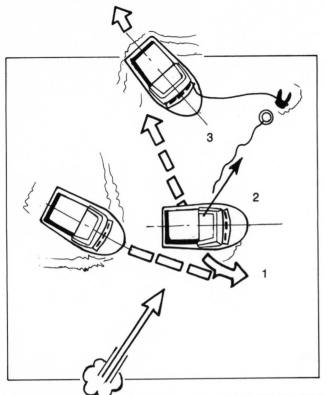

Therefore, the boat is brought up a few yards to windward of the target on a course at right angles to the direction of the wind **(1)** and briefly stopped. It drifts down very quickly toward the swimmer and the bow swings to leeward at the same time. At this moment, heave the ring **(2)**. As soon as it has been caught, back off slowly, steering away from the man overboard. Only when the boat is downwind of the man is he hauled in **(3)**. Bring him around the bow to the windward side and lead him to the quarter, where he can climb aboard on the ladder.

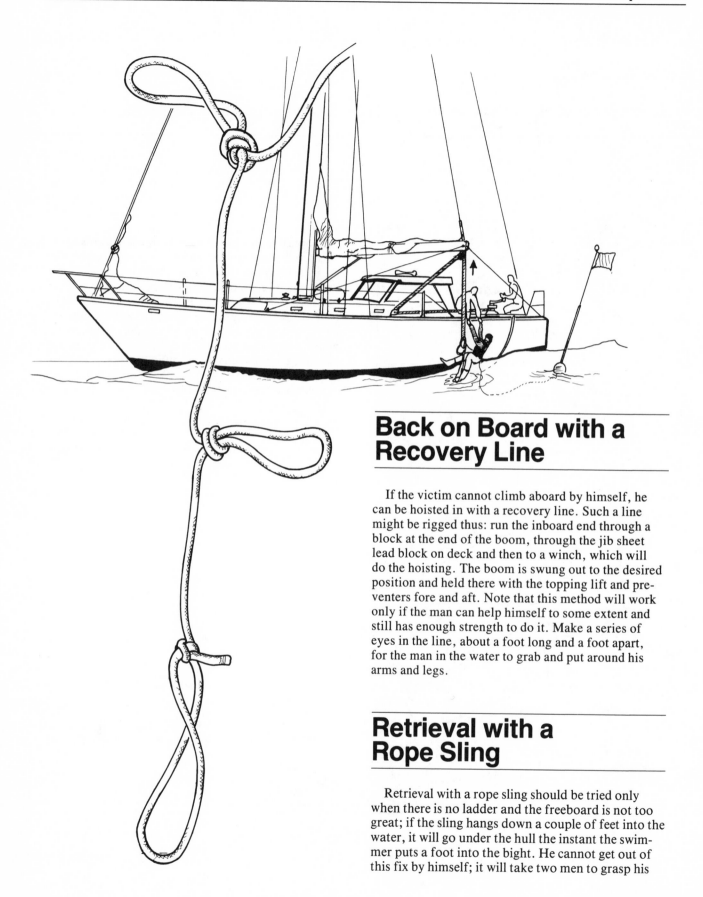

Back on Board with a Recovery Line

If the victim cannot climb aboard by himself, he can be hoisted in with a recovery line. Such a line might be rigged thus: run the inboard end through a block at the end of the boom, through the jib sheet lead block on deck and then to a winch, which will do the hoisting. The boom is swung out to the desired position and held there with the topping lift and preventers fore and aft. Note that this method will work only if the man can help himself to some extent and still has enough strength to do it. Make a series of eyes in the line, about a foot long and a foot apart, for the man in the water to grab and put around his arms and legs.

Retrieval with a Rope Sling

Retrieval with a rope sling should be tried only when there is no ladder and the freeboard is not too great; if the sling hangs down a couple of feet into the water, it will go under the hull the instant the swimmer puts a foot into the bight. He cannot get out of this fix by himself; it will take two men to grasp his

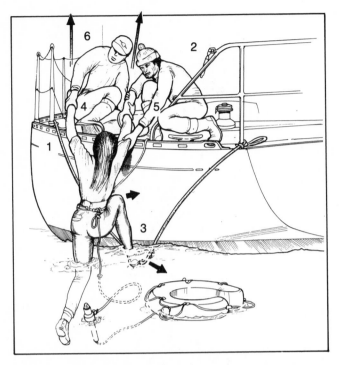

upstretched arms and haul him aboard. One does not get on deck from a rope sling without help! The sling is made fast at two points, which must not be too far apart, for instance at a stanchion and at the stern pulpit (**1**). Freeboard is generally lowest aft. Unhook the lifelines (**2**). Only one foot should go into the sling (**3**). Knee and leg should be braced against the hull while being lifted up; deck crew should find footholds against the toe rail (**4**), and/or jam themselves behind the pulpit supports (**5**). Now they can exert enough strength to heave the wet person up and inboard (**6**). But her active help is still needed . . .

Rescue of an Unconscious Person

If the person who has gone overboard is unconscious or has lost most of his strength, other methods of recovery must be used. If he is wearing neither a life jacket nor safety harness, the recovery line must be led under his armpits and behind his back. This will call for the help of someone in the water unless the freeboard is very low. This person will himself have to be well secured with a safety harness. Use a bowline to knot the line so that the eye will not slide closed.

The use of a jib to haul an unconscious or helpless person out of the water has often been recommended. The head of the sail is raised with the jib or main halyard using a winch. But the problem remains: How to roll the unconscious person under and through the lifeline to the deck? If there are enough crew, they should be able to pull him under the lifeline; otherwise it must be cut.

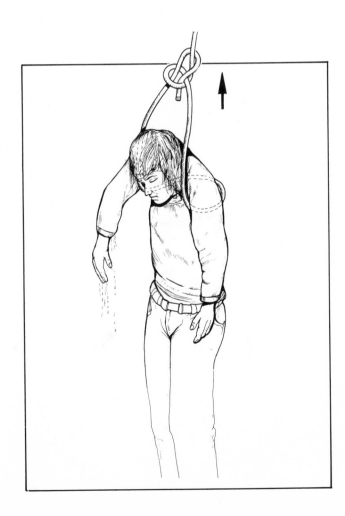

The hardest part of this job is to get the unconscious man into the bight of the rescue sail. First, he must be tied with a line in the water so he cannot drift off. Then he must be pulled into the right position over the sail, which has been sunk as far as possible.

Winching Up with Rescue Tackle and Halyard

Modern life jackets are available with safety harnesses sewn in, to which a strong rescue line can be attached. On a sailboat, the most satisfactory method of rescue is with the help of a halyard and the spinnaker pole with an extra tackle at its end. But this requires two or three men on deck. The boom, too, provides a powerful means of hoisting on board a hapless man overboard with his soaking wet clothing, if the mainsheet is led over a winch.

There is a special device for attaching a rescue tackle to the shroud. It is clamped to the shroud with four bolts as shown. It carries an eye, pointing outboard, for attaching the tackle; welded to the base, facing inboard, is a ring into which the boathook may be inserted. This placement of the tackle gives a suitable lead for the pull, so that the person can be hoisted up close to the topsides. Obviously this arrangement is suitable only for a larger yacht with correspondingly heavy shrouds.

The tackle should be at least four-part, preferably six, and should be led to a winch. If the tackle is not long enough, use a strop between it and the victim's life belt.

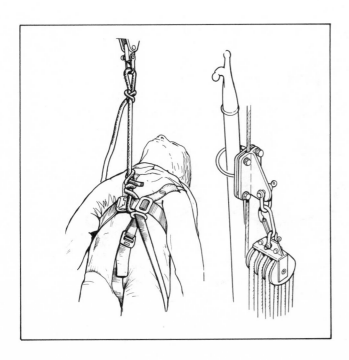

On Small Motorboats: Over the Motor Well

Small motorboats with outboards often have a motor well at the stern: One can get into the boat through this well. But don't fool yourself; your soggy clothes are so heavy that you will probably not be able to heave your body up over the edge of the well, even though it is relatively low. Instead, use the cavitation plate of the outboard as a step, or possibly step on some part of the propeller assembly.

Back Aboard the Day Sailer

In a two-man boat, the crew remaining in the boat can give valuable help. The handgrip is important: **(1)** Don't grab the man's hand this way; **(2)** shows the right grip. The swimmer assists the effort with a scissors kick **(3)**, while the sailor on the opposite side trims the boat as necessary by shifting her weight, bracing herself against the centerboard trunk **(4)**. The latter also serves as a handhold for the man as he climbs aboard **(5)**. Meanwhile the dinghy drifts with fully eased sheets as the wind takes her.

It's easier to climb back aboard over the stern in the case of a light boat or a one-man dinghy, because this doesn't heel the boat. In some of the older types with small afterdecks, the deck offers a good support for the body and the hands can reach inboard to grasp the coaming, which offers a handhold.

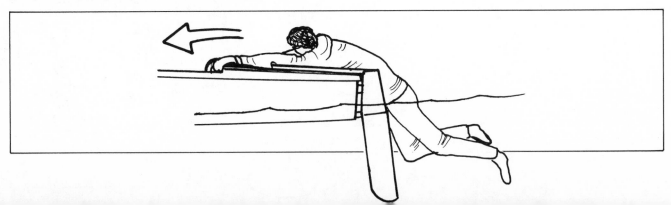

Safety Equipment for the Blue-Water Voyage

On long ocean passages, the boat must be provided with every safety device necessary against storm, shipwreck, emergency and man-overboard. The master is responsible to ensure that every safety device described here is on board for each member of the crew. He cannot assume that the casual shipmate will bring along his own PFD (Personal Flotation Device), safety harness, etc. The boat must be fitted out with all the safety equipment necessary for the largest crew expected. Even the size of the life raft depends on the size of the crew. A four-man raft will indeed accommodate six temporarily, but the chances of survival for every single one are slight if a long time elapses before they are found. The rule is this: Number of permanent bunks on board = maximum crew = available safety equipment.

1. Horseshoe buoy—solid, not inflatable, in strap or metal bracket to be thrown overboard instantly, carrying an attached light.

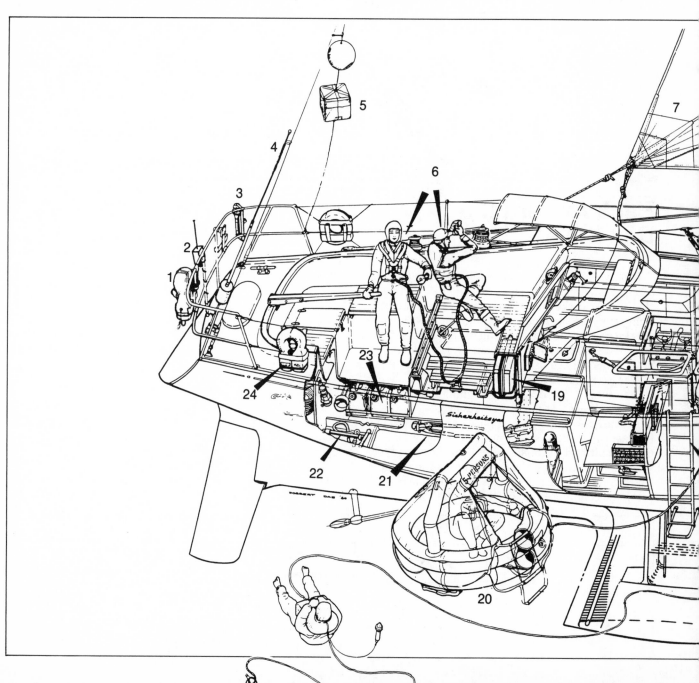

2. Emergency antenna on the stern pulpit for the VHF radio.

3. Floating light to help find a person overboard.

4. Man-overboard pole with red or signal letter ''O'' flag and marker light activated by contact with water. (The ''O'' flag consists of a rectangle divided once diagonally into an upper red and a lower yellow triangle.)

5. A ball and square shape signal, one shape above the other. If not available, any spherically shaped day signal and a square cushion, hung one above the other, will suffice.

6. Automatically inflated life vest and safety harness for each member of the crew, attached to a fixed pad eye in the cockpit by means of a line or strap.

7. Trysail for use during longer storms on the open sea.

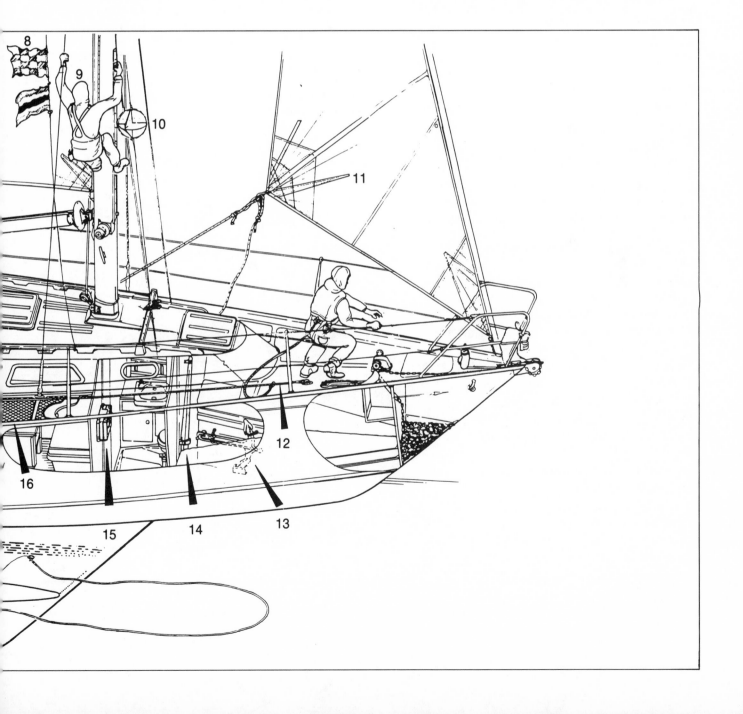

8. International distress signal flags "NC." These show that an emergency exists and that help is needed at once. It is recommended that every boat should carry a rectangular orange flag with a central black circle as a distress signal. Any signal carried should be as big as possible for maximum visibility.

9. Bosun's chair with solid seat and safety straps to prevent the user from slipping out.

10. If a fixed radar reflector cannot be attached at the masthead, then one that can be hoisted as required.

11. Storm jib with high-cut clew so that it can be trimmed very flat and so that it will not be damaged by a sea coming over the bow.

12. Jack line of steel cable run along the deck between solid pad eyes in case of bad weather. The crew snaps a line from his harness over the jack line and thus can safely get to the foredeck.

13. Spare anchor stowed below, but easily accessible.

14. Emergency tiller, quickly reached and installed.

15. Generous first-aid kit in an accessible wall bracket.

16. Non-skid patches on deck.

17. Floating emergency radio transmitter — EPIRB (Emergency Position Indicating Radio Beacon).

18. Rescue or boarding ladder, which should be carried on the side of larger yachts, because the stern pounds a great deal in a heavy sea and could drag a person under the transom.

19. Life raft, placed so that it can be reached without leaving the cockpit. Better still, on a bracket outboard of the stern pulpit.

20. Life raft with multiple buoyancy chambers and double bottom, sized for the maximum crew.

21. Bolt cutters large enough to cut the heaviest wire on board.

22. Large capacity spare hand pump.

23. Floating reserve water tank and container of emergency rations and other necessities for a long stay on the raft.

24. At least one additional horseshoe buoy within easy reach of the crew.

Life Vests for Continuous Wear

Unlike horseshoe buoys in brackets near the cockpit, solid life jackets are often stowed somewhere below-deck. Usually they are not worn at all or, if they are, put on too late. Inflatable vests that can be folded and kept in a flexible pouch which can readily be worn continuously over foul weather gear should be worn. They can be used for unconscious or helpless people as they automatically turn the wearer to a relatively safe position — lying on his back. They are designed to automatically self-inflate on contact with the water, using a gas bottle (**1**). A mouth-operated valve is also incorporated (**2**).

A whistle should be attached with a lanyard to help mark the wearer's position at night. Straps keep the vest from lifting up off the body.

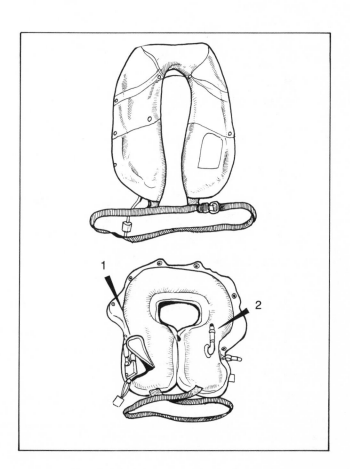

Horseshoe Buoys and Safety Lines

The modern horseshoe buoy has made the old life ring obsolete. It is indeed harder to heave as accurately or as far, but offers the man overboard greater safety; it can be put on in the water and worn like a life vest and it can be securely attached to the body with straps.

The horseshoe buoy is the safest because it has the most buoyancy and will support even a heavy unconscious person in a safe position. Disadvantage: It's very difficult to swim with.

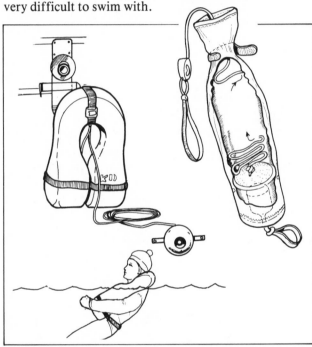

It's not a good idea to attach the horseshoe to a loosely coiled line; the latter will tangle as soon as the buoy is heaved. Thus the expected additional safety is turned into a disadvantage.

Instead, a light, strong heaving line ending in a weighted float is bracketed on the stern pulpit and coiled so that it runs out smoothly when the weighted float is heaved. The float adds buoyancy at the end of the line so that it is easily grasped in the water. Such devices are available commercially.

Available commercially is a cable spool that is bolted to the stern pulpit. It carries about 100 yards of line, which is fastened to the horseshoe so that it runs out when the buoy is thrown. It is protected by a Velcro® cover that keeps it from running out until needed; heaving the horse-shoe rips the closure open. Because of the length of this line, it is possible for the boat to make a circle around the man in the water in case it is felt unsafe or impossible to approach him directly. This enables the line to be grasped at any convenient place.

Emergency Light on Board

There should be on board at least two watertight flashlights of much higher power than that of the run-of-the-mill unit. One should be hung from a carabiner on the stern pulpit near the cockpit, always ready to be grabbed. It may also be clipped to the life belt at night so that it will be handy at any time.

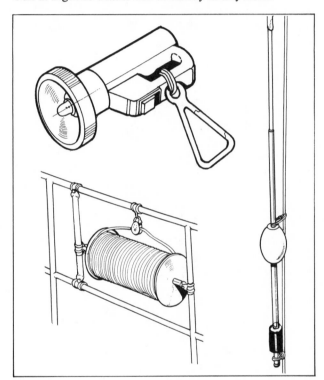

Marking the Spot!

If the luckless fellow is not reached at once with horseshoe or line, a man-overboard pole must be launched instantly! Poles are available with "O" flags for daylight visibility, powerful lights for night use or both. The pole is so designed that a counter weight at the lower end makes the pole float upright, while a float about one-third of the way up provides buoyancy. The flag is visible a long way off, while the water-activated lamp serves as an effective locator if the rescue continues into the night.

Prevention of Man-Overboard Accidents

Every skipper who is keenly aware of his responsibilities strives to prevent such accidents. Safety lines and life jackets are the best life insurance.

There are harness systems that are built into foul weather jackets or overalls. Less expensive and possibly safer are harnesses to be worn over the oilskins. In buying these, be sure that the straps are wide enough to give a good load-bearing surface and resist twisting.

Locking devices and/or hooks must be easy to operate at the chest level and should be of generous size. There are good reports of harnesses with solid backs. These sit firmly on the body and, in case of a fall overboard that causes a sudden heavy load, they distribute the load over a large area. The so-called "walking harness" is no good because it can lead to injury. One has to put on two separate leg loops in advance to keep the harness in its proper position on the seat. Every harness should have one long and one short line, so that one may snap on at the right length according to need. Then, as one goes up on the foredeck, one line can be left attached with its carabiner until the other has been snapped on.

Safest of all is a steel eye thru-bolted to the cockpit sole; to this the carabiner is hooked, eliminating the danger of being flung out of the cockpit. Never secure the harness line to the boat's lifeline; the thin steel cable will not always stand up to the load of a man falling backward over the side.

Useful are little pads of a rubber and cork composition that are stuck to the deck; these are better non-skid materials than any other. There are various shapes, all equally good. Stick these on the side decks unless these are of teak and on the most used areas of the cabin top.

The Boom Brake

Since an involuntary jibe can knock a man overboard, a preventer should be used on courses off the wind. It is rigged from the end of the boom to a cleat on the foredeck. Fairly simple and quickly available is a boom brake, a commercial device. Two lines are made fast to the chain plates or to special deck fittings. These lead to a gear system at the boom. The device acts as a brake, slowing down the movement of the boom.

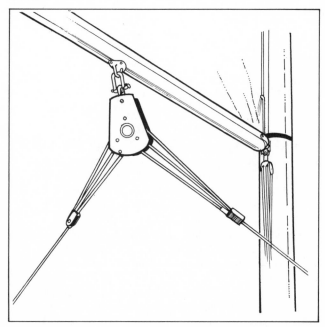

Assistance Via Radio

A VHF radio is no longer a luxury, even on small yachts. Such a set will reach large areas of coastal and lakes waters in case of emergency. Channel 16 is the internationally recognized distress frequency. Many sets have special knobs or systems for instantly switching to this channel. There should be an emergency antenna at the stern pulpit so that one can transmit even after a dismasting. A VHF set is shown.

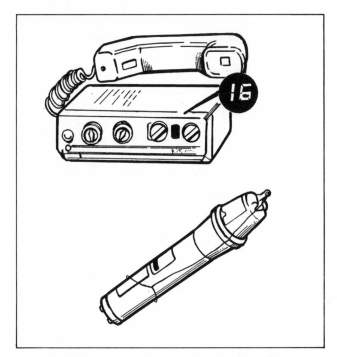

Illustrated also is an EPIRB (Emergency Position Indicating Radio Beacon). It is a radio distress signal transmitter operating on two frequencies, 121.5 MHz (monitored by commercial aircraft) and 243 MHz (monitored by the military). It should be taken aboard the life raft or attached to the horseshoe buoy to be thrown to a man overboard. It's essential function is to pinpoint the position of the distress by radio so that search and rescue vessels or helicopters can reach the spot quickly.

A radio beacon operating on 2182 kHz has a much greater range than does a VHF — about 150 miles compared to line of sight. Sets of this kind both transmit and receive. Various watertight units are available, suitalbe for yachts.

Radar Reflectors

Any yacht intending to cruise where there is commercial shipping should be fitted with a radar reflector. Tests have shown that only reflectors of adequate size will give useful echos. Each edge should be at least a foot long for the most reliable results, but smaller ones have worked on yachts. Note:

1. If it proves to be impossible to mount a reflector permanently at the masthead of a small yacht, then it must be hoisted during bad visibility or at night. Various models are available. Hoist the reflector so that one of its compartments is in the "catch water" position in order to achieve greatest possible efficiency.

2. The drawing at right shows an extremely light masthead reflector consisting merely of a pair of triple reflecting surfaces facing forward and aft. This configuration is not as good as that just described.

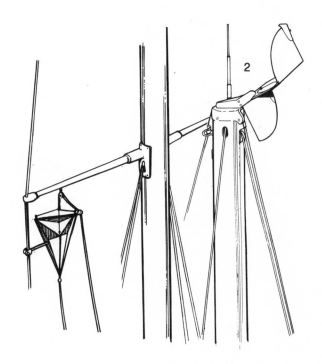

The Life Raft

If the yacht is in a sinking condition as the result of collision, storm or fire on the high seas, the life raft provides the last and safest means of rescue. But the best raft is useless if it can't be launched in time. Critical in this connection is its location on board. On motorboats:

1. In the cockpit near the pilothouse or on the cockpit sole is not good because the heavy raft would have to be raised a considerable way before it could be heaved over.

2. On the roof of the pilothouse is no good either because in a heavy sea and resulting heavy rolling, it is almost impossible to free it from its retainer by hand. In addition, there is the danger that the crewman may go over instead of the raft.

3. On the cabin top is somewhat safer, but also difficult to reach in a heavy sea.

4. On the afterdeck or after cabin top is the best place because the raft is easily launched from here under any conditions.

On sailboats:

1. In the cockpit just abaft the bridge deck, or in a special compartment under the after athwartships locker lid. The same considerations apply here as to the equivalent location on the motorboat.

2. On the cabin top. This is the place most often chosen on sailing yachts. It has two disadvantages. First, the raft interferes with vision forward, and second, it must be carried a certain distance before it can be heaved over the lifelines.

3. Before the mast. Same problem as on the cabin top. In a storm, or if the cabin is on fire, it may be extremely difficult to get from the cockpit to the raft.

4. In a special bracket outboard of the stern pulpit is the best place on board.

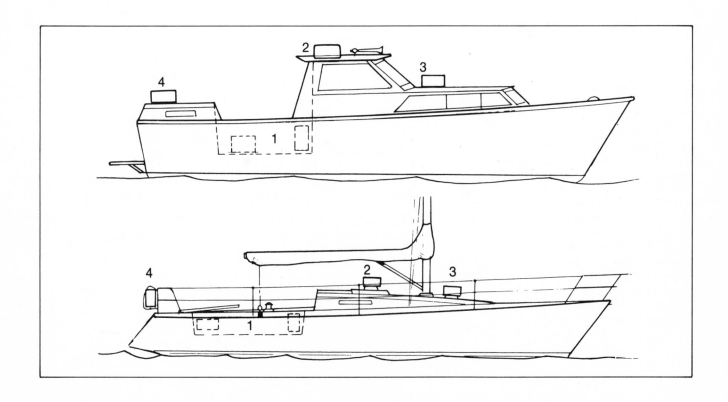

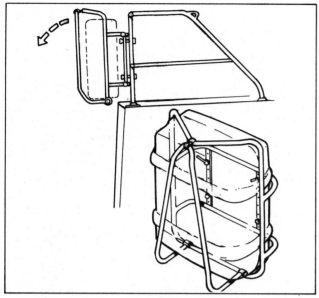

There are several kinds of life raft retaining devices for the stern pulpit. A latched locking ring allows the life raft to fall into the water of its own weight. It is essential that this be reachable from the cockpit and easily unlatched. Some devices have theft-proof locks

that prevent the latch from being lifted. All too often one forgets to unlock it before taking off. Besides, one way or another the key could be inaccessible or even somewhere in a burning cabin.

Life rafts should get the attention of an authorized service station every two years. A one-year interval is even better. This measure is necessary to ensure that the equipment will inflate and to renew supplies of water and emergency rations. A well-equipped raft will carry the following emergency items: Signal rockets, handheld flares, Morse signal light, flashlights, canteen of drinking water, emergency rations, first-aid kit, blankets, seasickness tablets, rainwater collector, sea anchor, paddle, life ring with lines, fishing equipment, identification light on the canopy, repair materials, leak plugs, bailer, sponge, bellows for maintaining air pressure, whistle and the appropriate instruction sheets.

Very necessary is a rigger's knife with which to cut the painter. It should always be kept in a special holster on the outside of the canopy near the entrance. The painter has but one good chance to be cut loose from the sinking yacht or the raft will be dragged down with it. Besides, you may want to get away from the boat as quickly as possible, for instance if it is on fire.

Beware of inflating the raft too early, because there is a danger of the attachment line pulling free or damaging the raft, as happened in the 1979 Fastnet. Delay boarding until the last moment, then go quickly.

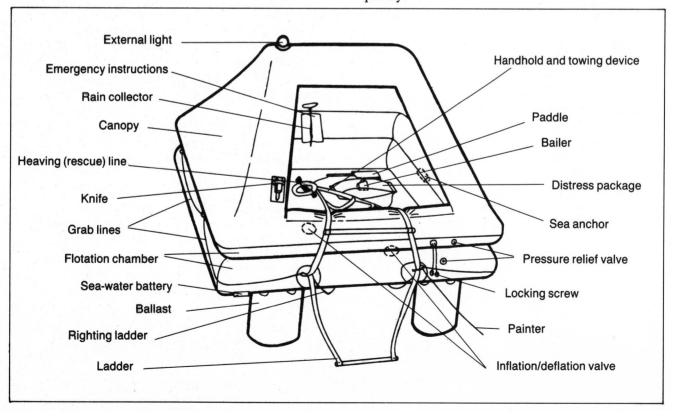

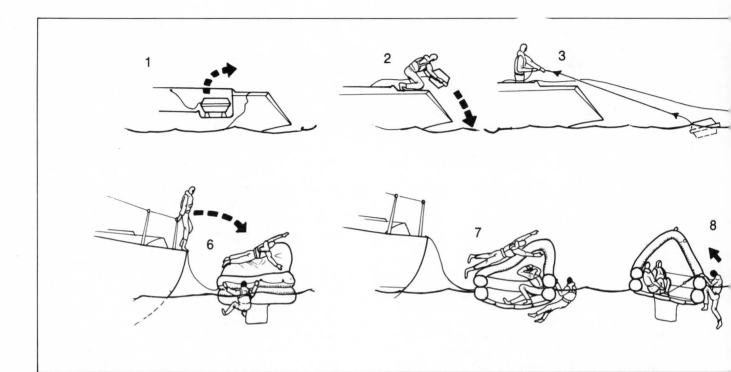

You Must Practice Boarding!

It is not easy to launch a life raft in a seaway and then get into it. Every owner must familiarize himself with it by hands-on practice. For this purpose the manufacturers stage demonstrations and there are also club arrangements for practice in a swimming pool.

1. The most important inspection before launching the raft is to determine that the painter (which activates the inflation) is made fast on board. Forget this item and both raft and safety disappear forever!

2. It's best to get the raft into the water over the stern if you can; thus it will be near the ladder.

3. The length of the painter is such that a certain amount must be drawn out before it will activate the automatic inflation. As soon as you feel some resistance, give the line a good jerk.

4. In most cases the life raft will be fully inflated automatically within 10 to 60 seconds, depending on the maker. It will be right side up.

5. But if this is not the case, then a crewmember must right it. Jump onto the raft and get to its leeward side. Grab the righting line (it's installed for the purpose), lean your body far outboard and haul the raft over. And of course you will fall into the water while doing it . . .

6. The best way to board the raft is to jump on the canopy. The air-filled structure that holds the canopy up is designed to take the load imposed by the jumper's landing and gives with him.

7. Once a crewman is inside the raft, have him move to its far side so that the next person can jump on unhindered. And if someone is already in the water, he can try to keep the raft in the right position.

8. Finally those in the water climb aboard using the webbing ladder that must be on board, as well as the auxiliary hand lines. The rest of the people on the raft form a counterweight by squeezing together on the side opposite the entry.

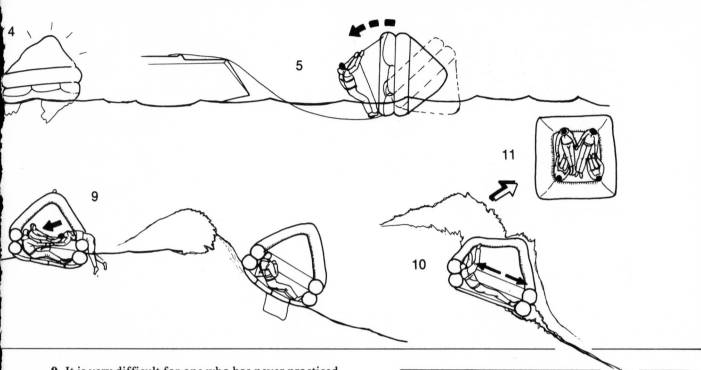

9. It is very difficult for one who has never practiced it to climb into the raft from the water. His shipmates already aboard must help him. They brace their feet, grab his arms and haul him aboard with all their might.

As soon as the raft is free of the mother craft, the crew should deploy the sea anchor that is, or ought to be, part of the raft's standard equipment.

10. In a heavy sea, a life raft is roughly knocked about. Breaking crests constantly threaten to push the raft or the canopy out of shape, especially if the air pressure is low. The crew will soon learn how to stabilize the raft with arms and legs under extreme conditions.

11. Accommodations in a four-man raft can hardly be called luxurious. If a long time has passed and still no rescue, the people will have to keep changing positions so that at least two will always be able to stretch their legs.

And Finally . . .

This book has discoursed upon accidents, disasters and emergencies on the water. After reading it, many a new owner may possibly view his forthcoming boating with anxiety, and will ask himself whether boating is indeed the activity he had always hoped would bring him pleasure and recreation. The authors would like, hereby, to dispel these doubts: From their own experience, they know that the disasters they have pictured and described very rarely come to pass and that most situations are much less dramatic than made to appear by the condensed format of the drawings and text. But it is good to know how to react when the exceptional event really does happen. To this end we hope that these examples and seaman-like practices have shown the way.